The
Brief
Pocket Reader

David Munger

LONGMAN

An imprint of Addison Wesley Longman, Inc.

New York • Reading, Massachusetts • Menlo Park, California • Harlow, England
Don Mills, Ontario • Sydney • Mexico City • Madrid • Amsterdam

Acquisitions Editor: Lynn M. Huddon
Marketing Manager: Carlise Paulson
Cover Design: John Callahan
Cover Photo: PhotoDisc
Interior Design: Dianne Hall, The Davidson Group
Electronic Page Makeup: Dianne Hall, The Davidson Group
Senior Manufacturing Buyer: Dennis J. Para

For permission to use copyrighted material, grateful acknowledgement is made to the copyright holders on pp. 241–243, which are hereby made part of this copyright page.

Library of Congress Cataloging-in-Publication Data

The Brief Pocket Reader [compiled by] David Munger.
  p. cm.
  "Based on 80 readings"—Pref.
  ISBN 0-321-07669-9
  1. College readers. 2. English language—Rhetoric—Problems, exercises, etc.
  3. Report writing—Problems, exercises, etc. 1. Munger, David.

PE1417 B713 1999
808'.0427dc21

                                                          99-056570

Please visit our website at http://www.awlonline.com

ISBN: 0-321-07669-9

12345678910—DOC—03020100

Contents

Example   47

Comparison & Contrast   65

Process Analysis   97

Classification   115

Cause & Effect   137

Analogy   161

Definition   187

Argument   209

Thematic Contents

Customs and Habits

Education

Family

Growing Up/Aging

Nature and the Environment

Poverty/Social Issues

Race and Culture

Science and Society

Women and Men

Writing and Language

Preface

The *Brief Pocket Reader* provides high-interest, teachable readings organized in the rhetorical arrangement preferred by thousands of instructors. *The Brief Pocket Reader* is based on *80 Readings*, but the selection of readings has been completely updated, it is more concise, and it offers an organization many instructors prefer—one motivated by the writing strategies they teach their students to use in class and expect them to utilize throughout their college career. By focusing each chapter on a particular rhetorical strategy, the text highlights the relationship between reading and writing and allows students to build writing skills in a methodical, step-by-step manner.

However, *The Brief Pocket Reader* does not ignore the context for the readings. Many common threads extend throughout the text: race in America, nature and the environment, gender, medical ethics, as well as many essays on the process of writing itself. While these connections are summarized in the Thematic Contents, they are also embedded in the structure of the book, through strategic juxtaposition of readings.

And, since different instructors place varying degrees of emphasis on readings, and since school terms vary in length, the text is also available in an expanded version: *The Pocket Reader*.

Summary of features
- Two different lengths: *The Brief Pocket Reader* and *The Pocket Reader*.
- Organized according to the most common writing strategies used by college writers.
- Brief and accessible selections for first-year college writers.
- Each chapter begins with writing guidelines for the rhetorical strategy featured in the chapter.

- Each chapter contains a student-written essay.
- Engaging headnotes give students the background they need to appreciate each reading.
- Budget pricing gives instructors the flexibility to assign more than one text.

Acknowledgments

This book could not have been completed without the dedication and attention contributed by many individuals. Lynn Huddon conceived of the project and gave unwavering support as it proceeded to completion. Rich Woll always encouraged me to think bigger. Deanna Campbell provided valuable research and suggestions both for headnotes and the selection of readings. Lisa Dressler was vigilant in seeking permissions for the works that were selected. Heather Hulett contributed research, words, and work, work, work. Dianne Hall and Mike Shelton did great work in production in the face of ever-changing deadlines. Greta, Jimmy, and Nora Munger contributed inspiration in volumes too great to be measured.

Finally, I offer my gratitude to the teachers and scholars who reviewed the manuscript for this book: Marge Bartelt, Edison Community College; James V. Cervantes, Mesa Community College; Pat Davis, Pima Community College; Norine Ryan, Briar Cliff College; Terry Scambray, Fresno City College; Richard Tomlinson, Richland Community College; Kathryn White, Pima Community College; and Russel Wiebe, Felician College.

—DAVID MUNGER

1

Narration

Narration

1. **Write for a purpose.** While you may think of narration as simply telling a story, no story is interesting unless it has a point. If your story is about trying to recover lost baggage, your point might be "Airline X's customer service department is unprofessional and rude," or it might be "If you're polite and friendly, people will do amazing things to help you out."

2. **Organize your narrative to make your point.** Most narration is told in chronological order. Usually this strategy is easiest for your readers to understand, and it can often help your purpose by leading directly to your main point. However, sometimes you might want to start in the middle of the story, or even near its end, surprising your reader at key points with details from earlier in the story.

3. **Give plenty of details.** Without details, most stories can be told in just a sentence or two. For example, the airline story could be told as concisely as this: "The airline lost my bags and it took me three days to recover them." The story gains power through its well-chosen details: the empty feeling as you watched the last bag being lifted from the carousel, the cab driver who waited to make sure you found a hotel room, the friendly hotel manager who let you borrow a tie for a business meeting, the shock of watching ice cream dribble down your one clean shirt.

4. **Use a consistent point of view.** If you're telling your story from the first person point of view (I lost my bags, etc.), don't suddenly shift perspectives (Dave went to the baggage counter, etc.). While this advice may seem obvious, it's an easy mistake to make, especially if you're writing your draft over the course of several days. A less obvious and even more common error is to shift tenses. If you're writing in the past tense, keep your entire story in the past. For an excellent example of an essay that maintains a consistent point of view, take a look at Brent Staples' "Black Men and Public Space." Here Staples recounts his story from the perspective of a writer many years later, jumping seamlessly from his descriptions of events which occurred long ago to his current reflections on the subject. Though the strategy is complex, it works because Staples is careful to keep his point of view consistent.

Annie Dillard

The Chase

Annie Dillard (b. 1945) is probably best known for writing that grapples with her relationship with God and the natural world in such books as *Holy the Firm* and *Pilgrim at Tinker Creek*, which won a Pulitzer Prize in 1975. Although written with the same intense emotion, her book *An American Childhood* takes a different direction from her earlier works, drawing on her memories of growing up in a middle-class neighborhood in Pittsburgh, Pennsylvania. In this selection, Dillard describes one of the adventures of her childhood—writing from a child's perspective, with a little adult wisdom seeping through.

SOME BOYS TAUGHT ME TO PLAY FOOTBALL. This was fine sport. You thought   1
up a new strategy for every play and whispered it to the others. You went out
for a pass, fooling everyone. Best, you got to throw yourself mightily at someone's running legs. Either you brought him down or you hit the ground flat
out on your chin, with your arms empty before you. It was all or nothing. If
you hesitated in fear, you would miss and get hurt: you would take a hard fall
while the kid got away, or you would get kicked in the face while the kid got
away. But if you flung yourself wholeheartedly at the back of his knees—if you
gathered and joined body and soul and pointed them diving fearlessly—then
you likely wouldn't get hurt, and you'd stop the ball. Your fate, and your
team's score, depended on your concentration and courage. Nothing girls did
could compare with it. Boys welcomed me at baseball, too, for I had, through
enthusiastic practice, what was weirdly known as a boy's arm. In winter, in the
snow, there was neither baseball nor football, so the boys and I threw snowballs at passing cars. I got in trouble throwing snowballs, and have seldom
been happier since.

On one weekday morning after Christmas, six inches of new snow had   2
just fallen. We were standing up to our boot tops in snow on a front yard on
trafficked Reynolds Street, waiting for cars. The cars traveled Reynolds Street
slowly and evenly; they were targets all but wrapped in red ribbons, cream
puffs. We couldn't miss. I was seven; the boys were eight, nine, and ten. The
oldest two Fahey boys were there—Mikey and Peter—polite blond boys who
lived near me on Lloyd Street, and who already had four brothers and sisters.
My parents approved of Mikey and Peter Fahey. Chickie McBride was there, a
tough kid, and Billy Paul and Mackie Kean too, from across Reynolds, where
the boys grew up dark and furious, grew up skinny, knowing, and skilled. We
had all drifted from our houses that morning looking for action, and had
found it here on Reynolds Street.

3   It was cloudy but cold. The cars' tires laid behind them on the snowy street a complex trail of beige chunks like crenellated castle walls. I had stepped on some earlier; they squeaked. We could have wished for more traffic. When a car came, we all popped it one. In the intervals between cars we reverted to the natural solitude of children.

4   I started making an iceball—a perfect iceball, from perfectly white snow, perfectly spherical, and squeezed perfectly translucent so no snow remained all the way through. (The Fahey boys and I considered it unfair actually to throw an iceball at somebody, but it had been known to happen.) I had just embarked on the iceball project when we heard tire chains come clanking from afar. A black Buick was moving toward us down the street. We all spread out, banged together some regular snowballs, took aim, and, when the Buick drew nigh, fired.

5   A soft snowball hit the driver's windshield right before the driver's face. It made a smashed star with a hump in the middle.

6   Often, of course, we hit our target, but this time, the only time in all of life, the car pulled over and stopped. Its wide black door opened; a man got out of it, running. He didn't even close the car door.

7   He ran after us, and we ran away from him, up the snowy Reynolds sidewalk. At the corner, I looked back; incredibly, he was still after us. He was in city clothes: a suit and tie, street shoes. Any normal adult would have quit, having sprung us into flight and made his point. This man was gaining on us. He was a thin man, all action. All of a sudden, we were running for our lives.

8   Wordless, we split up. We were on our turf; we could lose ourselves in the neighborhood backyards, everyone for himself. I paused and considered. Everyone had vanished except Mikey Fahey, who was just rounding the corner of a yellow brick house. Poor Mikey, I trailed him. The driver of the Buick sensibly picked the two of us to follow. The man apparently had all day. He chased Mikey and me around the yellow house and up a backyard path we knew by heart: under a low tree, up a bank, through a hedge, down some snowy steps, and across the grocery store's delivery driveway. We smashed through a gap in another hedge, entered a scruffy backyard and ran around its back porch and tight between houses to Edgerton Avenue; we ran across Edgerton to an alley and up our own sliding woodpile to the Halls' front yard; he kept coming. We ran up Lloyd Street and wound through mazy backyards toward the steep hilltop at Willard and Lang.

9   He chased us silently, block after block. He chased us silently over picket fences, through thorny hedges, between houses, around garbage cans, and across streets. Every time I glanced back, choking for breath, I expected he would have quit. He must have been as breathless as we were. His jacket strained over his body. It was an immense discovery, pounding into my hot head with every sliding, joyous step, that this ordinary adult evidently knew

what I thought only children who trained at football knew: that you have to fling yourself at what you're doing, you have to point yourself, forget yourself, aim, dive.

Mikey and I had nowhere to go, in our own neighborhood or out of it, but 10 away from this man who was chasing us. He impelled us forward; we compelled him to follow our route. The air was cold; every breath tore my throat. We kept running, block after block; we kept improvising, backyard after backyard, running a frantic course and choosing it simultaneously, failing always to find small places or hard places to slow him down, and discovering always, exhilarated, dismayed, that only bare speed could save us—for he would never give up, this man—and we were losing speed. He chased us through the backyard labyrinths of ten blocks before he caught us by our jackets. He caught us and we all stopped.

We three stood staggering, half blinded, coughing, in an obscure hilltop 11 backyard: a man in his twenties, a boy, a girl. He had released our jackets, our pursuer, our captor, our hero: he knew we weren't going anywhere. We all played by the rules. Mikey and I unzipped our jackets. I pulled off my sopping mittens. Our tracks multiplied in the backyard's new snow. We had been breaking new snow all morning. We didn't look at each other. I was cherishing my excitement. The man's lower pants legs were wet; his cuffs were full of snow, and there was a prow of snow beneath them on his shoes and socks. Some trees bordered the little flat backyard, some messy winter trees. There was no one around: a clearing in a grove, and we the only players.

It was a long time before he could speak. I had some difficulty at first re- 12 calling why we were there. My lips felt swollen; I couldn't see out of the sides of my eyes; I kept coughing.

"You stupid kids," he began perfunctorily. 13

We listened perfunctorily indeed, if we listened at all, for the chewing out 14 was redundant, a mere formality, and beside the point. The point was that he had chased us passionately without giving up, and so he had caught us. Now he came down to earth. I wanted the glory to last forever.

But how could the glory have lasted forever? We could have run through 15 every backyard in North America until we got to Panama. But when he trapped us at the lip of the Panama Canal, what precisely could he have done to prolong the drama of the chase and cap its glory? I brooded about this for the next few years. He could only have fried Mikey Fahey and me in boiling oil, say, or dismembered us piecemeal, or staked us to anthills. None of which I really wanted, and none of which any adult was likely to do, even in the spirit of fun. He could only chew us out there in the Panamanian jungle, after months or years of exalting pursuit. He could only begin, "You stupid kids," and continue in his ordinary Pittsburgh accent with his normal righteous anger and the usual common sense.

16   If in that snowy backyard the driver of the black Buick had cut off our heads, Mikey's and mine, I would have died happy, for nothing has required so much of me since as being chased all over Pittsburgh in the middle of winter—running terrified, exhausted—by this sainted, skinny, furious redheaded man who wished to have a word with us. I don't know how he found his way back to his car.

Russell Baker

from *Growing Up*

Russell Baker is a journalist whose ideas were shaped as he grew up in a poor family during the Great Depression. He spent his adolescent years in Baltimore, and after college landed a job as a reporter for the *Baltimore Sun.* Eventually he moved to the *New York Times,* where in 1962, he began writing his famous "Observer" column, which he continues to write today. His wry, incisive commentary in "Observer" earned him the Pulitzer Prize in 1979. Shortly thereafter, he began work on his own autobiography, conducting exhaustive interviews with family members in order to create a more accurate picture of depression-era America. The result, in 1983, was the Pulitzer Prize-winning *Growing Up,* which covers Baker's childhood, followed in 1989 by *The Good Times,* which describes the early years of Baker's career in journalism. In this excerpt from *Growing Up,* he recounts the shame of "going on relief" and contrasts it with the joy of Christmas.

1   [MY] PAPER ROUTE EARNED ME THREE DOLLARS A WEEK, sometimes four, and my mother, in addition to her commissions on magazine sales, also had her monthly check coming from Uncle Willie, but we'd been in Baltimore a year before I knew how desperate things were for her. One Saturday morning she told me she'd need Doris and me to go with her to pick up some food. I had a small wagon she'd bought me to make it easier to move the Sunday papers, and she said I'd better bring it along. The three of us set off eastward, passing the grocery stores we usually shopped at, and kept walking until we came to Fremont Avenue, a grim street of dilapidation and poverty in the heart of the West Baltimore black belt.

2   "This is where we go," she said when we reached the corner of Fremont and Fayette Street. It looked like a grocery, with big plate-glass windows and people lugging out cardboard cartons and bulging bags, but it wasn't. I knew very well what it was.

3   "Are we going on relief?" I asked her.

4   "Don't ask questions about things you don't know anything about," she said. "Bring that wagon inside."

I did, and watched with a mixture of shame and greed while men filled   5
it with food. None of it was food I liked. There were huge cans of grape-
fruit juice, big paper sacks of cornmeal, cellophane bags of rice and prunes.
It was hard to believe all this was ours for no money at all, even though
none of it was very appetizing. My wonder at this free bounty quickly
changed to embarrassment as we headed home with it. Being on relief was
a shameful thing. People who accepted the government's handouts were
scorned by everyone I knew as idle no-accounts without enough self-respect
to pay their own way in the world. I'd often heard my mother say the same
thing of families in the neighborhood suspected of being on relief. These,
I'd been taught to believe, were people beyond hope. Now we were as low
as they were.

Pulling the wagon back toward Lombard Street, with Doris following be-   6
hind to keep the edible proof of our disgrace from falling off, I knew my
mother was far worse off than I'd suspected. She'd never have accepted such
shame otherwise. I studied her as she walked along beside me, head high as
always, not a bit bowed in disgrace, moving at her usual quick, hurry-up pace.
If she'd given up on life, she didn't show it, but on the other hand she was un-
happy about something. I dared to mention the dreaded words only once on
that trip home.

"Are we on relief now, Mom?"   7

"Let me worry about that," she said.   8

What worried me most as we neared home was the possibility we'd be seen   9
with the incriminating food by somebody we knew. There was no mistaking
government-surplus food. The grapefruit-juice cans, the prunes and rice, the
cornmeal—all were ostentatiously unlabeled, thus advertising themselves as
"government handouts." Everybody in the neighborhood could read them
easily enough, and our humiliation would be gossiped through every parlor by
sundown. I had an inspiration.

"It's hot pulling this wagon," I said. "I'm going to take my sweater off."   10

It wasn't hot, it was on the cool side, but after removing the sweater I laid   11
it across the groceries in the wagon. It wasn't a very effective cover, but my
mother was suddenly affected by the heat too.

"It is warm, isn't it, Buddy?" she said. Removing her topcoat, she draped   12
it over the groceries, providing total concealment. "You want to take your coat
off, Doris?" asked my mother.

"I'm not hot, I'm chilly," Doris said.   13

It didn't matter. My mother's coat was enough to get us home without being   14
exposed as three of life's failures.

From then on I assumed we were paupers. . . .   15

[My mother] was a magician at stretching a dollar. That December, with   16
Christmas approaching, she was out at work and Doris was in the kitchen

when I barged into her bedroom one afternoon in search of a safety pin. Since her bedroom opened onto a community hallway, she kept the door locked, but needing the pin, I took the key from its hiding place, unlocked the door, and stepped in. Standing against the wall was a big, black bicycle with balloon tires. I recognized it instantly. It was the same second-hand bike I'd been admiring in a Baltimore Street shop window. I'd even asked about the price. It was horrendous. Something like $15. Somehow my mother had scraped together enough for a down payment and meant to surprise me with the bicycle on Christmas morning.

17   I was overwhelmed by the discovery that she had squandered such money on me and sickened by the knowledge that, bursting into her room like this, I had robbed her of the pleasure of seeing me astonished and delighted on Christmas day. I hadn't wanted to know her lovely secret; still, stumbling upon it like this made me feel as though I'd struck a blow against her happiness. I backed out, put the key back in its hiding place, and brooded privately.

18   I resolved that between now and Christmas I must do nothing, absolutely nothing, to reveal the slightest hint of my terrible knowledge. I must avoid the least word, the faintest intonation, the weakest gesture that might reveal my possession of her secret. Nothing must deny her the happiness of seeing me stunned with amazement on Christmas day.

19   In the privacy of my bedroom I began composing and testing exclamations of delight: "Wow!" "A bike with balloon tires! I don't believe it!" "I'm the luckiest boy alive!" And so on. They all owed a lot to movies in which boys like Mickey Rooney had seen their wildest dreams come true, and I realized that, with my lack of acting talent, all of them were going to sound false at the critical moment when I wanted to cry out my love spontaneously from the heart. Maybe it would be better to say nothing but appear to be shocked into such deep pleasure that speech had escaped me. I wasn't sure, though. I'd seen speechless gratitude in the movies too, and it never really worked until the actors managed to cry a few quiet tears. I doubted I could cry on cue, so I began thinking about other expressions of speechless amazement. In front of a hand-held mirror in my bedroom I tried the whole range of expressions: mouth agape and eyes wide; hands slapped firmly against both cheeks to keep the jaw from falling off; ear-to-ear grin with all teeth fully exposed while hugging the torso with both arms. These and more I practiced for several days without acquiring confidence in any of them. I decided to wait until Christmas morning and see if anything came naturally. . . .

20   That Christmas morning she roused us early, "to see what Santa Claus brought," she said with just the right tone of irony to indicate we were all old enough to know who Santa Claus was. I came out of my bedroom with my presents for her and Doris, and Doris came with hers. My mother's had been

placed under the tree during the night. There were a few small glittering packages, a big doll for Doris, but no bicycle. I must have looked disappointed.

"It looks like Santa Claus didn't do too well by you this year, Buddy," she   21
said, as I opened packages. A shirt. A necktie. I said something halfhearted like, "It's the thought that counts," but what I felt was bitter disappointment. I supposed she'd found the bike intolerably expensive and sent it back.

"Wait a minute!" she cried, snapping her fingers. "There's something in   22
my bedroom I forgot all about."

She beckoned to Doris, the two of them went out, and a moment later   23
came back wheeling between them the big black two-wheeler with balloon tires. I didn't have to fake my delight, after all. The three of us—Doris, my mother, and I—were people bred to repress the emotional expressions of love, but I did something that startled both my mother and me. I threw my arms around her spontaneously and kissed her.

"All right now, don't carry on about it. It's only a bicycle," she said.   24

Still, I knew that she was as happy as I was to see her so happy.   25

Amy Tan

Fish Cheeks

Amy Tan is a gifted storyteller whose first novel, *The Joy Luck Club* (1989), met with critical acclaim and huge success. The relationships it details between immigrant Chinese mothers and their Chinese American daughters came from Tan's firsthand experience. She was born in 1952 in Oakland, California, the daughter of immigrants who had fled China's Cultural Revolution in the late 1940s. She majored in English and linguistics at San Jose State University, where she received a B.A. in 1973 and an M.A. in 1974. After two more years of graduate work, Tan became a consultant in language development for disabled children and then started her own company writing reports and speeches for business corporations. Tan began writing fiction to explore her ethnic ambivalence and to find a voice for herself. After *The Joy Luck Club,* she published *The Kitchen God's Wife* (1991), a fictional account of her mother's harrowing life in China, and *The Hundred Secret Senses* (1995), a novel. Tan has also written children's books and contributed essays to *McCall's, Life, Glamour, The Atlantic Monthly,* and other magazines. In this very brief narrative, Tan deftly portrays the ambivalence—the contradictory feelings—of a child with feet in different cultures. "Fish Cheeks" first appeared in *Seventeen* in 1987.

I FELL IN LOVE WITH THE MINISTER'S SON the winter I turned fourteen. He was   1
not Chinese, but as white as Mary in the manger. For Christmas I prayed for this blond-haired boy, Robert, and a slim new American nose.

2   When I found out that my parents had invited the minister's family over for Christmas Eve dinner, I cried. What would Robert think of our shabby Chinese Christmas? What would he think of our noisy Chinese relatives who lacked proper American manners? What terrible disappointment would he feel upon seeing not a roasted turkey and sweet potatoes but Chinese food?

3   On Christmas Eve I saw that my mother had outdone herself in creating a strange menu. She was pulling black veins out of the backs of fleshy prawns. The kitchen was littered with appalling mounds of raw food: A slimy rock cod with bulging eyes that pleaded not to be thrown into a pan of hot oil. Tofu, which looked like stacked wedges of rubbery white sponges. A bowl soaking dried fungus back to life. A plate of squid, their backs crisscrossed with knife markings so they resembled bicycle tires.

4   And then they arrived—the minister's family and all my relatives in a clamor of doorbells and rumpled Christmas packages. Robert grunted hello, and I pretended he was not worthy of existence.

5   Dinner threw me deeper into despair. My relatives licked the ends of their chopsticks and reached across the table, dipping them into the dozen or so plates of food. Robert and his family waited patiently for platters to be passed to them. My relatives murmured with pleasure when my mother brought out the whole steamed fish. Robert grimaced. Then my father poked his chopsticks just below the fish eye and plucked out the soft meat. "Amy, your favorite," he said, offering me the tender fish cheek. I wanted to disappear.

6   At the end of the meal my father leaned back and belched loudly, thanking my mother for her fine cooking. "It's a polite Chinese custom to show you are satisfied," explained my father to our astonished guests. Robert was looking down at his plate with a reddened face. The minister managed to muster up a quiet burp. I was stunned into silence for the rest of the night.

7   After everyone had gone, my mother said to me, "You want to be the same as American girls on the outside." She handed me an early gift. It was a miniskirt in beige tweed. "But inside you must always be Chinese. You must be proud you are different. Your only shame is to have shame."

8   And even though I didn't agree with her then, I knew that she understood how much I had suffered during the evening's dinner. It wasn't until many years later—long after I had gotten over my crush on Robert—that I was able to fully appreciate her lesson and the true purpose behind our particular menu. For Christmas Eve that year, she had chosen all my favorite foods.

Brent Staples

Black Men and Public Space

The son of a truck driver, Brent Staples grew up in a family of eleven that was constantly on the move due to hard economic times in his hometown of Chester, Pennsylvania. At one point uncertain as to whether he would finish high school, he eventually parlayed a college scholarship into a Ph.D. from the University of Chicago. After an unrewarding career as a lecturer in behavioral science, he found his niche as a writer, first for the *Chicago Sun Times,* then for the *New York Times,* where he continues to work as an editorial writer. While he acknowledges that his race has had a tremendous impact on his life, Staples refuses to let race define him. In this essay, which was originally published in *Harper's* magazine, Staples examines the moment that he discovered that others didn't share his views about his race.

MY FIRST VICTIM WAS A WOMAN—WHITE, well-dressed, probably in her early   1
twenties. I came upon her late one evening on a deserted street in Hyde Park, a relatively affluent neighborhood in an otherwise mean, impoverished section of Chicago. As I swung onto the avenue behind her, there seemed to be a discreet, uninflammatory distance between us. Not so. She cast back a worried glance. To her, the youngish black man—a broad six feet two inches with a beard and billowing hair, both hands shoved into the pockets of a bulky military jacket—seemed menacingly close. After a few more quick glimpses, she picked up her pace and was soon running in earnest. Within seconds she disappeared into a cross street.

That was more than a decade ago. I was twenty-two years old, a graduate   2
student newly arrived at the University of Chicago. It was in the echo of that terrified woman's footfalls that I first began to know the unwieldy inheritance I'd come into—the ability to alter public space in ugly ways. It was clear that she thought herself the quarry of a mugger, a rapist, or worse. Suffering a bout of insomnia, however, I was stalking sleep, not defenseless wayfarers. As a softy who is scarcely able to take a knife to a raw chicken—let alone hold it to a person's throat—I was surprised, embarrassed, and dismayed all at once. Her flight made me feel like an accomplice in tyranny. It also made it clear that I was indistinguishable from the muggers who occasionally seeped into the area from the surrounding ghetto. That first encounter, and those that followed, signified that a vast, unnerving gulf lay between nighttime pedestrians—particularly women—and me. And I soon gathered that being perceived as dangerous is a hazard in itself. I only needed to turn a corner into a dicey situa-

tion, or crowd some frightened, armed person in a foyer somewhere, or make an errant move after being pulled over by a policeman. Where fear and weapons meet—and they often do in urban America—there is always the possibility of death.

3   In that first year, my first away from my hometown, I was to become thoroughly familiar with the language of fear. At dark, shadowy intersections in Chicago, I could cross in front of a car stopped at a traffic light and elicit the *thunk, thunk, thunk, thunk* of the driver—black, white, male, or female—hammering down the door locks. On less traveled streets after dark, I grew accustomed to but never comfortable with people who crossed to the other side of the street rather than pass me. Then there were the standard unpleasantries with policemen, doormen, bouncers, cab drivers, and others whose business it is to screen out troublesome individuals *before* there is any nastiness.

4   I moved to New York nearly two years ago and I have remained an avid night walker. In central Manhattan, the near-constant crowd cover minimizes tense one-on-one street encounters. Elsewhere—visiting friends in SoHo, where sidewalks are narrow and tightly spaced buildings shut out the sky— things can get very taut indeed.

5   Black men have a firm place in New York mugging literature. Norman Podhoretz in his famed (or infamous) 1963 essay, "My Negro Problem—And Ours," recalls growing up in terror of black males; they "were tougher than we were, more ruthless," he writes—and as an adult on the Upper West Side of Manhattan, he continues, he cannot constrain his nervousness when he meets black men on certain streets. Similarly, a decade later, the essayist and novelist Edward Hoagland extols a New York where once "Negro bitterness bore down mainly on other Negroes." Where some see mere panhandlers, Hoagland sees "a mugger who is clearly screwing up his nerve to do more than just *ask* for money." But Hoagland has "the New Yorker's quick-hunch posture for broken-field maneuvering," and the bad guy swerves away.

6   I often witness that "hunch posture," from women after dark on the warrenlike streets of Brooklyn where I live. They seem to set their faces on neutral and, with their purse straps strung across their chests bandolier style, they forge ahead as though bracing themselves against being tackled. I understand, of course, that the danger they perceive is not a hallucination. Women are particularly vulnerable to street violence, and young black males are drastically overrepresented among the perpetrators of that violence. Yet these truths are no solace against the kind of alienation that comes of being ever the suspect, against being set apart, a fearsome entity with whom pedestrians avoid making eye contact.

7   It is not altogether clear to me how I reached the ripe old age of twenty-two without being conscious of the lethality nighttime pedestrians attributed to me. Perhaps it was because in Chester, Pennsylvania, the small, angry in-

dustrial town where I came of age in the 1960s, I was scarcely noticeable against a backdrop of gang warfare, street knifings, and murders. I grew up one of the good boys, had perhaps a half-dozen fistfights. In retrospect, my shyness of combat has clear sources.

Many things go into the making of a young thug. One of those things is the consummation of the male romance with the power to intimidate. An infant discovers that random flailings send the baby bottle flying out of the crib and crashing to the floor. Delighted, the joyful babe repeats those motions again and again, seeking to duplicate the feat. Just so, I recall the points at which some of my boyhood friends were finally seduced by the perception of themselves as tough guys. When a mark cowered and surrendered his money without resistance, myth and reality merged—and paid off. It is, after all, only manly to embrace the power to frighten and intimidate. We, as men, are not supposed to give an inch of our lane on the highway; we are to seize the fighter's edge in work and in play and even in love; we are to be valiant in the face of hostile forces. ⁸

Unfortunately, poor and powerless young men seem to take all this nonsense literally. As a boy, I saw countless tough guys locked away; I have since buried several, too. They were babies, really—a teenage cousin, a brother of 22, a childhood friend in his mid-twenties—all gone down in episodes of bravado played out in the streets. I came to doubt the virtues of intimidation early on. I chose, perhaps even unconsciously, to remain a shadow—timid, but a survivor. ⁹

The fearsomeness mistakenly attributed to me in public places often has a perilous flavor. The most frightening of these confusions occurred in the late 1970s and early 1980s when I worked as a journalist in Chicago. One day, rushing into the office of a magazine I was writing for with a deadline story in hand, I was mistaken for a burglar. The office manager called security and, with an *ad hoc* posse, pursued me through the labyrinthine halls, nearly to my editor's door. I had no way of proving who I was. I could only move briskly toward the company of someone who knew me. ¹⁰

Another time I was on assignment for a local paper and killing time before an interview. I entered a jewelry store on the city's affluent Near North Side. The proprietor excused herself and returned with an enormous red Doberman pinscher straining at the end of a leash. She stood, the dog extended toward me, silent to my questions, her eyes bulging nearly out of her head. I took a cursory look around, nodded, and bade her good night. Relatively speaking, however, I never fared as badly as another black male journalist. He went to nearby Waukegan, Illinois, a couple of summers ago to work on a story about a murderer who was born there. Mistaking the reporter for the killer, police hauled him from his car at gunpoint and but for his press credentials would probably have tried to book him. Such episodes are not uncommon. Black men trade tales like this all the time. ¹¹

12   In "My Negro Problem—And Ours," Podhoretz writes that the hatred he feels for blacks makes itself known to him through a variety of avenues—one being his discomfort with that "special brand of paranoid touchiness" to which he says blacks are prone. No doubt he is speaking here of black men. In time, I learned to smother the rage I felt at so often being taken for a criminal. Not to do so would surely have led to madness—via that special "paranoid touchiness" that so annoyed Podhoretz at the time he wrote the essay.

13   I began to take precautions to make myself less threatening. I move about with care, particularly late in the evening. I give a wide berth to nervous people on subway platforms during the wee hours, particularly when I have exchanged business clothes for jeans. If I happen to be entering a building behind some people who appear skittish, I may walk by, letting them clear the lobby before I return, so as not to seem to be following them. I have been calm and extremely congenial on those rare occasions when I've been pulled over by the police.

14   And on late-evening constitutionals along streets less traveled by, I employ what has proved to be an excellent tension-reducing measure. I whistle melodies from Beethoven and Vivaldi and the more popular classical composers. Even steely New Yorkers hunching toward nighttime destinations seem to relax, and occasionally they even join in the tune. Virtually everybody seems to sense that a mugger wouldn't be warbling bright, sunny selections from Vivaldi's *Four Seasons*. It is my equivalent of the cowbell that hikers wear when they know they are in bear country.

Student Essay

Katherine Crane

Handling Room 15

Katherine wrote this essay in response to an assignment asking her to write a personal essay about an illness that she or someone she knew had experienced. It offers a very realistic glimpse into the world of mentally retarded children.

1   "ARE YOU SURE YOU ARE INTERESTED IN THIS, KATIE?" Mr. Becker asked. "Not everyone can handle what you are going to witness this afternoon." My math teacher's tone matched his expression: precise, pointed, cold and pensive.

Years of right triangles and permutations made him a calculating man, confident in his assessment of students and their potential. When he wasn't solving equations or summing up students, Mr. Becker took volunteers to the Hattie Larlham Foundation, a home for severely retarded children, a place especially significant to him. I didn't understand why he cared about HLF until I heard his daughter spent the short five years of her life there, fluttering between life and death, stricken with a rare brain-deteriorating condition. Seeing my name on the volunteer list obviously surprised him. He knew I wasn't a mathematician or a "visually minded student," and I knew I only took his class to pass it, so we were not especially close.

I grimaced. I took offense at his doubts about my ability to "handle" the children at the Hattie Larlham Foundation. My impeccable self-confidence as a "spring senior" prohibited me from envisioning myself as weak and vulnerable to a bunch of kids, no matter what their condition. I effectively "handled" the school newspaper, AP European History, a boyfriend, the college application process, my worried mother, fickle friends, and the Moore Street Mens' Shelter, so the prospect of baby-sitting a retarded child did not seem like a daunting task, much less one I would be incapable of handling.

I did not see any patients, or "special children," as they called them, when I entered the warm lobby, which smelled of the tangible "Band-Aid" stench of health care. Four of us stood there, I the only female, chatting idly until a male nurse, dressed in street clothes, welcomed us to the Foundation. He thanked us in advance for volunteering to work with a "special child" two days a week. He explained that the rest of our experience would come naturally, that there was not anything he could really instruct us to do. "Love them," he politely asked, or maybe he instructed, and he pointed at me to follow. I do not know now what I expected then to see behind the door to Room 15, but I was fairly confident that my job would be to rock a small, sickly infant until he fell asleep.

"His name is Daniel," the nurse explained before we entered, "we don't make it practice to reveal any information about our children, but I will tell you that Daniel is an exception at HLF. He's been here the longest of anyone, including staff. He's exceeded our age limitation by two years and we're not sure if Medicare will cover him next after he turns twenty-one. He likes girls, hates his diaper, so if he tries to take it off, hold his hands. I'm going to let you go in alone."

I opened the door slowly, wishing there was an observation window like the ones in asylums so I could prepare myself for Daniel. A glance from a window would allow me to see without detection, experience without contact. I entered. His massive body had curled itself into fetal position on a large blue mat in the center of the room, between his crib, stuffed animals and television which played a "Barney" video. His face tucked itself away from me, so I gingerly circled his body to view him face to face, half out of curiosity, half out of respect. A foul odor emanated from him, a putrid combination of teenage body odor, feces, and the palpable, decrepit smell of my great-grandmother. A puddle of mucus and phlegm had gathered under his mouth and heaving, stuffy nose, and my disgust caused me to take a jerking step backwards into a neatly sorted pile of Curious George books. The sudden movement woke the man, and his crusted brown eyes stared at my disbelieving face, yet his head did not move from the blue mat. His features were grossly distorted, his brown hair matted and tangled, his mouth gaping and groping for words he had never spoken.

6   "I'm Katie," I said stupidly, "what's your name?"

7   Daniel let out a sickening grunt.

8   Not knowing whether to run or stay, speak or remain silent, I did nothing. I tried to suppress feelings of sympathy in order to shield myself from despair, sensing, yet not knowing for sure whether pity would help or harm the situation. I crouched down to the floor, held his chaffed, cold hand which reflexively held mine and started to tell him about my day; how I lost my keys that morning; how Mr. Becker's class bored me more than usual; how Jessie kissed another boy, making him the third of the week. He smiled, showing his tremendously stained, yellow, crooked teeth. Certain topics seemed funny to him, especially those which made my voice inflect and those which were appropriate to teenagers. He laughed and snorted while I spoke, still clutching my hand until I broke away during the end of the session. As I tried to disengage my hand from his, he held on tighter, and I had to use my other hand to pry his grip apart. Freed, I started to stand up when he let out a horrifying bellow and tears began streaming down his face. I ran towards the door expecting him to lash out at me physically, but all his body did was futilely attempt to swivel around to see me as I closed the door to Room 15.

9   Later the nurse would tell me the scientific name for Daniel's reaction, how he established some sort of bond with me they had never witnessed before in him. The nurse said he might have fallen in love on some basic, incomprehensible level, and he encouraged me to come back and see him if I wished. He congratulated me for handling the situation well, for making the effort to communicate with Daniel and effectively doing so.

10   "Please come back," he said, and I politely smiled, nodded my head, put on my coat, and left. Mr. Becker picked us up and asked how our experiences were; everyone told him about the sick babies they rocked to sleep. I said nothing. The next Thursday I "missed the bus." Tuesday I had "homework." The next week, the roads were "too icy." And the next week I just stayed home. Sometimes I wonder if he remembers me or if he's moved from the blue mat. And I worry.

2

Description

Description

1. **Tell your readers what to see.** The most effective descriptions frame themselves around a dominant impression. Do you want your readers to see a dark room, or the glistening Olympic medal in the corner? Do you want them to feel saddened by the gloom, or inspired by momentary achievement that may have occurred decades ago? Depending on how you frame your description, you can tell the story of a dedicated athlete now devoting herself to public service, or a wasted talent rotting away in a tenement.

2. **Give concrete details.** In grade school, we all learn that adjectives describe. While this may be true from a technical standpoint, the best descriptions don't tell, they show, using precise nouns and active verbs. Instead of "a shiny silver medal was in the corner," it's more effective to say "a trickle of light illuminated a silver medallion, which had been carefully propped in the corner of the room."

3. **Choose words that express your purpose.** The English language contains a tremendous variety of words that each convey subtle (or not-so-subtle) connotations. As you compose and revise, select words that not only convey the meaning you intend, but also the subjective feeling or emotions you want your readers to experience. Was the medal *casually tossed* in the corner or *carefully propped* there? Was the woman *reclining* or *sprawled* on the sofa?

4. **Use a consistent method to organize details.** When describing a physical object or space, don't jerk the reader from side to side or back to front—select a method and stick to it. You might go from left to right, top to bottom, or outside to inside, but whatever method you choose, make sure you give your reader enough clues to create an image of the space in their mind. Martin Gansberg uses both a chronological and physical arrangement of details to achieve a chilling effect in "38 Who Saw Murder Didn't Call the Police." By tracing the path Kitty Genovese took as she was brutally attacked and murdered, Gansberg makes the objective details of the story come to life. Organization is equally important when describing abstract concepts such as *time* or *love*. If you don't proceed through your description in a methodical manner, your readers will get lost.

Martin Gansberg

38 Who Saw Murder Didn't Call the Police

After starting as a reporter for the *New York Times* in 1942, Martin Gansberg worked his way up through many editorial positions, rising to the level of editor of the *Times'* international edition. This column, based on a 1964 incident that shocked even the most jaded New Yorkers, merited Gansberg several journalism awards for the "vivid picture" it created. Reprinted to the sobered readers of newspapers across the country, it remains one of the most elegantly crafted pieces of journalistic writing in American history. Note how Gansberg makes his dramatic point simply by describing the events that happened that morning.

FOR MORE THAN HALF AN HOUR 38 RESPECTABLE, law-abiding citizens in   1
Queens watched a killer stalk and stab a woman in three separate attacks in
Kew Gardens.

Twice their chatter and the sudden glow of their bedroom lights inter-   2
rupted him and frightened him off. Each time he returned, sought her out,
and stabbed her again. Not one person telephoned the police during the assault; one witness called after the woman was dead.

That was two weeks ago today.   3

Still shocked is Assistant Chief Inspector Frederick M. Lussen, in charge   4
of the borough's detectives and a veteran of 25 years of homicide investigations. He can give a matter-of-fact recitation on many murders. But the Kew
Gardens slaying baffles him—not because it is a murder, but because the "good
people" failed to call the police.

"As we have reconstructed the crime," he said, "the assailant had three   5
chances to kill this woman during a 35-minute period. He returned twice to
complete the job. If we had been called when he first attacked, the woman
might not be dead now."

This is what the police say happened beginning at 3:20 A.M. in the staid,   6
middle-class, tree-lined Austin Street area:

Twenty-eight-year-old Catherine Genovese, who was called Kitty by al-   7
most everyone in the neighborhood, was returning home from her job as
manager of a bar in Hollis. She parked her red Fiat in a lot adjacent to the
Kew Gardens Long Island Rail Road Station, facing Mowbray Place. Like
many residents of the neighborhood, she had parked there day after day since
her arrival from Connecticut a year ago, although the railroad frowns on the
practice.

8   She turned off the lights of her car, locked the door, and started to walk the 100 feet to the entrance of her apartment at 82-70 Austin Street, which is in a Tudor building, with stores in the first floor and apartments on the second.

9   The entrance to the apartment is in the rear of the building because the front is rented to retail stores. At night the quiet neighborhood is shrouded in the slumbering darkness that marks most residential areas.

10   Miss Genovese noticed a man at the far end of the lot, near a seven-story apartment house at 82-40 Austin Street. She halted. Then, nervously, she headed up Austin Street toward Lefferts Boulevard, where there is a call box to the 102nd Police Precinct in nearby Richmond Hill.

11   She got as far as a street light in front of a bookstore before the man grabbed her. She screamed. Lights went on in the 10-story apartment house at 82-67 Austin Street, which faces the bookstore. Windows slid open and voices punctuated the early-morning stillness.

12   Miss Genovese screamed: "Oh, my God, he stabbed me! Please help me! Please help me!"

13   From one of the upper windows in the apartment house, a man called down: "Let that girl alone!"

14   The assailant looked up at him, shrugged and walked down Austin Street toward a white sedan parked a short distance away. Miss Genovese struggled to her feet.

15   Lights went out. The killer returned to Miss Genovese, now trying to make her way around the side of the building by the parking lot to get to her apartment. The assailant stabbed her again.

16   "I'm dying!" she shrieked, "I'm dying!"

17   Windows were opened again, and lights went on in many apartments. The assailant got into his car and drove away. Miss Genovese staggered to her feet. A city bus, Q-10, the Lefferts Boulevard line to Kennedy International Airport, passed. It was 3:35 A.M.

18   The assailant returned. By then, Miss Genovese had crawled to the back of the building, where the freshly painted brown doors to the apartment house held out hope for safety. The killer tried the first door; she wasn't there. At the second door, 82-62 Austin Street, he saw her slumped on the floor at the foot of the stairs. He stabbed her a third time—fatally.

19   It was 3:50 by the time the police received their first call, from a man who was a neighbor of Miss Genovese. In two minutes they were at the scene. The neighbor, a 70-year-old woman, and another woman were the only persons on the street. Nobody else came forward.

20   The man explained that he had called the police after much deliberation.

He had phoned a friend in Nassau County for advice and then he had crossed the roof of the building to the apartment of the elderly woman to get her to make the call.

"I didn't want to get involved," he sheepishly told the police.   21

Six days later, the police arrested Winston Moseley, a 29-year-old business-   22 machine operator, and charged him with homicide. Moseley had no previous record. He is married, has two children and owns a home at 133-19 Sutter Avenue, South Ozone Park, Queens. On Wednesday, a court committed him to Kings County Hospital for psychiatric observation.

When questioned by the police, Moseley also said that he had slain Mrs.   23 Annie May Johnson, 24, of 146-12 133rd Avenue, Jamaica, on Feb. 29 and Barbara Kralik, 15, of 174-17 140th Avenue, Springfield Gardens, last July. In the Kralik case, the police are holding Alvin L. Mitchell, who is said to have confessed to that slaying.

The police stressed how simple it would have been to have gotten in touch   24 with them. "A phone call," said one of the detectives, "would have done it." The police may be reached by dialing "O" for operator or SPring 7-3100.

Today witnesses from the neighborhood, which is made up of one-family   25 homes in the $35,000 to $60,000 range with the exception of the two apartment houses near the railroad station, find it difficult to explain why they didn't call the police.

A housewife, knowingly if quite casually, said, "We thought it was a lover's   26 quarrel." A husband and wife both said, "Frankly, we were afraid." They seemed aware of the fact that events might have been different. A distraught woman, wiping her hands on her apron, said, "I didn't want my husband to get involved."

One couple, now willing to talk about that night, said they heard the first   27 screams. The husband looked thoughtfully at the bookstore where the killer first grabbed Miss Genovese.

"We went to the window to see what was happening," he said, 'but the   28 light from our bedroom made it difficult to see the street." The wife, still apprehensive, added: "I put out the light and we were able to see better."

Asked why they hadn't called the police, she shrugged and replied: "I don't   29 know."

A man peeked out from the slight opening in the doorway to his apart-   30 ment and rattled off an account of the killer's second attack. Why hadn't he called the police at the time? "I was tired," he said without emotion. "I went back to bed."

It was 4:25 A.M. when the ambulance arrived to take the body of Miss   31 Genovese. It drove off. "Then," a solemn police detective said, "the people came out."

George Simpson

The War Room at Bellevue

George Simpson, who runs a public relations firm specializing in Internet and online communications, has been public affairs director for *Newsweek* and vice president of corporate communications for Simon & Schuster. He writes stories for newspapers and magazines such as the *New York Times*, *Glamour*, and *Sport* in his spare time. Simpson wrote "The War Room at Bellevue" for *New York* magazine while he was still working for *Newsweek*.

1   BELLEVUE. THE NAME CONJURES UP IMAGES of an indoor war zone: the wounded and bleeding lining the halls, screaming for help while harried doctors in blood-stained smocks rush from stretcher to stretcher, fighting a losing battle against exhaustion and the crushing number of injured. "What's worse," says a longtime Bellevue nurse, "is that we have this image of being a hospital only for. . ." She pauses, then lowers her voice, "for crazy people."

2   Though neither battlefield nor Bedlam is a valid image, there is something extraordinary about the monstrous complex that spreads for five blocks along First Avenue in Manhattan. It is said best by the head nurse in Adult Emergency Service: "If you have any chance for survival, you have it here." Survival—that is why they come. Why do injured cops drive by a half-dozen other hospitals to be treated at Bellevue? They've seen the Bellevue emergency team in action.

3   9:00 P.M. It is a Friday night in the Bellevue emergency room. The after-work crush is over (those who've suffered through the day, only to come for help after the five-o'clock whistle has blown) and it is nearly silent except for the mutter of voices at the admitting desk, where administrative personnel discuss who will go for coffee. Across the spotless white-walled lobby, ten people sit quietly, passively, in pastel plastic chairs, waiting for word of relatives or to see doctors. In the past 24 hours, 300 people have come to the Bellevue Adult Emergency Service. Fewer than 10 percent were true emergencies. One man sleeps fitfully in the emergency ward while his heartbeat, respiration, and blood pressure are monitored by control consoles mounted over his bed. Each heartbeat trips a tiny bleep in the monitor, which attending nurses can hear across the ward. A half hour ago, doctors in the trauma room withdrew a six-inch stiletto blade from his back. When he is stabilized, the patient will be moved upstairs to the twelve-bed Surgical Intensive Care Unit.

4   9:05 P.M. An ambulance backs into the receiving bay, its red and yellow lights flashing in and out of the lobby. A split second later, the glass doors

burst open as a nurse and an attendant roll a mobile stretcher into the lobby. When the nurse screams, "Emergency!" the lobby explodes with activity as the way is cleared to the trauma room. Doctors appear from nowhere and transfer the bloodied body of a black man to the treatment table. Within seconds his clothes are stripped away, revealing a tiny stab wound in his left side. Three doctors and three nurses rush around the victim, each performing a task necessary to begin treatment. Intravenous needles are inserted into his arms and groin. A doctor draws blood for the lab, in case surgery is necessary. A nurse begins inserting a catheter into the victim's penis and continues to feed in tubing until the catheter reaches the bladder. Urine flows through the tube into a plastic bag. Doctors are glad not to see blood in the urine. Another nurse records pulse and blood pressure.

The victim is in good shape. He shivers slightly, although the trauma room   5
is exceedingly warm. His face is bloodied, but shows no major lacerations. A third nurse, her elbow propped on the treatment table, asks the man a series of questions, trying to quickly outline his medical history. He answers abruptly. He is drunk. His left side is swabbed with yellow disinfectant and a doctor injects a local anesthetic. After a few seconds another doctor inserts his finger into the wound. It sinks in all the way to the knuckle. He begins to rotate his finger like a child trying to get a marble out of a milk bottle. The patient screams bloody murder and tries to struggle free.

Meanwhile in the lobby, a security guard is ejecting a derelict who has   6
begun to drink from a bottle hidden in his coat pocket. "He's a regular, was in here just two days ago," says a nurse. "We checked him pretty good then, so he's probably okay now. Can you believe those were clean clothes we gave him?" The old man, blackened by filth, leaves quietly.

9:15 P.M. A young Hispanic man interrupts, saying his pregnant girl   7
friend, sitting outside in his car, is bleeding heavily from her vagina. She is rushed into an examination room, treated behind closed doors, and rolled into the observation ward, where, much later in the night, a gynecologist will treat her in a special room—the same one used to examine rape victims. Nearby, behind curtains, the neurologist examines an old white woman to determine if her headaches are due to head injury. They are not.

9:45 P.M. The trauma room has been cleared and cleaned mercilessly. The   8
examination rooms are three-quarters full—another overdose, two asthmatics, a young woman with abdominal pains. In the hallway, a derelict who has been sleeping it off urinates all over the stretcher. He sleeps on while attendants change his clothes. An ambulance—one of four that patrol Manhattan for Bellevue from 42nd Street to Houston, river to river—delivers a middle-aged white woman and two cops, the three of them soaking wet. The woman has escaped from the psychiatric floor of a nearby hospital and tried to drown herself in the East River. The cops fished her out. She lies on a stretcher shiver-

ing beneath white blankets. Her eyes stare at the ceiling. She speaks clearly when an administrative worker begins routine questioning. The cops are given hospital gowns and wait to receive tetanus shots and gamma globulin—a hedge against infection from the befouled river water. They will hang around the E.R. for another two hours, telling their story to as many as six other policemen who show up to hear it. The woman is rolled into an examination room, where a male nurse speaks gently: "They tell me you fell into the river." "No," says the woman, "I jumped. I have to commit suicide." "Why?" asks the nurse. "Because I'm insane and I can't help [it]. I have to die." The nurse gradually discovers the woman has a history of psychological problems. She is given dry bedclothes and placed under guard in the hallway. She lies on her side, staring at the wall.

9   The pace continues of increase. Several more overdose victims arrive by ambulance. One, a young black woman, had done a striptease on the street just before passing out. A second black woman is semiconscious and spends the better part of her time at Bellevue alternately cursing at and pleading with the doctors. Attendants find a plastic bottle coated with methadone in the pocket of a Hispanic O.D. The treatment is routinely the same, and sooner or later involves vomiting. Just after doctors begin to treat the O.D., he vomits great quantities of wine and methadone in all directions. "Lovely business, huh?" laments one of the doctors. A young nurse confides that if there were other true emergencies, the overdose victims would be given lower priority. "You can't help thinking they did it to themselves," she says, "while the others are accident victims."

10   10:30 P.M. A policeman who twisted his knee struggling with an "alleged perpetrator" is examined and released. By 10:30, the lobby is jammed with friends and relatives of patients in various stages of treatment and recovery. The attendant who also functions as a translator for Hispanic patients adds chairs to accommodate the overflow. The medical walk-in rate stays steady—between eight and ten patients waiting. A pair of derelicts, each with battered eyes, appear at the admitting desk. One has a dramatically swollen face laced with black stitches.

11   11:30 P.M. The husband of the attempted suicide arrives. He thanks the police for saving his wife's life, then talks at length with doctors about her condition. She continues to stare into the void and does not react when her husband approaches her stretcher.

12   Meanwhile, patients arrive in the lobby at a steady pace. A young G.I. on leave has lower-back pains; a Hispanic man complains of pains in his side; occasionally parents hurry through the adult E.R. carrying children to the pediatric E.R. A white woman of about 50 marches into the lobby from the walk-in entrance. Dried blood covers her right eyebrow and upper lip. She begins to perform. "I was assaulted on 28th and Lexington, I was," she says grandly,

"and I don't have to take it *anymore*. I was a bride 21 years ago and, God, I was beautiful then." She has captured the attention of all present. "I was there when the boys came home—on Memorial Day—and I don't have to take this kind of treatment."

As midnight approaches, the nurses prepare for the shift change. They   13 must brief the incoming staff and make sure all reports are up-to-date. One young brunet says, "Christ, I'm gonna go home and take a shower—I smell like vomit."

11:50 P.M. The triage nurse is questioning an old black man about chest   14 pains, and a Hispanic woman is having an asthma attack, when an ambulance, its sirens screaming full tilt, roars into the receiving bay. There is a split-second pause as everyone drops what he or she is doing and looks up. Then all hell breaks loose. Doctors and nurses are suddenly sprinting full-out toward the trauma room. The glass doors burst open and the occupied stretcher is literally run past me. Cops follow. It is as if a comet has whooshed by. In the trauma room it all becomes clear. A half-dozen doctors and nurses surround the lifeless form of a Hispanic man with a shotgun hole in his neck the size of your fist. Blood pours from a second gaping wound in his chest. A respirator is slammed over his face, making his chest rise and fall as if he were breathing. "No pulse," reports one doctor. A nurse jumps on a stool and, leaning over the man, begins to pump his chest with her palms. "No blood pressure," screams another nurse. The ambulance driver appears shaken, "I never thought I'd get here in time," he stutters. More doctors from the trauma team upstairs arrive. Wrappings from syringes and gauze pads fly through the air. The victim's eyes are open yet devoid of life. His body takes on a yellow tinge. A male nurse winces at the gunshot wound. "This guy really pissed off somebody," he says. This is no ordinary shooting. It is an execution. IV's are jammed into the body in the groin and arms. One doctor has been plugging in an electrocardiograph and asks everyone to stop for a second so he can get a reading. "Forget it," shouts the doctor in charge. "No time." "Take it easy, Jimmy," someone yells at the head physician. It is apparent by now that the man is dead, but the doctors keep trying injections and finally they slit open the chest and reach inside almost up to their elbows. They feel the extent of the damage and suddenly it is all over. "I told 'em he was dead," says one nurse, withdrawing. "They didn't listen." The room is very still. The doctors are momentarily disgusted, then go on about their business. The room clears quickly. Finally there is only a male nurse and the still-warm body, now waxy-yellow, with huge ribs exposed on both sides of the chest and giant holes in both sides of the neck. The nurse speculates that this is yet another murder in a Hispanic political struggle that has brought many such victims to Bellevue. He marvels at the extent of the wounds and repeats, "This guy was really blown away."

15   MIDNIGHT. A hysterical woman is hustled through the lobby into an examination room. It is the dead man's wife, and she is nearly delirious. "I know he's dead, I know he's dead," she screams over and over. Within moments the lobby is filled with anxious relatives of the victim, waiting for word on his condition. The police are everywhere asking questions, but most people say they saw nothing. One young woman says she heard six shots, two louder than the other four. At some point, word is passed that the man is, in fact, dead. Another woman breaks down in hysterics; everywhere young Hispanics are crying and comforting each other. Plainclothes detectives make a quick examination of the body, check on the time of pronouncement of death, and begin to ask questions, but the bereaved are too stunned to talk. The rest of the uninvolved people in the lobby stare dumbly, their injuries suddenly paling in light of a death.

16   12:30 A.M. A black man appears at the admissions desk and says he drank poison by mistake. He is told to have a seat. The ambulance brings in a young white woman, her head wrapped in white gauze. She is wailing terribly. A girl friend stands over her, crying, and a boyfriend clutches the injured woman's hands, saying, "I'm here, don't worry, I'm here." The victim has fallen downstairs at a friend's house. Attendants park her stretcher against the wall to wait for an examination room to clear. There are eight examination rooms and only three doctors. Unless you are truly an emergency, you will wait. One doctor is stitching up the eyebrow of a drunk who's been punched out. The friends of the woman who fell down the stairs glance up at the doctors anxiously, wondering why their friend isn't being treated faster.

17   1:10 A.M. A car pulls into the bay and a young Hispanic asks if a shooting victim has been brought here. The security guard blurts out, "He's dead." The young man is stunned. He peels his tires leaving the bay.

18   1:20 A.M. The young woman of the stairs is getting stitches in a small gash over her left eye when the same ambulance driver who brought in the gunshot victim delivers a man who has been stabbed in the back on East 3rd Street. Once again the trauma room goes from 0 to 60 in five seconds. The patient is drunk, which helps him endure the pain of having the catheter inserted through his penis into his bladder. Still he yells, "That hurts like a bastard," then adds sheepishly, "Excuse me, ladies." But he is not prepared for what comes next. An X-ray reveals a collapsed right lung. After just a shot of local anesthetic, the doctor slices open his side and inserts a long plastic tube. Internal bleeding had kept the lung pressed down and prevented it from reinflating. The tube releases the pressure. The ambulance driver says the cops grabbed the guy who ran the eight-inch blade into the victim's back. "That's not the one," says the man. "They got the wrong guy." A nurse reports that there is not much of the victim's type

blood available at the hospital. One of the doctors says that's okay, he won't need surgery. Meanwhile blood pours from the man's knife wound and the tube in his side. As the nurses work, they chat about personal matters, yet they respond immediately to orders from either doctor. "How ya doin'?" the doctor asks the patient. "Okay," he says. His blood spatters on the floor.

So it goes into the morning hours. A Valium overdose, a woman who 19 fainted, a man who went through the windshield of his car. More overdoses. More drunks with split eyebrows and chins. The doctors and nurses work without complaint. "This is nothing, about normal, I'd say," concludes the head nurse. "No big deal."

Student Essay

Adam Burrell

Time Torture

In this essay, Adam describes what truly must be every student's object of hatred—the clock radio. Notice how he uses the device of personification to make his loathing of his clock seem more . . . well, personal. Adam uses hyperbole—like the "millions" of dials—to excellent comic effect. You must be brave to use comedy well: there are many situations where it may be seen as inappropriate.

DON'T GET ME WRONG—I'M REALLY NOT PARANOID. I mean, my alarm clock 1 looks like a typical generic style clock radio. Nothing appears outwardly abnormal at all. In fact, it doesn't have any truly distinguishing features at all, and I'm tempted to say that it's an average, run-of-the-mill, nondescript clock radio. But, since it's a cop-out to describe something as "nondescript" (if not outright contradictory), I'll give a quick rundown of it. I've owned this clock radio, a Realistic Chronomatic 213, for a month now, and it's still difficult to remember exactly what it looks like. There it is, a rectangular box sitting on my desk in the corner, six feet from my bed, with a bright red digital readout saying 9:39. The colon between the 9 and the 39—no, now 40—flashes on and off once per second, 24 hours a day. To the right of the time display is the radio tuning dial, set near 97 FM, probably KBCO Boulder. Also on the rectangular front face, just below the clock display and the radio tuning dial, is a row of four small round switches, used to set the time and the alarm. The top and the sides of the radio are an artificial wood-grain finish, trimmed with black and separated from the front panel by a chrome strip. Centered on its top is a small square speaker grill.

2   Yeah, this alarm clock would seem like a normal, well-adjusted appliance to most people, but that's because they don't have to live with it. Just by looking at it, a person wouldn't sense that this clock radio carried a grudge and had general anti-social tendencies. Even I didn't notice anything strange until recently. First, small irritating things became apparent. For instance, the way it stares at night, annoyingly blinking its stupid red colon. After a half-hour of watching the clock gaze back, it's obvious that the stare isn't a benign one; it has the qualities of an unpleasant sneer, that certain executioner's look of someone in ultimate control. Then, I noticed how time always seemed to speed up at night while I slept. I could almost hear that damn blood-red colon flashing faster and faster, but as soon as I would open my eyes it would skid back down to once per second, once per second. The unnerving part, though, is that the clock speeds up in direct proportion to the amount of sleep that I need—so even if I go to bed early the night before a big exam, I still wake up with severe jetlag.

3   This clock's attitude problem doesn't become blatantly apparent until early morning, however. The hours of darkness slowly convert it into a remorseless predatory creature, primed to terrorize. Yes, terrorize. Remaining utterly silent and motionless so as not to stir its unsuspecting comatose victim, the clock waits. Mercilessly it savors its position of power as the final seconds slip by. And then it strikes. Noise and chaos, resembling the detonation of a medium-sized nuclear device in the corner of my room, slam out of its tiny speaker. At five in the morning. Actually, at five in the morning, the sound has more of a physical quality, roughly equivalent to a chainsaw being started in the left ear while a rake crashes into the jaw. Instinctively, my body, instantly brought from suspended animation to adrenaline overload, lunges in the general direction of the demonic box on the desk. My hand swats at every small knob—there are now millions of them—until it slaps the right switch in the right direction, snuffing out the noise and the pain.

4   Every morning, as I lie limply on the floor, I can see the clock display staring straight ahead, blinking its damned red colon in the morning sun, once per second, once per second, and I know it's trying not to snicker. I'm not paranoid—the clock really does hate me.

Lani Kwon Meilgaard

An "Other" American

On Being Multiracial-American

Lani Kwon Meilgaard grew up on the islands of Oahu and Maui, where being multi-ethnic was not unusual. She graduated with honors from the University of Hawaii at Manoa with a degree in English. She received her M.A. in Creative Writing from the University of Colorado at Boulder, where she wrote this essay, which originally appeared in the e-zine *Interracial Voice*. Meilgaard lives in California where she is a professor of English writing. She has just completed her first novel, *A Place Without Regret*.

San Bernardino, California
December 1967

"But Sharon," said my grandmother, sitting across from Mom at the dinner table, buttering a piece of white bread, "won't your children be. . . ." She paused, searching for the right words, ". . . confused?"   1

It was incredibly hot in the kitchen, and Mom could feel rivulets of sweat running down her sides under her pullover and in the waistband of pink pedal pushers. Heat continued to radiate from the gas oven. Mom's mind was only half on the conversation. She was thinking of the most recent letter she had received. She was thinking of Dad, who was no longer a music major at Redlands University and had narrowly escaped being drafted into the Army. They had both realized that he could have been mistaken for Vietnamese and shot in "friendly fire" if he was fighting on the ground. Enlisted in the Navy instead, he was at boot camp in San Diego, soon to be 2nd class petty officer/ machinist mate on the U.S.S. Hancock, stationed off the northern coast of Vietnam.   2

"Don't you think it will be difficult for your children?" Grandma held the slice of bread out as if it were a crystal ball or flattened palm in which Mom would certainly see her future.   3

"What do you mean, Mom?"   4

"Getting married to this . . . this . . . Japanese person." Grandma's thin lips shriveled as if she had tasted something bitter.   5

"Mom," she sighed long-sufferingly, "Michael's an American, not Japa . . ."   6

"He's dark, Sharon." Grandma hissed what she had up until that point kept to herself.   7

"So?" Mom said, only realizing she had spoken aloud when she saw her mother's pursed lips.   8

Grandma sighed, "Don't you see?"   9

10   "We've already set the date. January 26th."

11   "Sharon, I'm trying to help you . . ."

12   Mom stabbed at the dry roast chicken breast on her plate. She didn't look up as she said,

13   "The best way to help is to give me your blessing."

14   "Your children will hate you."

15   Grandma spat out the words.

16   Mom sat there stunned. She heard the screen door slam behind her and exhaled, not realizing that she had been holding her breath. She turned to her father.

17   It had been a rough day for him, working construction in Riverside County. He carefully wiped his face, bald head and neck with an old red bandanna—an indication of his reluctance to get involved—before saying, "It's your choice."

18   It was my parents' choice. California was the first state, in 1948, to decide that interracial marriages were *not* unconstitutional. It took almost twenty years, until 1967, for anti-miscegenation laws to be struck down nationwide in the aptly named Supreme Court decision, *Loving vs. Virginia.*

19   Grandma did not "forgive" Mom for marrying my father until after I was born, until after she got to know my father and his family. It wasn't easy for her. I think she genuinely believed she had been trying to help, offering my mother "good" advice. I became the living symbol of what my grandmother had feared most—World War II propaganda come to life—"the enemy" marrying into the family, changing the blood, changing the future.

20   I am not sure if I have forgiven *her* yet.

21   I look into the mirror and try to see myself as a stranger might: dark brown eyes and hair, full lips and light skin. I can see in the slight curving of my eyes my paternal grandparents' Asian faces, my mother's Native American features. Under bright, artificial light, I can see the slight yellow cast of my skin, my irises so dark that I can only see the pupil if I look close.

22   In Hawaii, I grew up *hapa haole*, of *mixed race.* But in England and in Colorado, the identity *hapa* was taken from me; I was labeled *white*, rather than being categorized as *other*, like many of my darker-skinned friends. In California, I am once again *hapa* and difficult to conveniently categorize, although here, often other Asian-Americans (unless they are originally from Hawaii) do not recognize me as another Asian. Never before was my race and ethnicity an issue to me, and I have tried to discover why. How has my racial identity shifted? It wasn't a change from the inside, but rather from the outside. It is based upon other people's assumptions, differing in each of the places I have lived.

23   For many years, the cultural model of assimilation, "the melting pot," was touted as the only way to be an American. Yet the standard for this model was based on the politically and economically more powerful European settlers'

values and cultural norms. In the 1960s and '70s, a more inclusive ideology was suggested—"a stew" or "mixed salad"—whereby immigrants to America might maintain their distinct cultures, languages and traditions, their *ethnicity* or *ancestry*, while at the same time recognizing their "Americanness."

Today, rising numbers of Americans are, like myself, of mixed ethnicity. 24 Many of us are proud of this heritage and interested in our multiple ancestries. We do not fit the limiting, artificial categories of race—White, Black or Negro, American Indian or Alaskan Native, and Asian or Pacific Islander—outlined in Statistical Directive 15, which was adopted in 1978 by the Office of Management and Budget and used in the 1990 U.S. Census of the Population. We are "Multiracial-Americans."

Nationality is a complex and often shifting set of political, historical and 25 socio-economic circumstances. A group of people recognize themselves as a country. They identify themselves by their country of origin. At the birth of our relatively young nation, perhaps people wanted to be known *only* by their new national identity—American.

Yet saying I am simply "American" not only fails to address the complex- 26 ity of my being: It nullifies the elements that make me whole. It disregards my ethnicity and ancestry and the many cultural values attached. When I am labeled *white*, I am not seen in relation to the other parts of myself I value. For in addition to being of several European ethnicities—Scottish, Irish, Dutch, German, English, French, and Spanish—I am also Japanese, Korean, Chinese, and Native American (Iroquois and Delaware).

When your veins flow with the blood of twelve nations, you belong to 27 none, yet are encompassed by all.

Brunswick, Georgia
March 30, 1969

When Mom filled out the application for my birth certificate, she was faced 28 with the following question:

Race of child: 29
__White __Black.   30

"But my baby's half-Asian."   31
The nurse, a Caucasian matriarch dressed in starched white, many shades 32 lighter than her skin, replied, "Honey, that baby ain't Black, so she's White." And so I am, according to Georgia Department of Public Health records.

My father, too, was classified *"White"* on my birth certificate, but he gained 33 none of the privileges whites at this time took for granted—something as simple as the right to walk by or to go into a store without being stared at by others.

34   Lea, the middle sister, was born in Jacksonville, Florida and was classified "Malaysian," even though she has no Malay blood. This practice was apparently discontinued in 1971, when my youngest sister, Laura, was born in Lamar, California. According to my mother, she is not classified by race.

35   Have these slips of paper changed who we are?

36   A paper that says you're white means nothing when your dark-skinned, Asian father moves back to Hawaii—where many Asian-Americans live—taking his family with him just to feel he belongs.

Makakilo, Hawaii 1978
Defining the "Other," Hawaiian Style

37   *Haole* n. White person, American, Englishman, Caucasian; formerly, any foreigner.

38   v. ["To be haole"] To act like a white person, to ape the white people, or assume airs of superiority, often said disparagingly, especially of half-whites. (Pukui 58)

39   At my elementary school, the last day of school was called "Kill Haole Day." It was when kids of the non-white races, who were in the majority, would pick on white kids—call them names, throw rotten eggs at them, beat them up.

40   I don't remember anything ever actually happening on this day; most of the white kids stayed at home, and most of the kids talking about participating were part-white themselves. All I remember was trying to fit in, being a tomboy, acting as if I were tough. I did not know that there were decades of suppressed rage behind what we were doing.

41   We were unaware of the implications behind racial jokes—which in Hawaii were common but not taken seriously or intended to offend. Everybody made fun of everybody, knew all the local stereotypes—that Chinese were *pake*, interested only in money; that Japanese were xenophobic and ambitious; that whites were greedy and loud; while Hawaiians were labeled lazy. In some ways, these racial jokes provided a safety valve for the unnamed feelings many of us did not acknowledge.

42   Our persecution of white children re-enacted on a smaller scale the resentment of some of our parents, grandparents and great-grandparents, the collective anger against generations of oppression by white *lunas*, overseers on the plantations, and white missionaries. We were emulating a dangerous precedent about which we knew nothing, and yet we somehow remained ignorant that this was racism—in our own school, our own neighborhood.

43   Would I have held down little Aaron—the boy whose breath was tinged with the sour odor of milk and fear—while Kaui beat his white skin red and

purple? These were the colors of our anger, of misunderstanding and revenge. For what? The fact that Aaron did better in class than we? Or that his clothes were newer and more expensive? Or was it his Southern accent that we disliked, his way of ignoring the taunts and jeers every day as he got off the bus?

Aaron does not exist. He is all the children who did not fit in, some white, some black, but more often defined as *from the Mainland*, a place that was too far away and alien for many of us to understand. 44

"Racism" was something that happened on the Mainland: Whites against Blacks. We did not think that racism could happen in Hawaii. We did not think. 45

Pearl City, Hawaii
Christmas 1982

Christmas festivities in my family consisted of a mixture of American tradition and several local customs unique to the region: eating *kim chee* and sushi with our Christmas turkey or ham, making a gingerbread house garnished with imported Japanese candy bought at Shirokiya, and sometimes having a picnic of hamburgers and *lomi lomi* salmon at the beach. 46

On this occasion, my sisters and I had decorated our living room with the usual Christmas finery. In one corner a Douglas Fir (one of the trees shipped in by the thousands from the mainland U.S. in refrigerated Matson shipping containers, the oddity of which we took for granted) wilted in its solution of sugar water. We made a construction paper fireplace where we hung our stockings. Antique hand-blown glass ornaments and handicrafts we had made in school (like the blue sequin-covered eggshell ornament which held my front-toothless 5th grade portrait) were in positions of prestige on the tree. 47

On Christmas morning we woke our parents up at 5 a.m. and began digging into our loot. The room smelled of Christmas pine and excitement. There are several gifts I remember from that year: a pink Barbie sportscar, silly putty and, from our paternal grandparents on Maui, dolls in costumes from around the world. 48

The card was inscribed, "To the girls. Value your ancestors. Love, Grandma and Grandpa Kwon." 49

Each doll stood about six inches tall and, as promised, was dressed in a "traditional" costume. Miss Japan wore a kimono adorned with a cherry blossom pattern and a golden *obi*, and she had an elaborate hairstyle. Was she from Tokyo or Osaka? The box did not specify. Miss America wore leather buckskin and beaded moccasins. She was an amalgam of popular images of Native Americans, like the Disneyfied Pocahontas would be years later. Miss Spain had a long flamenco-style dress, and in her hair there was a veil held by 50 a miniature carved wooden comb. She was not from Galicia, the Northwestern region of Spain (once a part of Portugal) from whence our great-grandmother came. Yet we thought of her as being Spanish.

51   Each doll had some item of clothing that made her representative of her nation, and each doll had the appropriately colored skin and eyes to match the perceived norm of her country of origin. But each doll failed to fully represent the ethnic and cultural diversity within each country.

52   What I discovered later is something difficult to explain. My sisters and I are Japanese, Native American, Spanish, etc. . . . , but who we are as people, as "individuals," differs greatly from each of the nations represented by the dolls.

53   We have an identity, but it is not determined by country of origin. It is based on what our family has done together or what we have done individually—like driving to Hanauma Bay to snorkel, or taking a Kentucky Fried Chicken picnic up to the mountains of Aiea, or helping Grandma Kwon prepare *bul go gi*, Korean bar-be-cue beef—that makes us who we are.

54   Growing up was a mish-mash of cultural traditions. We'd watch Disney movies like *The Jungle Book* and *Cinderella* on one day and dance hula the next. Hawaii's multiethnic "culture" offered us these choices, choices we could make according to individual taste and inclination. The cultural activities I enjoyed, like the Japanese *Obon* festivals in the summer at the local Hongwanji to honor our dead relatives, were sometimes different than those my sisters chose to attend.

55   My sisters and I are *individuals.* Doesn't the intrinsic meaning of that word allow for difference?

Oxford, England
1992

56 Justin, my husband, had been working in England for about two years. He was responsible for arranging housing, excursions and social events for an American agency which brought American students to Oxford to study. Justin's father is Danish, his mother English, Irish and Huguenot French. He is a British citizen by birth but grew up in Monterrey, Mexico and Detroit, Michigan. He, like myself, has always felt "different." But for him this feeling has come from inside—the feeling of being an observer, antsider—a person who has adapted to living in many different countries. It is an altogether different experience when this feeling of being an outsider is imposed on you from the outside.

57   On a typically gray evening, Justin and I were invited to a dinner party by an estate agent ("real estate agent" in American-English) with whom Justin often consulted. The night air smelled of ivy and dampness. The estate agent and his mother had offered to pick us up.

"So, how're you adjusting to our weather?"   58

At first I did not realize that the estate agent was speaking to me. He   59
glanced at me in the rearview mirror, his horn-rimmed glasses and balding
pate glowing slightly red from a traffic light. He and Justin had been talking
business, while I was looking out the window at the rapidly passing landscape,
lights whizzing by. "Oh, yes . . . I am. Thank you," I replied, uncertain as to
why I had become unaccountably shy and withdrawn since I had come to England—a 180 degree turn from my usual personality.

The estate agent continued talking with Justin. His mother—a woman   60
roughly in her sixties, wearing an old-fashioned overcoat, wool dress and
stockings, whom I (knowing it was a stereotype) imagined knitted, owned a
cat and never turned up the heat in her house—offered a word or two occasionally. I tuned in and out on what they were saying: "Yes, housing starts
these days . . . outrageous. . . . New apartments available? . . . Oxford's growing too fast. . . . students. . . . would be a suburb of London if not for the
zoning laws. . . ."

We spun around one of the freeway medians, which in England are cir-   61
cular and called "roundabouts." Suddenly, I heard the words, ". . . Japanese
. . . yes, my wife is part Asian." Justin said this proudly, holding my hand. I
noticed the mother's shoulders stiffen. Her son said nothing until we arrived
at the house.

For the rest of the evening the estate agent's mother refused to speak with   62
me, avoided my gaze. Her son eyed me strangely from under his bushy eyebrows.

At the time I racked my brain to discover what I might have said or done   63
to offend them. Later, I realized it was nothing I had done, but simply who I
was.

USA 1990 Census of Population Form: When it comes to the question of   64
race, here's what you see:

RACE
Fill ONE circle for the race that the person considers himself/herself to be.

○ White   ○ Black or Negro   ○ Indian (Amer.)
         If Indian (Amer.), print the name of the enrolled or principal tribe
○ Eskimo   ○ Chinese   ○ Japanese
○ Asian Indian If Other Asian or Pacific Islander (API),
○ Aleut Asian or Pacific Islander (API)
○ Other API (Print below) Cambodian, and so on.
○ Samoan print one group, for example: Hmong, Guamanian Fijian, Laotian,
    Thai, Tongan, Pakistani

○ Filipino   ○ Hawaiian   ○ Korean
○ Vietnamese   ○ Other race (Print below)

65   Census records are kept as statistical data for a variety of Federal and State Government uses—educational funding, city and state grants, to enforce the Voting Rights Act and equal employment regulations, just to name a few. People are asked to "Fill ONE circle for the race each person considers himself/herself to be" (Census E-2). But the race categorizations seem so arbitrary when you read:

66   White—Includes persons who indicated their race as "White" or reported entries such as Canadian, German, Italian, Lebanese, Near Easterner, Arab, or Polish.

67   Black—Includes persons who indicated their race as "Black or Negro" or reported entries such as African American, Afro-American, Black Puerto Rican, Jamaican, Nigerian, West Indian, or Haitian (B-29).

68   If you consider yourself of European or even Middle Eastern descent, you are categorized by the government as "White." If you consider yourself African or Caribbean (which historically has also had interracial children born to parents of African, Indian and/or European races), you are categorized "Black."

69   An article entitled "The 'Other' Americans" in the June 1994 issue of American Demographics, illustrates how outdated this thinking is:

70   The 1990 census questionnaire asked respondents to put themselves into a racial category and to indicate their ethnicity and ancestry elsewhere. Respondents who felt that they didn't fit into one of the four categories checked a box marked "other race." The number of people who checked that box increased 45 percent between the 1980 and 1990 censuses, to 9.8 million. That's about 1 in 25 Americans (37).

71   Part of this increase is due to the fact that if you write in a "race" which is categorized by the government as an "ethnicity," your responses are categorized "other race." According to American Demographics, Statistical Directive 15 "defines Hispanic origin as an ethnic category separate from race" (37). People of Hispanic ethnicity are often categorized as either "white" or "black."

72   But if you are of multiracial heritage, like myself, you cannot list more than one "race" in the box marked "other." The box and classificatory system are too narrow.

73   You cannot, for example, check each and every box that applies to you. If you do so, according to the U.S. Census and Department of Commerce,

either "the race of the mother [is] used" or "the first race reported by the person [is] used" (B-28) to define your race. You may fill in "multiethnic" or "multiracial," but you are categorized anonymously as "other." If you choose to rebel and fill in nothing, "race [is] assigned based upon the re-ported entries of race by other household members" (B-30). In most cases "White" is used. It just happens to be the first category provided on the census form.

Denver, Colorado
October 29, 1994

It was chilly, though still unseasonably warm that fall; the steam vents in the   74
Denver streets released masses of white cloud. I was standing outside Curri-gan Exhibition Hall, site of the 2nd Annual Rocky Mountain Book Festival, with several friends—to see Linda Hogan, a professor of ours at the University of Colorado, and other writers we admired.

Linda arrived, wearing a black velvet tunic, long flowing pants and silver   75
hoop earrings, which brushed against her shoulders. She smiled as she recog-nized our group.

There was a communal shout. "Linda!" "It's good to see you!" "How are   76
you?"

"Linda, you're the only woman I'd get up at six to see," I said laughing as   77
I gave her a hug.

"Me, too," she said, and we all laughed.   78

Linda was swept aside by one of the organizers of the festival toward the   79
author's entrance, as we dashed up the stairs and into the "Agatha Christie" room for her reading.

Our room was full of rows of black, uncomfortable-looking chairs. The   80
ceiling was high, and there was a raised stage before which stood an inauspi-cious wooden podium. We took seats in the second and third rows, amazed that we were so close to the front, having expected mobs for this first reading of the day.

I looked around the room, noticing a few others who had come to hear   81
Linda read: a couple of older men—white hair, denim; a group of women in broomstick skirts and fancy embroidered blouses; a newspaper reporter from the *Rocky Mountain News* who had interviewed Linda a couple of weeks ear-lier about her Colorado Book Award and Lannan Literary Prize; and Sher-man Alexie, the next reader in the room, another writer whom I had come to meet.

The room was too large, yet I felt as if I was in class. Linda was only about   82
five feet away, and her soothing voice reassured me. She read from *Dwellings*, a book of essays about nature she had just completed, then several poems

from *The Book of Medicines.* She read well, slowly, yet with a rhythmic cadence. I blinked with surprise when it was over.

83   The question and answer session that followed was fairly straightforward: How long have you been writing? Who have been your influences? What procedure do you follow when you write? Do you write on a computer or longhand? What inspires your writing? etc. . . . etc. . . .

84   Then, suddenly, one of the men in denim, a throwback, an anachronistic cowboy, asked "the question." His tone of voice was skeptical, as if he thought he was exposing a fraud: a woman who identifies herself as a Native American writer, but who is really white. He asked, "What kind of Indian are you, if you are an Indian . . . and do you pray . . . How do you pray?"

85   Linda took a deep breath, and I saw the anger flash briefly across her eyes. This all occurred in less than a second.

86   I have felt the same twisting in my gut, the blood burning in my veins, at being labeled a fake by those who have read my writing and thought my work "exploitive" and "presumptuous," that I am cashing in on the popularity of minority literature.

87   I have often felt an odd sort of guilt, as well. For by being labeled white by others when I know myself to be part Asian, I have been granted privileges my friends have not. I have felt like an impostor or a spy.

88   Linda's answer was one I wish I could emulate at times like these, full of grace and dignity. She did not get into a lengthy argument. She described herself in terms of the culture with which she most closely identifies. She responded in an even tone of voice, "I am Chickasaw, and my poems are my prayers."

Palo Alto, California
April 13, 1996

89   Filling out applications in order to teach English Composition in local community colleges, I find the following at the end of each questionnaire:

90   The information that you provide will be used for statistical record keeping and reporting only. You will not be identified by name when these statistics are reported, and this information will not be forwarded as part of your application materials.

What is your Racial/Ethnic Group? (Check one)

○ Caucasian   ○ Black   ○ Native American
○ Hispanic/Latino   ○ Asian/Pacific Islander

I could check Asian/Pacific Islander and Caucasian. I am both, but the in-   91
structions clearly say, "Check one." And what does it mean to be Asian/Pa-
cific Islander anyway? The cultures in this region, the "Pacific Rim," are as different and unique from one another as Canada, the United States and Mexico are from each other. Within these countries there are many distinct linguistic and cultural differences.

According to U.S. Census Statistics, published in a February 13, 1995 ar-   92
ticle in *Newsweek*, there were 310,000 interracial married couples in 1970. In
1993 that number grew to 1,195,000 (72). It is estimated by the National Center for Health Statistics that the total number of interracial births from 1970
to 1990 has increased from 39,012 to 124,468 (Sandor 39). "If current trends
continue, minorities will be approaching half of the total U.S. population as
early as 2050" (Sandor 37).

Race is an artificial category, imposed by governments or political interest   93
groups—easily altered and incapable of fully classifying everyone. Should this
be an argument to abolish race or race-based issues in America? While race is
an artificial categorization of a group of people by another group of people, it
is still an inescapable issue in a country that wants to ignore what it is not willing to confront or understand.

I add the following to some of the applications: 94

__Multiracial or __Multiethnic.   95

On others, if there is room, I list my entire ethnic heritage. I check these   96
twelve boxes in dark ink and press the pen down firmly.

Works Cited

"The Loving Generation." *Newsweek*. February 13, 1995. 72.

Pukui, Mary Kawena and Samuel H. Elbert. *Hawaiian Dictionary: Hawaiian-
English, English-Hawaiian*. Revised and Enlarged Edition. Honolulu: University of Hawaii Press, 1986.

Sandor, Gabrielle. "The 'Other' Americans." *American Demographics*. June
1994. 36–42.

United States Department of Commerce. *1990 Census of Population: Social and
Economic Characteristics*. Washington: Government Printing Office, No-
vember 1993.

Gordon Parks

Flavio's Home

Gordon Parks emerged from the poverty and racial isolation of a large Midwestern family to become one of the most influential photographers in American history. The youngest of 15 children, Parks departed home at the age of 16 after his mother died. He supported himself through odd jobs until the early 1930s, when he became inspired by the work of the social documentary photographers of the Great Depression. He bought an inexpensive camera and obtained a position taking photographs for the federal government. Working his way up through jobs at *Vogue* and *Life* magazine, he gradually built a reputation for himself. By the time he wrote "Flavio's Home" in 1961, he was already one of the most admired photographers in the nation. On its publication with its accompanying photographs, "Flavio's Home" elicited a groundswell of public support that eventually allowed Flavio to be brought to the U.S. for treatment and to buy a new home for his family.

1   I'VE NEVER LOST MY FIERCE GRUDGE AGAINST POVERTY. It is the most savage of all human afflictions, claiming victims who can't mobilize their efforts against it, who often lack strength to digest what little food they scrounge up to survive. It keeps growing, multiplying, spreading like a cancer. In my wanderings I attack it wherever I can—in barrios, slums and favelas.

2   Catacumba was the name of the favela where I found Flavio da Silva. It was wickedly hot. The noon sun baked the mud-rot of the wet mountainside. Garbage and human excrement clogged the open sewers snaking down the slopes. José Gallo, a *Life* reporter, and I rested in the shade of a jacaranda tree halfway up Rio de Janeiro's most infamous deathtrap. Below and above us were a maze of shacks, but in the distance alongside the beach stood the gleaming white homes of the rich.

3   Breathing hard, balancing a tin of water on his head, a small boy climbed toward us. He was miserably thin, naked but for filthy denim shorts. His legs resembled sticks covered with skin and screwed into his feet. Death was all over him, in his sunken eyes, cheeks and jaundiced coloring. He stopped for breath, coughing, his chest heaving as water slopped over his bony shoulders. Then jerking sideways like a mechanical toy, he smiled a smile I will never forget. Turning, he went on up the mountainside.

4   The detailed *Life* assignment in my back pocket was to find an impoverished father with a family, to examine his earnings, political leanings, religion, friends, dreams and frustrations. I had been sent to do an essay on poverty. This frail boy bent under his load said more to me about poverty than a dozen poor fathers. I touched Gallo, and we got up and followed the boy to where he entered a shack near the top of the mountainside. It was a leaning crum-

pled place of old plankings with a rusted tin roof. From inside we heard the babblings of several children. José knocked. The door opened and the boy stood smiling with a bawling naked baby in his arms.

Still smiling, he whacked the baby's rump, invited us in and offered us a box to sit on. The only other recognizable furniture was a sagging bed and a broken baby's crib. Flavio was twelve, and with Gallo acting as interpreter, he introduced his younger brothers and sisters: "Mario, the bad one; Baptista, the good one; Albia, Isabel and the baby Zacarias." Two other girls burst into the shack, screaming and pounding on one another. Flavio jumped in and parted them. "Shut up, you two." He pointed at the older girl. "That's Maria, the nasty one." She spit in his face. He smacked her and pointed to the smaller sister. "That's Luzia. She thinks she's pretty."

Having finished the introductions, he went to build a fire under the stove—a rusted, bent top of an old gas range resting on several bricks. Beneath it was a piece of tin that caught the hot coals. The shack was about six by ten feet. Its grimy walls were a patchwork of misshapen boards with large gaps between them, revealing other shacks below stilted against the slopes. The floor, rotting under layers of grease and dirt, caught shafts of light slanting down through spaces in the roof. A large hole in the far corner served as a toilet. Beneath that hole was the sloping mountainside. Pockets of poverty in New York's Harlem, on Chicago's south side, in Puerto Rico's infamous El Fungito seemed pale by comparison. None of them had prepared me for this one in the favela of Catacumba.

Flavio washed rice in a large dishpan, then washed Zacarias's feet in the same water. But even that dirty water wasn't to be wasted. He tossed in a chunk of lye soap and ordered each child to wash up. When they were finished he splashed the water over the dirty floor, and, dropping to his knees, he scrubbed the planks until the black suds sank in. Just before sundown he put beans on the stove to warm, then left, saying he would be back shortly. "Don't let them burn," he cautioned Maria. "If they do and Poppa beats me, you'll get it later." Maria, happy to get at the licking spoon, switched over and began to stir the beans. Then slyly she dipped out a spoonful and swallowed them. Luzia eyed her. "I see you. I'm going to tell on you for stealing our supper."

Maria's eyes flashed anger. "You do and I'll beat you, you little bitch." Luzia threw a stick at Maria and fled out the door. Zacarias dropped off to sleep. Mario, the bad one, slouched in a corner and sucked his thumb. Isabel and Albia sat on the floor clinging to each other with a strange tenderness. Isabel held onto Albia's hair and Albia clutched at Isabel's neck. They appeared frozen in an act of quiet violence.

Flavio returned with wood, dumped it beside the stove and sat down to rest for a few minutes, then went down the mountain for more water. It was dark when he finally came back, his body sagging from exhaustion. No longer smiling, he suddenly had the look of an old man and by now we could see that he kept the family going. In the closed torment of that pitiful shack, he was waging a hopeless battle against starvation. The da Silva children were living in a coffin.

10   When at last the parents came in, Gallo and I seemed to be part of the family. Flavio had already told them we were there. "Gordunn Americano!" Luzia said, pointing at me. José, the father, viewed us with skepticism. Nair, his pregnant wife, seemed tired beyond speaking. Hardly acknowledging our presence, she picked up Zacarias, placed him on her shoulder and gently patted his behind. Flavio scurried about like a frightened rat, his silence plainly expressing the fear he held of his father. Impatiently, José da Silva waited for Flavio to serve dinner. He sat in the center of the bed with his legs crossed beneath him, frowning, waiting. There were only three tin plates. Flavio filled them with black beans and rice, then placed them before his father. José da Silva tasted them, chewed for several moments, then nodded his approval for the others to start. Only he and Nair had spoons; the children ate with their fingers. Flavio ate off the top of a coffee can. Afraid to offer us food, he edged his rice and beans toward us, gesturing for us to take some. We refused. He smiled, knowing we understood.

11   Later, when we got down to the difficult business of obtaining permission from José da Silva to photograph his family, he hemmed and hawed, wallowing in the pleasant authority of the decision maker. He finally gave in, but his manner told us that he expected something in return. As we were saying good night Flavio began to cough violently. For a few moments his lungs seemed to be tearing apart. I wanted to get away as quickly as possible. It was cowardly of me, but the bluish cast of his skin beneath the sweat, the choking and spitting were suddenly unbearable.

12   Gallo and I moved cautiously down through the darkness trying not to appear as strangers. The Catacumba was no place for strangers after sundown. Desperate criminals hid out there. To hunt them out, the police came in packs, but only in daylight. Gallo cautioned me. "If you get caught up here after dark it's best to stay at the da Silvas' until morning." As we drove toward the city the large white buildings of the rich loomed up. The world behind us seemed like a bad dream. I had already decided to get the boy Flavio to a doctor, and as quickly as possible.

13   The plush lobby of my hotel on the Copacabana waterfront was crammed with people in formal attire. With the stink of the favela in my clothes, I hurried to the elevator hoping no passengers would be aboard. But as the door was closing a beautiful girl in a white lace gown stepped in. I moved as far away as possible. Her escort entered behind her, swept her into his arms and they indulged in a kiss that lasted until they exited on the next floor. Neither of

them seemed to realize that I was there. The room I returned to seemed to be oversized; the da Silva shack would have fitted into one corner of it. The steak dinner I had would have fed the da Silvas for three days.

Billowing clouds blanketed Mount Corcovado as we approached the favela   14
the following morning. Suddenly the sun burst through, silhouetting Cristo Redentor, the towering sculpture of Christ with arms extended, its back turned against the slopes of Catacumba. The square at the entrance to the favela bustled with hundreds of favelados. Long lines waited at the sole water spigot. Others waited at the only toilet on the entire mountainside. Women, unable to pay for soap, beat dirt from their wash at laundry tubs. Men, burdened with lumber, picks and shovels and tools important to their existence threaded their way through the noisy throngs. Dogs snarled, barked and fought. Woodsmoke mixed with the stench of rotting things. In the mist curling over the higher paths, columns of favelados climbed like ants with wood and water cans on their heads.

We came upon Nair bent over her tub of wash. She wiped away sweat with   15
her apron and managed a smile. We asked for her husband and she pointed to a tiny shack off to her right. This was José's store, where he sold kerosene and bleach. He was sitting on a box, dozing. Sensing our presence, he awoke and commenced complaining about his back. "It kills me. The doctors don't help because I have no money. Always talk and a little pink pill that does no good. Ah, what is to become of me?" A woman came to buy bleach. He filled her bottle. She dropped a few coins and as she walked away his eyes stayed on her backside until she was out of sight. Then he was complaining about his back again.

"How much do you earn a day?" Gallo asked.   16

"Seventy-five cents. On a good day maybe a dollar."   17

"Why aren't the kids in school?"   18

"I don't have money for the clothes they need to go to school."   19

"Has Flavio seen a doctor?"   20

He pointed to a one-story wooden building. "That's the clinic right there.   21
They're mad because I built my store in front of their place. I won't tear it down so they won't help my kids. Talk, talk, talk and pink pills." We bid him good-bye and started climbing, following mud trails, jutting rock, slime-filled holes and shack after shack propped against the slopes on shaky pilings. We sidestepped a dead cat covered with maggots. I held my breath for an instant, only to inhale the stench of human excrement and garbage. Bare feet and legs with open sores climbed above us—evils of the terrible soil they trod every day, and there were seven hundred thousand or more afflicted people in favelas around Rio alone. Touching me, Gallo pointed to Flavio climbing ahead of us carrying firewood. He stopped to glance at a man descending with a small cof-

fin on his shoulder. A woman and a small child followed him. When I lifted my camera, grumbling erupted from a group of men sharing beer beneath a tree.

22   "They're threatening," Gallo said. "Keep moving. They fear cameras. Think they're evil eyes bringing bad luck." Turning to watch the funeral procession, Flavio caught sight of us and waited. When we took the wood from him he protested, saying he was used to carrying it. He gave in when I hung my camera around his neck. Then, beaming, he climbed on ahead of us.

23   The fog had lifted and in the crisp morning light the shack looked more squalid. Inside the kids seemed even noisier. Flavio smiled and spoke above their racket. "Someday I want to live in a real house on a real street with good pots and pans and a bed with sheets." He lit the fire to warm leftovers from the night before. Stale rice and beans—for breakfast and supper. No lunch; midday eating was out of the question. Smoke rose and curled up through the ceiling's cracks. An air current forced it back, filling the place and Flavio's lungs with fumes. A coughing spasm doubled him up, turned his skin blue under viscous sweat. I handed him a cup of water, but he waved it away. His stomach tightened as he dropped to his knees. His veins throbbed as if they would burst. Frustrated, we could only watch; there was nothing we could do to help. Strangely, none of his brothers or sisters appeared to notice. None of them stopped doing whatever they were doing. Perhaps they had seen it too often. After five interminable minutes it was over, and he got to his feet, smiling as though it had all been a joke. "Maria, it's time for Zacarias to be washed!"

24   "But there's rice in the pan!"

25   "Dump it in another pan—and don't spill water!"

26   Maria picked up Zacarias, who screamed, not wanting to be washed. Irritated, Maria gave him a solid smack on his bare bottom. Flavio stepped over and gave her the same, then a free-for-all started with Flavio, Maria and Mario slinging fists at one another. Mario got one in the eye and fled the shack calling Flavio a dirty son-of-a-bitch. Zacarias wound up on the floor sucking his thumb and escaping his washing. The black bean and rice breakfast helped to get things back to normal. Now it was time to get Flavio to the doctor.

27   The clinic was crowded with patients—mothers and children covered with open sores, a paralytic teenager, a man with an ear in a state of decay, an aged blind couple holding hands in doubled darkness. Throughout the place came wailings of hunger and hurt. Flavio sat nervously between Gallo and me. "What will the doctor do to me?" he kept asking.

28   "We'll see. We'll wait and see."

29   In all, there were over fifty people. Finally, after two hours, it was Flavio's turn and he broke out in a sweat, though he smiled at the nurse as he passed

through the door to the doctor's office. The nurse ignored it; in this place of misery, smiles were unexpected.

The doctor, a large, beady-eyed man with a crew cut, had an air of impa- 30 tience. Hardly acknowledging our presence, he began to examine the fright- ened Flavio. "Open your mouth. Say 'Ah.' Jump up and down. Breathe out. Take off those pants. Bend over. Stand up. Cough. Cough louder. Louder." He did it all with such cold efficiency. Then he spoke to us in English so Flavio wouldn't understand. "This little chap has just about had it." My heart sank. Flavio was smiling, happy to be over with the examination. He was handed a bottle of cough medicine and a small box of pink pills, then asked to step outside and wait.

"This the da Silva kid?" Yes. 31

"What's your interest in him?" 32

"We want to help in some way." 33

"I'm afraid you're too late. He's wasted with bronchial asthma, malnutri- 34 tion and, I suspect, tuberculosis. His heart, lungs and teeth are all bad." He paused and wearily rubbed his forehead. "All that at the ripe old age of twelve. And these hills are packed with other kids just as bad off. Last year ten thou- sand died from dysentery alone. But what can we do? You saw what's waiting outside. It's like this every day. There's hardly enough money to buy aspirin. A few wealthy people who care help keep us going." He was quiet for a mo- ment. "Maybe the right climate, the right diet, and constant medical care might. . . ." He stopped and shook his head. "Naw. That poor lad's finished. He might last another year—maybe not." We thanked him and left.

"What did he say?" Flavio asked as we scaled the hill. 35

"Everything's going to be all right, Flav. There's nothing to worry about." 36

It had clouded over again by the time we reached the top. The rain swept 37 in, clearing the mountain of Corcovado. The huge Christ figure loomed up again with clouds swirling around it. And to it I said a quick prayer for the boy walking beside us. He smiled as if he had read my thoughts. "Papa says 'El Cristo' has turned his back on the favela."

"You're going to be all right, Flavio." 38

"I'm not scared of death. It's my brothers and sisters I worry about. What 39 would they do?"

"You'll be all right, Flavio." 40

3

Example

Writing Guidelines:

Example

1. **Use examples to support a major point.** Without examples, it would be nearly impossible to write a persuasive essay. Readers aren't convinced by "artists these days create too many works that are vulgar and profane." The point becomes much more persuasive when supported by an example: "One 'artist' dumped elephant dung on a portrait of the Virgin Mary—an act considered blasphemous by millions of Catholics worldwide." The same logic holds true in reverse—examples are worthless if you don't use them to make a point.

2. **Think of a variety of examples.** Your work is most effective when you use a variety of examples to support your point. Use brainstorming techniques such as freewriting, listing, and clustering to come up with as many examples as you can. At this stage, just write down every idea you come up with—you'll winnow down your list later.

3. **Select the most relevant examples for your purpose.** While well-selected examples persuade and engage your readers, too many examples will put them to sleep. In her essay on pickup lines, Stephanie Crocket offers just enough examples to tempt the reader. Rather than continuing on and on, she simply stops, and leaves the rest to imagination.

4. **Arrange the examples effectively.** Unlike narration and description, examples can be presented in almost any order without disorienting your reader. But while you have many choices for organizing your examples, some strategies work better than others. One tried and true method is to finish with your most effective example to drive your point home. If you're worried that readers won't be engaged in your topic, you might want to lead off with your best example. Finally, you can use almost any strategy in this book (narration, comparison and contrast, analogy, etc.) to arrange examples.

Barbara Ehrenreich

In Defense of Talk Shows

Best known for her wry and witty essays in *Time* magazine, Barbara Ehrenreich has been a social critic since the early 1970s, when she burst onto the scene with *Complaints and Disorders: The Sexual Politics of Sickness,* a bitter critique of America's health care system coauthored with Dierdre English. A self-described "socialist and feminist," much of Ehrenreich's work is framed by her politics. In *The Hearts of Men* she suggests that men have simply abandoned their familial obligations, freed from guilt by publications like *Playboy.* Her essays often touch on issues of feminist politics, but in this essay, which originally appeared in *Time,* she tackles a wider issue of society's voyeuristic tendencies, with typical wit.

UP UNTIL NOW, the targets of Bill (*The Book of Virtues*) Bennett's crusades have   1
at least been plausible sources of evil. But the latest victim of his wrath—TV
talk shows of the *Sally Jessy Raphael* variety—are in a whole different category
from drugs and gangsta rap. As anyone who actually watches them knows, the
talk shows are one of the most excruciatingly moralistic forums the culture
has to offer. Disturbing and sometimes disgusting, yes, but their very business
is to preach the middle-class virtues of responsibility, reason and self-control.

Take the case of Susan, recently featured on *Montel Williams* as an exam-   2
ple of a woman being stalked by her ex-boyfriend. Turns out Susan is also
stalking the boyfriend and—here's the sexual frisson—has slept with him only
days ago. In fact Susan is neck deep in trouble without any help from the
boyfriend: She's serving a year-long stretch of home incarceration for assault-
ing another woman, and home is the tiny trailer she shares with her nine-year-
old daughter.

But no one is applauding this life spun out of control. Montel scolds   3
Susan roundly for neglecting her daughter and failing to confront her role in
the mutual stalking. A therapist lectures her about this unhealthy "obsessive
kind of love." The studio audience jeers at her every evasion. By the end Susan
has lost her cocky charm and dissolved into tears of shame.

The plot is always the same. People with problems—"husband says she looks   4
like a cow," "pressured to lose her virginity or else," "mate wants more sex than
I do"—are introduced to rational methods of problem solving. People with
moral failings—"boy crazy," "dresses like a tramp," "a hundred sex partners"—
are introduced to external standards of morality. The preaching—delivered alternately by the studio audience, the host and the ever present guest therapist—
is relentless. "This is wrong to do this," Sally Jessy tells a cheating husband.
"Feel bad?" Geraldo asks the girl who stole her best friend's boyfriend. "Any

sense of remorse?" The expectation is that the sinner, so hectored, will see her way to reform. And indeed, a Sally Jessy update found "boy crazy," who'd been a guest only weeks ago, now dressed in schoolgirlish plaid and claiming her "attitude [had] changed"—thanks to the rough-and-ready therapy dispensed on the show.

5   All right, the subjects are often lurid and even bizarre. But there's no part of the entertainment spectacle, from *Hard Copy* to *Jade,* that doesn't trade in the lurid and bizarre. At least in the talk shows, the moral is always loud and clear: Respect yourself, listen to others, stop beating on your wife. In fact it's hard to see how *The Bill Bennett Show,* if there were to be such a thing, could deliver a more pointed sermon. Or would he prefer to see the reckless Susan, for example, tarred and feathered by the studio audience instead of being merely booed and shamed?

6   There *is* something morally repulsive about the talks, but it's not anything Bennett or his co-crusader Senator Joseph Lieberman has seen fit to mention. Watch for a few hours, and you get the claustrophobic sense of lives that have never seen the light of some external judgment, of people who have never before been listened to, and certainly never been taken seriously if they were. "What kind of people would let themselves be humiliated like this?" is often asked, sniffily, by the shows' detractors. And the answer, for the most part, is people who are so needy—of social support, of education, of material resources and self-esteem—that they mistake being the center of attention for being actually loved and respected.

7   What the talks are about, in large part, is poverty and the distortions it visits on the human spirit. You'll never find investment bankers bickering on *Rolonda,* or the host of *Gabrielle* recommending therapy to sobbing professors. With few exceptions the guests are drawn from trailer parks and tenements, from bleak streets and narrow, crowded rooms. Listen long enough, and you hear references to unpaid bills, to welfare, to twelve-hour workdays and double shifts. And this is the real shame of the talks: that they take lives bent out of shape by poverty and hold them up as entertaining exhibits. An announcement appearing between segments of *Montel* says it all: The show is looking for "pregnant women who sell their bodies to make ends meet."

8   This is class exploitation, pure and simple. What next—"homeless people so hungry they eat their own scabs"? Or would the next step be to pay people outright to submit to public humiliation? For $50 would you confess to adultery in your wife's presence? For $500 would you reveal your thirteen-year-old's girlish secrets on *Ricki Lake?* If you were poor enough, you might.

9   It is easy enough for those who can afford spacious homes and private therapy to sneer at their financial inferiors and label their pathetic moments of stardom vulgar. But if I had a talk show, it would feature a whole different cast of characters and category of crimes than you'll ever find on the talks:

"CEOs who rake in millions while their employees get downsized" would be an obvious theme, along with "Senators who voted for welfare and Medicaid cuts"—and, if he'll agree to appear, "well-fed Republicans who dithered about talk shows while trailer-park residents slipped into madness and despair."

Stephanie A. Crockett

"Haven't We Met . . . ?":
The Pickup Line Just Goes On and On

"Picking up" a member of the opposite sex has never been easy. It's even harder in these times of political correctness, where a wrong move can be interpreted as a moral affront. In "Haven't We Met . . . ?" Stephanie Crockett, a reporter for the *Washington Post*, covers the basics of meeting people in today's extra-sensitive dating environment.

IT'S A PHENOMENON AS OLD AS THE BATTLE BETWEEN THE SEXES. The pickup line.   1

"What's up, sexy."   2

"I know my name, what's yours?"   3

Or the oldest line in the book—"Can I talk to you for a minute?"   4

Walter Cloud, "30-ish," divorced owner of a graphic design company in   5
Arlington, has it down to a science. He enters the club, rakes his eyes over the crowd until he spots a subject, then moves in.

He chooses his words carefully, tailoring them to the way the woman is   6
dressed, the event and the atmosphere. A woman in pearls or a business suit gets the gentle approach—polite conversation about the weather, the president, the O. J. trial.

"I would like to make them feel like the effort that they made to put that   7
all together is well-deserved," explains Cloud.

But for sisters in sexier garb, no telling. "The base is the dress, that's how   8
you decide what you're going to say to a woman," he says. "Believe it or not, people wear clothes that are appropriate for the event. If she's wearing something that is raunchy just to show off, you don't have as much respect for them."

Judson Tallandier, 22, a senior at Howard University majoring in telecom-   9 munications, says the key to his pickup lines is getting a woman to smile. "I say, 'Would you be offended if I ask you a personal question?' Then they have to tell me yes or no. Most girls say no, they wouldn't be offended," Tallandier says. Then he continues. "'Would you be offended if I asked you what your name was?' Then they smile. If they break a smile, a smile says so much."

10 Next thing, he says, he's buying her a drink or a hamburger and they're getting acquainted. Hopefully, he gets a telephone number.

11 Pickup lines are as varied as the people who deliver them. Some men and women looking to meet someone they have spotted across a room, in a grocery store aisle or along a trail in the park simply walk up, say hello and introduce themselves.

12 That's how Tony Mack, a 25-year-old administrative assistant at the National Institutes of Health, does it. He says pickup lines don't work. "Basically, I just say, 'How are you, what's your name, where are you from?' . . . stuff like that," says Mack. "Then I tell them a little about myself."

13 But for others, the pickup line is alive and well in an intricate series of verbal volleys and return shots that will either be entertaining enough to elicit a positive response or stupid enough to ensure rejection.

14 "Don't I know you from somewhere?" almost always results in an answer of "I don't think so," "I hope not," or "No, and you won't."

15 A typical response to "What's your sign?" is almost always "A stop sign."

16 "Can I go with you?" is sure to receive a curt "No."

17 Several pickup artists say the delivery is the key element to success in the introduction: "Everybody uses the same lines. It's like sex. Sex is sex, but lovers make it what it is," says Cloud, using a comparison to a familiar subject.

18 The general consensus, among several unscientifically polled people, is that men are more prone to use pickup lines than women, even in comparable social situations. "I have tried every trick in the book," says Cloud. "Guys have a whole head full of pickup lines."

19 Kimberly Turrentine, 24, an administrative assistant at Bolling Air Force Base, doesn't use lines on men in an effort to gain their affection. "Pickup lines are a last resort or desperate plea for attention for women," says Turrentine, turning up her nose at the thought of using one.

20 "Women should never put themselves in positions where they can be rejected," she goes on. "If a man approaches me or I see a man that I am attracted to, I will give him eye contact in the hope that he will notice that I am interested in him."

21 Men always are the ones who have to set themselves up for rejection, complains Dale Rudolph, a 28-year-old delivery driver.

22 "Girls want to look nice so guys can talk to them, then when we talk to them, they shove us away," he says. "You [women] shoot us down, but you can't do our job," he says. "Then you wonder why we get so mad."

Flattery, they say, will get you nowhere. But unabashed flattery is what 23
Bernard Sumlin, a 30-year-old copyright technician, recommends.

"I say, 'Do you know that you are the most beautiful woman in the 24
world?'" Sumlin says, lowering his voice seductively and moving closer, for a
second assuming the pickup role.

Then he straightens up and his voice returns to its normal tone: 25

"And it works, I guarantee you, that works," he says. 26

Donald M. Murray

The Maker's Eye: Revising Your Own Manuscript

"My writing day begins about eleven-thirty in the morning when I turn off the computer and go out to lunch," says Donald Murray about his means of inspiration. "I have written and now I will allow the well to refill." He hasn't stopped writing—at least 500 words a day—since he got his first job at the *Boston Herald* in 1948. In the interim he's won the Pulitzer Prize, published two novels, and written a number of books about writing. He also founded the journalism program at the University of New Hampshire, where he is professor emeritus of English. In this essay, which first appeared in *The Writer* and was then rewritten for a different anthology, he analyzes the processes he and other great writers use to revise their work.

WHEN STUDENTS COMPLETE A FIRST DRAFT, they consider the job of writing 1
done—and their teachers too often agree. When professional writers complete
a first draft, they usually feel that they are at the start of the writing process.
When a draft is completed, the job of writing can begin.

That difference in attitude is the difference between amateur and profes- 2
sional, inexperience and experience, journeyman and craftsman. Peter F.
Drucker, the prolific business writer, calls his first draft the "zero draft"—after
that he can start counting. Most writers share the feeling that the first draft,
and all of those which follow, are opportunities to discover what they have to
say and how best they can say it.

To produce a progression of drafts, each of which says more and says it 3
more clearly, the writer has to develop a special kind of reading skill. In school
we are taught to decode what appears on the page as finished writing. Writers, however, face a different category of possibility and responsibility when

they read their own drafts. To them the words on the page are never finished. Each can be changed and rearranged, can set off a chain reaction of confusion or clarified meaning. This is a different kind of reading which is possibly more difficult and certainly more exciting.

4   Writers must learn to be their own best enemy. They must accept the criticism of others and be suspicious of it; they must accept the praise of others and be even more suspicious of it. Writers cannot depend on others. They must detach themselves from their own pages so that they can apply both their caring and their craft to their own work.

5   Such detachment is not easy. Science fiction writer Ray Bradbury supposedly puts each manuscript away for a year to the day and then rereads it as a stranger. Not many writers have the discipline or the time to do this. We must read when our judgment may be at its worst, when we are close to the euphoric moment of creation.

6   Then the writer, counsels novelist Nancy Hale, "should be critical of everything that seems to him most delightful in his style. He should excise what he most admires, because he wouldn't thus admire it if he weren't . . . in a sense protecting it from criticism." John Ciardi, the poet, adds, "The last act of the writing must be to become one's own reader. It is, I suppose, a schizophrenic process, to begin passionately and to end critically, to begin hot and to end cold; and, more important, to be passion-hot and critic-cold at the same time."

7   Most people think that the principal problem is that writers are too proud of what they have written. Actually, a greater problem for most professional writers is one shared by the majority of students. They are overly critical, think everything is dreadful, tear up page after page, never complete a draft, see the task as hopeless.

8   The writer must learn to read critically but constructively, to cut what is bad, to reveal what is good. Eleanor Estes, the children's book author, explains: "The writer must survey his work critically, coolly, as though he were a stranger to it. He must be willing to prune, expertly and hard-heartedly. At the end of each revision, a manuscript may look . . . worked over, torn apart, pinned together, added to, deleted from, words changed and words changed back. Yet the book must maintain its original freshness and spontaneity."

9   Most readers underestimate the amount of rewriting it usually takes to produce spontaneous reading. This is a great disadvantage to the student writer, who sees only a finished product and never watches the craftsman who takes the necessary step back, studies the work carefully, returns to the task, steps back, returns, steps back, again and again. Anthony Burgess, one of the most prolific writers in the English-speaking world, admits, "I might revise a page twenty times." Roald Dahl, the popular children's writer, states, "By the time I'm nearing the end of a story, the first part will have been reread and al-

tered and corrected at least 150 times. . . . Good writing is essentially rewriting. I am positive of this."

Rewriting isn't virtuous. It isn't something that ought to be done. It is simply something that most writers find they have to do to discover what they have to say and how to say it. It is a condition of the writer's life. 10

There are, however, a few writers who do little formal rewriting, primarily because they have the capacity and experience to create and review a large number of invisible drafts in their minds before they approach the page. And some writers slowly produce finished pages, performing all the tasks of revision simultaneously, page by page, rather than draft by draft. But it is still possible to see the sequence followed by most writers most of the time in rereading their own work. 11

Most writers scan their drafts first, reading as quickly as possible to catch the larger problems of subject and form, then move in closer and closer as they read and write, reread and rewrite. 12

The first thing writers look for in their drafts is *information*. They know that a good piece of writing is built from specific, accurate, and interesting information. The writer must have an abundance of information from which to construct a readable piece of writing. 13

Next writers look for *meaning* in the information. The specifics must build to a pattern of significance. Each piece of specific information must carry the reader toward meaning. 14

Writers reading their own drafts are aware of *audience*. They put themselves in the reader's situation and make sure that they deliver information which a reader wants to know or needs to know in a manner which is easily digested. Writers try to be sure that they anticipate and answer the questions a critical reader will ask when reading the piece of writing. 15

Writers make sure that the *form* is appropriate to the subject and the audience. Form, or genre, is the vehicle which carries meaning to the reader, but form cannot be selected until the writer has adequate information to discover its significance and an audience which needs or wants that meaning. 16

Once writers are sure the form is appropriate, they must then look at the *structure*, the order of what they have written. Good writing is built on a solid framework of logic, argument, narrative, or motivation which runs through the entire piece of writing and holds it together. This is the time when many writers find it most effective to outline as a way of visualizing the hidden spine on which the piece of writing is supported. 17

The element on which writers may spend a majority of their time is *development*. Each section of a piece of writing must be adequately developed. It must give readers enough information so that they are satisfied. How much information is enough? That's as difficult as asking how much garlic belongs in a salad. It must be done to taste, but most beginning writers underdevelop, underestimating the reader's hunger for information. 18

19   As writers solve development problems, they often have to consider questions of *dimension*. There must be a pleasing and effective proportion among all the parts of the piece of writing. There is a continual process of subtracting and adding to keep the piece of writing in balance.

20   Finally, writers have to listen to their own voices. *Voice* is the force which drives a piece of writing forward. It is an expression of the writer's authority and concern. It is what is between the words on the page, what glues the piece of writing together. A good piece of writing is always marked by a consistent, individual voice.

21   As writers read and reread, write and rewrite, they move closer and closer to the page until they are doing line-by-line editing. Writers read their own pages with infinite care. Each sentence, each line, each clause, each phrase, each word, each mark of punctuation, each section of white space between the type has to contribute to the clarification of meaning.

22   Slowly the writer moves from word to word, looking through language to see the subject. As a word is changed, cut, or added, as a construction is rearranged, all the words used before that moment and all those that follow that moment must be considered and reconsidered.

23   Writers often read aloud at this stage of the editing process muttering or whispering to themselves, calling on the ear's experience with language. Does this sound right—or that? Writers edit, shifting back and forth from eye to page to ear to page. I find I must do this careful editing in short runs, no more than fifteen or twenty minutes at a stretch, or I become too kind with myself. I begin to see what I hope is on the page, not what actually is on the page.

24   This sounds tedious if you haven't done it, but actually it is fun. Making something right is immensely satisfying, for writers begin to learn what they are writing about by writing. Language leads them to meaning, and there is the joy of discovery, of understanding, of making meaning clear as the writer employs the technical skills of language.

25   Words have double meanings, even triple and quadruple meanings. Each word has its own potential for connotation and denotation. And when writers rub one word against the other, they are often rewarded with a sudden insight, an unexpected clarification.

26   The maker's eye moves back and forth from word to phrase to sentence to paragraph to sentence to phrase to word. The maker's eye sees the need for variety and balance, for a firmer structure, for a more appropriate form. It peers into the interior of the paragraph, looking for coherence, unity, and emphasis, which make meaning clear.

27   I learned something about this process when my first bifocals were prescribed. I had ordered a larger section of the reading portion of the glass because of my work, but even so, I could not contain my eyes within this new limit of vision. And I still find myself taking off my glasses and bending my

nose towards the page, for my eyes unconsciously flick back and forth across the page, back to another page, forward to still another, as I try to see each evolving line in relation to every other line.

When does this process end? Most writers agree with the great Russian writer Tolstoy, who said, "I scarcely ever reread my published writing. If by chance I come across a page, it always strikes me: all this must be rewritten; this is how I should have written it." 28

The maker's eye is never satisfied, for each word has the potential to ignite new meaning. This article has been twice written all the way through the writing process, and it was published four years ago. Now it is to be republished in a book. The editors made a few small suggestions, and then I read it with my maker's eye. Now it has been re-edited, revised, re-read, re-re-edited, for each piece of writing is to the writer full of potential and alternatives. 29

A piece of writing is never finished. It is delivered to a deadline, torn out of the typewriter on demand, sent off with a sense of accomplishment and shame and pride and frustration. If only there were a couple more days, time for just another run at it, perhaps then . . . 30

Alleen Pace Nilsen

Sexism and Language

Profoundly affected by the overt sexism she saw during a stay in Afghanistan in 1967, Alleen Pace Nilsen has since built a career out of examining the subtle ways the English language responds to and defines sexual roles and stereotypes. She is now a professor at the University of Arizona, and continues her work studying gender and language as it applies to literature for young adults.

OVER THE LAST HUNDRED YEARS, American anthropologists have travelled to the corners of the earth to study primitive cultures. They either became linguists themselves or they took linguists with them to help in learning and analyzing languages. Even if the culture was one that no longer existed, they were interested in learning its language because besides being tools of communication, the vocabulary and structure of a language tell much about the values held by its speakers. 1

However, the culture need not be primitive, nor do the people making observations need to be anthropologists and linguists. Anyone living in the United States who listens with a keen ear or reads with a perceptive eye can 2 come up with startling new insights about the way American English reflects our values.

Animal Terms for People—Mirrors of the Double Standard

3   If we look at just one semantic area of English, that of animal terms in relation to people, we can uncover some interesting insights into how our culture views males and females. References to identical animals can have negative connotations when related to a female, but positive or neutral connotations when related to a male. For example, a *shrew* has come to mean "a scolding, nagging, evil-tempered woman," while *shrewd* means "keen-witted, clever, or sharp in practical affairs; astute . . . businessman, etc." (*Webster's New World Dictionary of the American Language*, 1964).

4   A *lucky dog* or a *gay dog* may be a very interesting fellow, but when a woman is a *dog*, she is unattractive, and when she's a *bitch* she's the personification of whatever is undesirable in the mind of the speaker. When a man is self-confident, he may be described as *cocksure* or even *cocky*, but in a woman this same self-confidence is likely to result in her being called a *cocky bitch*, which is not only a mixed metaphor, but also probably the most insulting animal metaphor we have. *Bitch* has taken on such negative connotations—children are taught it is a swear word—that in everyday American English, speakers are hesitant to call a female dog a *bitch*. Most of us feel that we would be insulting the dog. When we want to insult a man by comparing him to a dog, we call him a *son of a bitch*, which quite literally is an insult to his mother rather than to him.

5   If the female is called a *vixen* (a female fox), the dictionary says this means she is "an ill-tempered, shrewish, or malicious woman." The female seems both to attract and to hold on longer to animal metaphors with negative connotations. A *vampire* was originally a corpse that came alive to suck the blood of living persons. The word acquired the general meaning of an unscrupulous person such as a blackmailer and then, the specialized meaning of "a beautiful but unscrupulous woman who seduces men and leads them to their ruin." From this latter meaning we get the word *vamp*. The popularity of this term and of the name *vampire bat* may contribute to the idea that a female being is referred to in a phrase such as *the old bat*.

6   Other animal metaphors do not have definitely derogatory connotations for the female, but they do seem to indicate frivolity or unimportance, as in *social butterfly* and *flapper*. Look at the differences between the connotations of participating in a *hen party* and in a *bull session*. Male metaphors, even when they are negative in connotation, still relate to strength and conquest. Metaphors related to aggressive sex roles, for example, *buck, stag, wolf,* and *stud,* will undoubtedly remain attached to males. Perhaps one of the reasons that in the late sixties it was so shocking to hear policemen called *pigs* was that the con-

notations of *pig* are very different from the other animal metaphors we usually apply to males.

When I was living in Afghanistan, I was surprised at the cruelty and un-   7
fairness of a proverb that said, "When you see an old man, sit down and take a lesson; when you see an old woman, throw a stone." In looking at Afghan folk literature, I found that young girls were pictured as delightful and enticing, middle-aged women were sometimes interesting but more often just tolerable, while old women were always grotesque and villainous. Probably the reason for the negative connotation of old age in women is that women are valued for their bodies while men are valued for their accomplishments and their wisdom. Bodies deteriorate with age but wisdom and accomplishments grow greater.

When we returned home from Afghanistan, I was shocked to discover that   8
we have remnants of this same attitude in America. We see it in our animal metaphors. If both the animal and the woman are young, the connotation is positive, but if the animal and the woman are old, the connotation is negative. Hugh Hefner might never have made it to the big time if he had called his girls *rabbits* instead of *bunnies*. He probably chose *bunny* because he wanted something close to, but not quite so obvious as *kitten* or *cat*—the all-time winners for connoting female sexuality. Also *bunny*, as in the skiers' *snow bunny*, already had some of the connotations Hefner wanted. Compare the connotations of *filly* to *old nag*; *bird* to *old crow* or *old bat*; and *lamb* to *crone* (apparently related to the early modern Dutch *kronje*, *old ewe* but now *withered old woman*).

Probably the most striking examples of the contrast between young and   9
old women are animal metaphors relating to cats and chickens. A young girl is encouraged to be *kittenish*, but not *catty*. And though most of us wouldn't mind living next door to a *sex kitten*, we wouldn't want to live next door to a *cat house*. Parents might name their daughter *Kitty* but not *Puss* or *Pussy*, which used to be a fairly common nickname for girls. It has now developed such sexual connotations that it is used mostly for humor, as in the James Bond movie featuring Pussy Galore and her flying felines.

In the chicken metaphors, a young girl is a *chick*. When she gets old   10
enough she marries and soon begins feeling *cooped up*. To relieve the boredom she goes to *hen parties* and *cackles* with her friends. Eventually she has her *brood*, begins to *henpeck* her husband, and finally turns into an *old biddy*.

How English Glorifies Maleness

Throughout the ages physical strength has been very important, and because   11
men are physically stronger than women, they have been valued more. Only now in the machine age, when the difference in strength between males and females pales into insignificance in comparison to the strength of earth-mov-

ing machinery, airplanes, and guns, males no longer have such an inherent advantage. Today a man of intellect is more valued than a physical laborer, and since women can compete intellectually with men, their value is on the rise. But language lags far behind cultural changes, so the language still reflects this emphasis on the importance of being male. For example, when we want to compliment a male, all we need to do is stress the fact that he is male by saying he is a *he-man*, or he is *manly*, or he is *virile*. Both *virile* and *virtuous* come from the Latin *vir*, meaning *man*.

12   The command or encouragement that males receive in sentences like "Be a man!" implies that *to be a man* is to be honorable, strong, righteous, and whatever else the speaker thinks desirable. But in contrast to this, a girl is never told to be a *woman*. And when she is told to be a *lady*, she is simply being encouraged to "act feminine," which means sitting with her knees together, walking gracefully, and talking softly.

13   The armed forces, particularly the Marines, use the positive masculine connotation as part of their recruitment psychology. They promote the idea that to join the Marines (or the Army, Navy, or Air Force) guarantees that you will become a man. But this brings up a problem, because much of the work that is necessary to keep a large organization running is what is traditionally thought of as *women's work*. Now, how can the Marines ask someone who has signed up for a *man-sized job* to do *women's work*? Since they can't, they euphemize and give the jobs titles that either are more prestigious or, at least, don't make people think of females. Waitresses are called *orderlies*, secretaries are called *clerk-typists*, nurses are called *medics*, assistants are called *adjutants*, and cleaning up an area is called *policing* the area. The same kind of word glorification is used in civilian life to bolster a man's ego when he is doing such tasks as cooking and sewing. For example, a *chef* has higher prestige than a *cook* and a *tailor* has higher prestige than a *seamstress*.

14   Little girls learn early in life that the boy's role is one to be envied and emulated. Child psychologists have pointed out that experimenting with the role of the opposite sex is much more acceptable for little girls than it is for little boys. For example, girls are free to dress in boys' clothes, but certainly not the other way around. Most parents are amused if they have a daughter who is a *tomboy*, but they are genuinely distressed if they have a son who is a *sissy*. The names we give to young children reflect this same attitude. It is all right for girls to have boys' names, but pity the boy who has a girl's name! Because parents keep giving boys' names to girls, the number of acceptable boys' names keeps shrinking. Currently popular names for girls include *Jo, Kelly, Teri, Chris, Pat, Shawn, Toni,* and *Sam* (short for *Samantha*). *Evelyn, Carroll, Gayle, Hazel, Lynn, Beverley, Marion, Francis,* and *Shirley* once were acceptable names for males. But as they were given to females, they became less and less acceptable. Today, men who are stuck with them

self-consciously go by their initials or by abbreviated forms such as *Haze,
Shirl, Frank,* or *Ev.* And they seldom pass these names on to their sons.

Many common words have come into the language from people's names. 15
These lexical items again show the importance of maleness compared to the
triviality of the feminine activities being described. Words derived from the
names of women include *Melba toast,* named for the Australian singer Dame
Nellie Melba; *Sally Lunn cakes,* named after an eighteenth-century woman who
first made them; *pompadour,* a hair style named after Madame Pompadour;
and the word *maudlin,* as in *maudlin sentiment,* from Mary Magdalene, who was
often portrayed by artists as displaying exaggerated sorrow.

There are trivial items named after men—*teddy bear* after Theodore Roo- 16
sevelt and *sideburns* after General Burnside—but most words that come from
men's names relate to significant inventions or developments. These include
pasteurization after Louis Pasteur, *sousaphone* after John Philip Sousa, *mason jar*
after John L. Mason, *boysenberry* after Rudolph Boysen, *pullman car* after
George M. Pullman, *braille* after Louis Braille, *franklin stove* after Benjamin
Franklin, *diesel engine* after Rudolf Diesel, *ferris wheel* after George W. G. Ferris, and the verb *to lynch* after William Lynch, who was a vigilante captain in
Virginia in 1780.

The latter is an example of a whole set of English words dealing with vio- 17
lence. These words have strongly negative connotations. From research using
free association and semantic differentials, with university students as subjects, James Ney concluded that English reflects both an anti-male and an anti-
female bias because these biases exist in the culture (*Etc.: A Review of General
Semantics,* March 1976, pp. 67–76). The students consistently marked as masculine such words as *killer, murderer, robber, attacker, fighter, stabber, rapist, assas-
sin, gang, hood, arsonist, criminal, hijacker, villain,* and *bully,* even though most of
these words contain nothing to specify that they are masculine. An example
of bias against males, Ney observed, is the absence in English of a pejorative
term for women equivalent to *rapist.* Outcomes of his free association test indicated that if "English speakers want to call a man something bad, there
seems to be a large vocabulary available to them but if they want to use a term
which is good to describe a male, there is a small vocabulary available. The reverse is true for women."

Certainly we do not always think positively about males; witness such 18
words as *jerk, creep, crumb, slob, fink,* and *jackass.* But much of what determines
our positive and negative feelings relates to the roles people play. We have very
negative feelings toward someone who is hurting us or threatening us or in
some way making our lives miserable. To be able to do this, the person has to
have power over us and this power usually belongs to males.

On the other hand, when someone helps us or makes our life more pleas- 19
ant, we have positive feelings toward that person or that role. *Mother* is one of

the positive female terms in English, and we see such extensions of it as *Mother Nature*, *Mother Earth*, *mother lode*, *mother superior*, etc. But even though a word like *mother* is positive, it is still not a word of power. In the minds of English speakers being female and being powerless or passive are so closely related that we use the terms *feminine* and *lady* either to mean female or to describe a certain kind of quiet and unobtrusive behavior.

Words Labeling Women as Things

20 Because of our expectations of passivity, we like to compare females to items that people acquire for their pleasure. For example, in a . . . commercial for the television show "Happy Days," one of the characters announced that in the coming season, they were going to have not only "cars, motorcycles, and girls," but also a band. Another example of this kind of thinking is the comparison of females to food since food is something we all enjoy, even though it is extremely passive. We describe females as such delectable morsels as a *dish*, a *cookie*, a *tart*, *cheesecake*, *sugar and spice*, a *cute tomato*, *honey*, a *sharp cookie*, and *sweetie pie*. We say a particular girl has a *peaches and cream complexion* or "she looks good enough to eat." And parents give their daughters such names as *Candy* and *Cherry*.

21   Other pleasurable items that we compare females to are toys. Young girls are called *little dolls* or *China dolls*, while older girls—if they are attractive—are simply called *dolls*. We might say about a woman, "She's pretty as a picture," or "She's a fashion plate." And we might compare a girl to a plant by saying she is a *clinging vine*, a *shrinking violet*, or a *wallflower*. And we might name our daughters after plants such as *Rose*, *Lily*, *Ivy*, *Daisy*, *Iris*, and *Petunia*. Compare these names to boys' names such as *Martin* which means warlike, *Ernest* which means resolute fighter, *Nicholas* which means victory, *Val* which means strong or valiant, and *Leo* which means lion. We would be very hesitant to give a boy the name of something as passive as a flower although we might say about a man that he is a *late-bloomer*. This is making a comparison between a man and the most active thing a plant can do, which is to bloom. The only other familiar plant metaphor used for a man is the insulting *pansy*, implying that he is like a woman.

Student Essay

Eleanor Belgin

Pets and Their Humans

For this essay, Eleanor's assignment asked her to respond to Alleen Pace Nilsen's essay on sexism using a strategy employing many examples. Eleanor chose to imitate Nilsen's style, but give it a humorous twist.

IN HER ESSAY "SEXISM AND LANGUAGE," ALLEEN PACE NILSEN examines the bi-   1
ases inherent in the English language. When animal words, for example, are applied to humans, men are typically favorably compared to animals ("he's a stud") while females are unfavorably compared ("she's a dog"). Nilsen subtly demonstrates that our language reflects our biases—thus showing that the road to gender equality is fraught not only with the prejudices that tradition hands down from generation to generation, but also the slant implicit in every word we speak.

Perhaps even more frightening than the biases Nilsen observes, however,   2
are the misdeeds of that most dastardly group of Americans—pet owners. Pet owners regularly and voluntarily compare their animals to humans, and the animals nearly always come out on top. At least people who use biased terms like "stud" and "dog" have the defense that these terms are ingrained in our language. Pet owners, through their words and actions, believe that animals are superior to humans.

For example, many dog owners clothe their animals in such human ap-   3
parel as coats, hats, and even shoes. You'll see a well-dressed woman strolling down the street with her corgi—and the dog is dressed in a beautiful wool coat and matching Timberland moccasins. Meanwhile homeless people shiver on the street wearing only plastic bags.

Another hypocrisy of pet owners is the idea that their pets have the right   4
to use any human's lawn as their own personal bathroom. While this practice is both disgusting and unhealthy, pet owners act like public restroom privileges for their animals is some sort of sacred freedom. If a human behaved this way in public, he or she would be fined, if not jailed. Pets, it seems, have more rights than humans.

If you listen to their owners, pets are also smarter than humans. Accord-   5
ing to its owner, a dog that can't be restrained from barking at a stranger isn't simply stupid, it's endowed with supernatural powers that enable it to sense when a stranger is afraid. When a human couple tells a charming story about

their baby's first word, the pet owners inevitably chime in with similar stories about their *animals*: "Fido understands every word I say," or "Spot can walk on her hind legs!"

6   Pet owners believe their pets experience the same emotions as humans. For example, pets are "depressed" when their owners leave town for a few days. There are even animal psychiatrists to help pets deal with such traumas as pet sibling rivalry, anxiety, and a death in the family. No doubt this service is covered by the many pet HMOs springing up across the country.

7   On television, pets now have their own game shows, athletic competitions, and yes, emergency room dramas. There is even an entire cable channel devoted to animals. What more evidence is necessary to show that pet owners have elevated their animals to superhuman importance? Perhaps only this—one of the worst insults you can level at a dog is to say that it "acts like a baby"!

4

Comparison & Contrast

Comparison & Contrast

1. **Identify an appropriate topic.** When writing a comparison and contrast essay, the topic is critical. Some topics beg to be covered using this strategy; others simply won't work at all. Essay exams often ask you quite directly to use this strategy: "Compare and contrast the reigns of Elizabeth I and Victoria." Other times, the assignment may be more subtle. You may be asked to simply "compare" two things, to examine the "similarities and differences," or you may simply want to evaluate two choices, such as books, college courses, or physical items like cars or computers. Comparison and contrast is an effective strategy for evaluating, analyzing, or assessing two things that have similarities and differences. It's not effective if the subjects you're comparing have little in common. Unless you're feeling very clever, don't try to compare and contrast milk with the Milky Way.

2. **Write a strong thesis.** Nothing is more dull than a simple list of similarities and differences. Unless you're making a point, your readers will quickly lose interest. Of course, as you write your essay, you may decide to modify your thesis or change it entirely. Remember that if you change your thesis, you'll also need to reassess your essay as a whole to make sure it's supporting your point.

3. **Narrow your comparison to the points that support your thesis.** Any comparison and contrast essay can easily be expanded to fill pages, even volumes. To be effective, you need to emphasize the examples that make your point best. Depending on your thesis, you could compare Elizabeth and Victoria's religious, political, and foreign policies, or you could compare their clothing, hairstyles, and love lives. Then make sure you cover these points using plenty of clear examples (see Chapter 3).

4. **Select the organization that fits your topic best.** Comparison and contrast usually follows either a point-by-point comparison model or a block pattern:

Point-by-point	**Block**	
Kennedy's clothes	Kennedy	Clinton
Clinton's clothes	clothes	clothes
Kennedy's hair	hair	hair
Clinton's hair	love life	love life
Kennedy's love life		
Clinton's love life		

   Point-by-point usually works better for longer essays when you're concerned readers might not remember your earlier points. Block can be more effective for shorter essays or when you're comparing more than two items.

Mark Twain

Two Views of the Mississippi

Mark Twain was born in 1835, the year of the appearance of Halley's comet, and foresaw his own death with the return of that comet in 1910. Like the comet that framed his life, Mark Twain's writing lurks as a shadow behind all of American literature, and then occasionally, inevitably, bursts onto the scene in a fire of relevance. This unusual essay, excerpted from *Life on the Mississippi*, reveals none of the wry wit usually associated with Mark Twain. It is, instead, a lyrical, pensive reflection on his view of the river before and after he was trained as a riverboat pilot.

THE FACE OF THE WATER, IN TIME, BECAME A WONDERFUL BOOK—a book that   1
was a dead language to the uneducated passenger, but which told its mind to
me without reserve, delivering its most cherished secrets as clearly as if it uttered them with a voice. And it was not a book to be read once and thrown
aside, for it had a new story to tell every day. Throughout the long twelve hundred miles there was never a page that was void of interest, never one that you
could leave unread without loss, never one that you would want to skip, thinking you could find higher enjoyment in some other thing. There never was so
wonderful a book written by man; never one whose interest was so absorbing,
so unflagging, so sparklingly renewed with every reperusal. The passenger who
could not read it was charmed with a peculiar sort of faint dimple on its surface (on the rare occasions when he did not overlook it altogether); but to the
pilot that was an *italicized* passage; indeed, it was more than that, it was a legend of the largest capitals, with a string of shouting exclamation points at the
end of it; for it meant that a wreck or a rock was buried there that could tear
the life out of the strongest vessel that ever floated. It is the faintest and simplest expression the water ever makes, and the most hideous to a pilot's eye.
In truth, the passenger who could not read this book saw nothing but all manner of pretty pictures in it, painted by the sun and shaded by the clouds,
whereas to the trained eye these were not pictures at all, but the grimmest and
most dead-earnest of reading matter.

Now when I had mastered the language of this water and had come to   2
know every trifling feature that bordered the great river as familiarly as I knew
the letters of the alphabet, I had made a valuable acquisition. But I had lost
something, too. I had lost something which could never be restored to me
while I lived. All the grace, the beauty, the poetry had gone out of the majes-
tic river! I still keep in mind a certain wonderful sunset which I witnessed
when steamboating was new to me. A broad expanse of the river was turned

to blood; in the middle distance the red hue brightened into gold, through which a solitary log came floating, black and conspicuous; in one place a long, slanting mark lay sparkling upon the water; in another the surface was broken by boiling, tumbling rings, that were as many-tinted as an opal; where the ruddy flush was faintest, was a smooth spot that was covered with graceful circles and radiating lines, ever so delicately traced; the shore on our left was densely wooded, and the somber shadow that fell from this forest was broken in one place by a long, ruffled trail that shone like silver; and high above the forest wall a clean-stemmed dead tree waved a single leafy bough that glowed like a flame in the unobstructed splendor that was flowing from the sun. There were graceful curves, reflected images, woody heights, soft distances; and over the whole scene, far and near, the dissolving lights drifted steadily, enriching it, every passing moment, with new marvels of coloring.

3   I stood like one bewitched. I drank it in, in a speechless rapture. The world was new to me, and I had never seen anything like this at home. But as I have said, a day came when I began to cease from noting the glories and the charms which the moon and the sun and the twilight wrought upon the river's face; another day came when I ceased altogether to note them. Then, if that sunset scene had been repeated, I should have looked upon it without rapture, and should have commented upon it, inwardly, after this fashion: This sun means that we are going to have wind tomorrow; that floating log means that the river is rising, small thanks to it; that slanting mark on the water refers to a bluff reef which is going to kill somebody's steamboat one of these nights, if it keeps on stretching out like that; those tumbling "boils" show a dissolving bar and a changing channel there; the lines and circles in the slick water over yonder are a warning that that troublesome place is shoaling up dangerously; that silver streak in the shadow of the forest is the "break" from a new snag, and he has located himself in the very best place he could have found to fish for steamboats; that tall dead tree, with a single living branch, is not going to last long, and then how is a body ever going to get through this blind place at night without the friendly landmark?

4   No, the romance and the beauty were all gone from the river. All the value any feature of it had for me now was the amount of usefulness it could furnish toward compassing the safe piloting of a steamboat. Since those days, I have pitied doctors from my heart. What does the lovely flush in a beauty's cheek mean to a doctor but a "break" that rippled above some deadly disease? Are not all her visible charms sown thick with what are to him the signs and symbols of hidden decay? Does he ever see her beauty at all, or doesn't he simply view her professionally, and comment upon her unwholesome condition all to himself? And doesn't he sometimes wonder whether he had gained most or lost most by learning his trade?

David M. Kennedy

Can We Still Afford to Be a Nation of Immigrants?

Comparing yesterday's immigration with today's, a historian is struck by the unprecedented nature of our present situation

A professor of history at Stanford University, David Kennedy has received awards both for his teaching and his writing. When asked to provide some tips to aspiring young history teachers, Kennedy characteristically quoted Theodore Roosevelt: "make it a cartoon, not a portrait." His point was that simpler points are easier for listeners (and readers) to comprehend. Kennedy has spent a lifetime making history easier for thousands to comprehend—he has written a popular history textbook, *The American Portrait*, helped with PBS historical documentaries, and penned articles appearing in *The New York Times* and *The Atlantic Monthly*, from which this selection was taken.

THE QUESTION IN MY TITLE IMPLIES A PREMISE: that historically the United   1
States has well afforded to be a nation of immigrants—indeed, has benefited handsomely from its good fortune as an immigrant destination. That proposition was once so deeply embedded in our national mythology as to be axiomatic. More than a century ago, for example, in the proclamation that made Thanksgiving Day a national holiday, Abraham Lincoln gave thanks to God for having "largely augmented our free population by emancipation and by immigration."

Lincoln spoke those words when there were but 34 million Americans and   2
half a continent remained to be settled. Today, however, the United States is a nation of some 264 million souls on a continent developed beyond Lincoln's imagination. It is also a nation experiencing immigration on a scale never before seen. In the past three decades, since the passage of the Immigration and Nationality Act Amendments of 1965, the first major revision in American immigration statutes since the historic closure of immigration in the 1920s, some 20 million immigrants have entered the United States. To put those numbers in perspective: prior to 1965 the period of heaviest immigration to the United States was the quarter century preceding the First World War, when some 17 million people entered the country—roughly half the total number of Europeans who migrated to the United States in the century after 1820 (along with several hundred thousand Asians). The last prewar census, in 1910, counted about 13.5 million foreign-born people in the American population, in contrast to about 22.5 million in 1994. Historians

know a great deal about those earlier immigrants—why they came, how they ended up, what their impact was on the America of their day. Whether America's historical experience with immigration provides a useful guide to thinking about the present case is the principal question I want to address. I want not only to explore the substantive issue of immigration but also to test the proposition that the discipline of history has some value as a way of knowing and thinking about the world.

3   With respect to immigration itself, I intend to explore two sets of questions.

4   • Why did people migrate to America in the past, and what were the consequences, for them and for American society, once they landed?

5   • Why are people migrating to America today, and what might be the consequences, for them and for American society, of their presence in such numbers?

The Pull of America

6   A generation or two ago upbeat answers to the first pair of questions so pervaded the culture that they cropped up in the most exotic places—in Tunisia, for example, on July 9, 1943. The occasion was the eve of the invasion of Sicily, and General George S. Patton Jr. was addressing his troops, who were about to embark for the battle. He urged, "When we land, we will meet German and Italian soldiers whom it is our honor and privilege to attack and destroy. Many of you have in your veins German and Italian blood, but remember that these ancestors of yours so loved freedom that they gave up home and country to cross the ocean in search of liberty. The ancestors of the people we shall kill lacked the courage to make such a sacrifice and continued as slaves."

7   In his own inimitable idiom Patton was invoking what for most Americans was—and still is—the standard explanation of who their immigrant forebears were, why they left their old countries, and what was their effect on American society. In this explanation immigrants were the main-chance-seeking and most energetic, entrepreneurial, and freedom-loving members of their Old World societies. They were drawn out of Europe by the irresistible magnet of American opportunity and liberty, and their galvanizing influence on American society made this country the greatest in the world.

8   A radically different explanation of immigration has also historically been at work in the American mind. As the noted social scientist Edward Alsworth Ross put it in 1914:

9   Observe immigrants not as they come travel-wan up the gang-plank, nor as they issue toil-begrimed from pit's mouth or mill-gate, but in their gatherings, washed, combed, and in their Sunday best. . . . [They]

are hirsute, low-browed, big-faced persons of obviously low mentality. . . . They simply look out of place in black clothes and stiff collar, since clearly they belong in skins, in wattled huts at the close of the Great Ice Age. These ox-like men are descendants of those who always stayed behind.

Ross was describing in these invidious terms what he and his turn-of-the-cen- 10 tury contemporaries called the "new" immigrants—new because they came predominantly from eastern and southern Europe, as distinct from the "old," early-and-mid-nineteenth-century immigrants, who had come mainly from northern and western Europe. Ironically, Ross was also talking about the parents of those very troops (at least the Italian-American troops) whom Patton addressed in 1943.

Between those two poles of explanation American views of immigration 11 have oscillated. On the one hand, as Patton reminds us, immigrants were judged to be noble souls, tugged by the lodestone of American opportunity, whose talents and genius and love of liberty account for the magnificent American character. On the other hand, as in Ross's view, especially if they had the misfortune to arrive on a more recent boat, immigrants were thought to be degraded, freeloading louts, a blight on the national character and a drain on the economy—the kind of people described all too literally, so the argument goes, by Emma Lazarus's famous inscription on the base of the Statue of Liberty: "your tired, your poor . . . the wretched refuse of your teeming shore."

Yet for all their differences, the two views have several things in common. 12 Both explain immigration in terms of the moral character of immigrants. Both understand immigration as a matter of individual choice. And both implicitly invoke the American magnet as the irresistible force that put people in motion, drawing them either to opportunity or to dependency.

Those concepts do not bear close analysis as adequate explanations for the 13 movement of some 35 million human beings over the course of a century. This was a historical phenomenon too huge and too specific in time to be sufficiently accounted for by summing 35 million decisions supposedly stimulated by the suddenly irresistible gravitational attraction of a far-off continent.

The Push of Europe

For the first three centuries or so after the European discovery of the New 14 World the principal source of immigrants to the two American continents and the Caribbean was not Europe but Africa. Only in the early nineteenth century did the accumulated total of European settlers in the New World exceed the approximately 10 million Africans who had made the trans-Atlantic voyage in the years since 1492. To explain the African diaspora by citing entrepreneurial instincts, the love of democracy, or the freely chosen decisions of migrants to follow the lodestar of American promise would be a mockery. Clearly, the involuntary movement of those 10 million Africans is best explained not in terms of their individual characters and choices but in terms of the catastrophically disruptive expansion of large-scale plantation agriculture and its accursed corollary, large-scale commercial slavery.

15   A comparable—though, to be sure, not identical—element of involuntariness characterized emigration from nineteenth-century Europe. Any generalization about what prompted a phenomenon as long-lived and complicated as the great European migration must, of course, be subject to many qualifications. All discussions of the migration process recognize both push and pull factors. But at bottom the evidence convincingly supports the argument that disruption is essential to the movement of people on such a scale. And, as in the African case, the best, most comprehensive explanation for a process that eventually put some 35 million people in motion is to be found in two convulsively disruptive developments that lay far beyond the control of individual Europeans. Those developments had their historical dynamic within the context of European, not American, history.

16   The first of these needs little elaboration. It was, quite simply, population growth. In the nineteenth century the population of Europe more than doubled, from some 200 million to more than 400 million, even after about 70 million people had left Europe altogether. (Only half of these, it should be noted, went to the United States—one among many clues that the American-magnet explanation is inadequate.) That population boom was the indispensable precondition for Europe to export people on the scale that it did. And the boom owed little to American stimulus; rather, it was a product of aspects of European historical evolution, especially improvements in diet, sanitation, and disease control.

17   The second development was more complex, but we know it by a familiar name: the Industrial Revolution. It includes the closely associated revolution in agricultural productivity. Wherever it occurred, the Industrial Revolution shook people loose from traditional ways of life. It made factory workers out of artisans and, even more dramatically, turned millions of rural farmers into urban wage-laborers. Most of those migrants from countryside to city, from agriculture to industry, remained within their country of origin, or at least within Europe. But in the early stages of industrialization the movement of people, like the investment of capital during the unbridled early days of industrialism, was often more than what the market could bear. In time most European societies reached a kind of equilibrium, absorbing their own work-

ers into their own wage markets. But in the typical transitional phase some workers who had left artisanal or agricultural employments could not be reabsorbed domestically in European cities. They thus migrated overseas.

The large scholarly literature documenting this process might be summarized as follows: Imagine a map of Europe. Across this map a time line traces the evolution of the Industrial Revolution. From a point in the British Isles in the late eighteenth century the line crosses to the Low Countries and Germany in the early and mid nineteenth century and to eastern and southern Europe in the late nineteenth and early twentieth centuries. Across the same map a second line traces the chronological evolution of migration to the United States. As it happens, the two lines are almost precisely congruent—migration came principally from the British Isles in the eighteenth and early nineteenth centuries, then mainly from Germany, and finally from the great watersheds of the Vistula and the Danube and the mountain ranges of the Apennines and Carpathians to the south and east. 18

The congruence of those lines is not coincidental. Industrialization, in this view, is *the* root cause and the most powerful single variable explaining the timing, the scale, the geographic evolution, and the composition of the great European migration. 19

For another perspective on the importance of understanding the European migration from a European point of view, consider the lyrics of a nineteenth-century Italian folk song called "The Wives of the Americans." In this case, the "Americans" were men who had gone off to America and left their wives behind in Italy—specifically, the southern region of Campania. In fact, men, young men in particular, predominated in the nineteenth-century migratory stream, and their predominance constitutes a reliable indicator of their purposes. Many of them never intended to settle permanently elsewhere but hoped to work abroad for a time and eventually return to the old country. Repatriation rates for European immigrants averaged nearly 40 percent. Only the Jews and the Irish did not go home again in significant numbers. For some later, "new" immigrant groups, especially from the southern Danube regions, repatriation rates ran as high as 80 percent. 20

The song describes the wives of the Americans going to church and praying, "Send money, my husband. Send more money. The money you sent earlier I have already spent. I spent it on my lover. I spent it with pleasure. Send more money, you *cornuto fottuto* [damnable cuckold]." Those lyrics conjure an image of immigration quite different from the one General Patton urged on his Italian-American troops in 1943. Together with the figures on repatriation, they offer a strong corrective to uncritical reliance on the American-magnet explanation for the past century's European migration. 21

The Immigrants in America

22   What happened to European immigrants, and to American society, once they arrived? Much historical inquiry on this point focuses on immigrant hardship and on recurrent episodes of nativism, anti-Semitism, anti-Catholicism, and anti-foreign-radicalism, from the Know-Nothing movement of the 1850s to the American Protective Association of the late nineteenth century and the revived Ku Klux Klan of the early twentieth century, culminating in the highly restrictive immigration legislation of the 1920s. Those are important elements in the history of American immigration, and we would forget them at our peril. But getting the question right is the most challenging part of any historical investigation, and there is an analytically richer question to be asked than Why did immigrants meet sometimes nasty difficulties?

23   An even more intriguing question is How did tens of millions of newcomers manage to accommodate themselves to America, and America to them, without more social disruption? How can we explain this society's relative success—and success I believe it was—in making space so rapidly for so many people?

24   The explanation is surely not wise social policy. Beyond minimal monitoring at the ports of entry, no public policy addressed the condition of immigrants once they were cleared off Castle Garden or Ellis Island. But three specific historical circumstances, taken together, go a long way toward composing an answer to the question.

25   First, somewhat surprisingly, for all their numbers, immigrants—even the 17 million who arrived from 1890 to 1914—never made up a very large component of the already enormous society that was turn-of-the-century America. The census of 1910 records the highest percentage of foreign-born people ever resident in the United States: 14.7 percent. Now, 14.7 percent is not a trivial proportion, but it is a decided minority, and relative to other societies that have received large numbers of immigrants, a small minority. The comparable figures in Australia and Canada at approximately the same time were 17 percent and more than 20 percent, and even higher in Argentina. So here is one circumstance accounting for the relative lack of social conflict surrounding immigration a century ago: at any given moment immigrants were a relatively small presence in the larger society.

26   A second circumstance was economic. Immigrants supplied the labor that a growing economy urgently demanded. What is more, economic growth allowed the accommodation of newcomers without forcing thorny questions of redistribution—always the occasion for social contest and upheaval. Here, as so often in American history, especially during the period of heavy immigration before the First World War, economic growth worked as a pre-emptive solution to potential social conflict.

27   The third circumstance was more complicated than sheer numbers or eco-

nomic growth. I call this circumstance "pluralism"—by which I mean simply that the European immigrant stream was remarkably variegated in its cultural, religious, national, and linguistic origins. These many subcurrents also distributed themselves over an enormous geographic region—virtually the entire northeastern quadrant of the United States—and through several political jurisdictions. By the 1920s immigrants were distributed widely across the great industrial belt that stretched from New England through New York, New Jersey, Pennsylvania, and beyond: Ohio, Indiana, Illinois, Michigan, Wisconsin, and Minnesota. The states with the most immigrants, not incidentally, also had per capita incomes higher than the national average—an important fact pertinent to understanding the relationship between immigration and economic vitality.

The varied composition and broad dispersal of the immigrant stream carried certain crucial implications, one being that no immigrant group could realistically aspire to preserve its Old World culture intact for more than a few generations at best. To be sure, many groups made strenuous efforts to do just that. Legend to the contrary, last century's immigrants did not cast their Old World habits and languages overboard before their ship steamed into New York Harbor. In fact, many groups heroically exerted themselves to sustain their religions, tongues, and ways of life. The Catholic school system, which for a generation or two in some American cities educated nearly as many students as the public school system, eloquently testified to the commitment of some immigrant communities to resist assimilation. But circumstances weighed heavily against the success of such efforts. The virtual extinction of the parochial school system in the past generation—the empty schools and dilapidated parish buildings that litter the inner cores of the old immigrant cities—bears mute witness both to the ambition and to the ultimate failure of those efforts to maintain cultural distinctiveness.   28

A second and no less important implication of pluralism was that neither any single immigrant group nor immigrants as a whole could realistically mount any kind of effective challenge to the existing society's way of doing things. No single group had sufficient weight in any jurisdiction larger than a municipality to dictate a new political order. And there was little likelihood that Polish Jews and Italian Catholics and Orthodox Greeks could find a common language, much less common ground for political action.   29

To recapitulate: The most comprehensive explanation of the causes of immigration a century ago is to be found in the disruptions visited on European society by population growth and the Industrial Revolution. The United States was, to use the language of the law, the incidental beneficiary of that upheaval. The swelling immigrant neighborhoods in turn-of-the-century American cities were, in effect, by-products of the urbanization of Europe. And once landed in America, immigrants accommodated themselves to the   30 larger society—not always easily assimilating, but at least working out a modus vivendi—without the kinds of conflicts that have afflicted other multinational societies. That mostly peaceful process of accommodation came about because of the relatively small numbers of immigrants at any given time, because of the health of the economy, and because of the constraints on alternatives to accommodation inherent in the plural and dispersed character of the immigrant stream.

31   Having lit this little lamp of historical learning, I would like to carry it forward and see if it can illuminate the present.

Today's Immigration

32   The biggest apparent novelty in current immigration is its source, or sources. Well over half of the immigration of the past thirty years has come from just seven countries: Mexico, the Philippines, China (I am including Taiwan), Vietnam, Korea, India, and the Dominican Republic.

33   Not a single European country is on that list. Here, it would seem, is something new under the historical sun. Europe has dried up as a source of immigration and been replaced by new sources in Latin America and Asia.

34   And yet if we remember what caused the great European migration, the novelty of the current immigration stream is significantly diminished. Though particular circumstances vary, most of the countries now sending large numbers of immigrants to the United States are undergoing the same convulsive demographic and economic disruptions that made migrants out of so many nineteenth-century Europeans: population growth and the relatively early stages of their own industrial revolutions.

35   Mexico, by far the leading supplier of immigrants to the United States, conforms precisely to that pattern. Since the Second World War the Mexican population has more than tripled—a rate of growth that recollects, indeed exceeds, that of nineteenth-century Europe. And as in Europe a century ago, population explosion has touched off heavy internal migration, from rural to urban areas. By some reckonings, Mexico City has become the largest city in the world, with 20 million inhabitants and an in-migration from the Mexican countryside estimated at 1,000 people a day.

36   Also since the Second World War the Mexican economy, despite periodic problems, has grown at double the average rate of the U.S. economy. Rapid industrialization has been accompanied by the swift and widespread commercialization of Mexican agriculture. A Mexican "green revolution," flowing from improvements in mechanical processing, fertilizers, and insecticides, has in fact exacerbated the usual disruptions attendant on rapid industrialization: depopulation of the countryside, urban in-migration, and movement across the national border. But as in nineteenth-century Europe, most of the move-

ment has been within Mexico itself. Since 1970 some five million Mexicans have entered the United States to stay; probably more than 10 million have moved to Mexico City alone.

Thus we are in the presence of a familiar historical phenomenon, impelled 37 by developments that are for all practical purposes identical to those that ignited the great European migration of a century ago.

What Does the Future Hold?

If the causes of present-day immigration are familiar, what will be the conse- 38 quences for today's immigrants and tomorrow's America?

I have suggested that three historical circumstances eased the accommoda- 39 tion between immigrants and the American society of a century ago—the relatively small number of immigrants present at any given time, the needs and vitality of the economy, and the plural and distributed character of the immigrant stream. How do those factors weigh in an analysis of immigration today?

With respect to numbers, the historical comparison gives a basis for con- 40 fidence that the answer to our original question—Can we still afford to be a nation of immigrants?—is yes. The U.S. Census Bureau reports that as of 1994 foreign-born people represented 8.7 percent of the American population, or just a bit more than half the proportion they made up in the census of 1910. (Comparable recent numbers for Canada and Australia, incidentally, are approximately 16 percent and 22 percent.) So, with reference to both American historical experience and contemporary experience in other countries, the *relative* incidence of current immigration to the United States is rather modest. Surely the United States at the end of the twentieth century is resourceful enough to deal with an immigrant inflow proportionally half what American society managed to deal with quite successfully in the early years of this century.

With reference to the needs and vitality of the economy, the historical 41 comparison is more complicated. Economic theory suggests that immigration is a bargain for any receiving society, because it augments the labor supply, one of the three principal factors of production (along with land and capital), essentially free of cost. The sending society bears the burden of feeding and raising a worker to the age when he or she can enter the labor market. If at that point the person emigrates and finds productive employment elsewhere, the source society has in effect subsidized the economy of the host society. That scenario essentially describes the historical American case, in which fresh supplies of immigrant labor underwrote the nation's phenomenal industrial surge in the half century after the Civil War.

The theory is subject to many qualifications. Unskilled immigrant work- 42 ers may indeed increase gross economic output, as they did from the Pittsburgh blast furnaces to the Chicago packinghouses a century ago, and as they do today in garment shops and electronic assembly plants from Los Angeles to Houston. But as productivity has become more dependent on knowledge and skill, the net value of unskilled immigrant labor has decreased, a point that informs much of the current case for restricting immigration. Yet it is important to note that argument on this point turns on the *relative* contribution of low-skill workers to overall output; the theory is still unimpeachable in its insistence on the *absolute* value of an additional worker, from whatever source, immigrant or native. Nevertheless, large numbers of unskilled immigrants may in the long run retard still higher potential outputs, because the inexpensive labor supply that they provide diminishes incentives to substitute capital and improved technology for labor, and thus inhibits productivity gains. On the other hand, just to complicate the calculation further, insofar as the host society continues to need a certain amount of low-skill work done, the availability of unskilled immigrants may *increase* the economy's overall efficiency by freeing significant numbers of better-educated native workers to pursue higher-productivity employment. And overhanging all this part of the immigration debate is the question of whose ox is gored. Low-skill immigrants may benefit the economy as a whole, but may at the same time impose substantial hardships on the low-skill native workers with whom they are in direct competition for jobs and wages.

43   Of course, the theory that immigration subsidizes the host economy is true only insofar as the immigrant in question is indeed a worker, a positive contributor to the productive apparatus of the destination society. Even the crude American immigration-control system of the nineteenth century recognized that fact, when it barred people likely to become social dependents, such as the chronically ill or known criminals. The issue of dependency is particularly vexatious in the United States today for two reasons. First, the 1965 legislation contained generous clauses providing for "family reunification," under the terms of which a significant portion of current immigrants are admitted not as workers but as the spouses, children, parents, and siblings of citizens or legally resident aliens. In 1993, a typical year, fewer than 20 percent of immigrants entered under "employment-based" criteria.

44   Because of family-reunification provisions, the current immigrant population differs from previous immigrant groups in at least two ways: it is no longer predominantly male and, even more strikingly, it is older. The percentage of immigrants over sixty-five exceeds the percentage of natives in that age group, and immigrants over sixty-five are two and a half times as likely as natives to be dependent on Supplemental Security Income, the principal federal program making cash payments to the indigent elderly. Newspaper accounts suggest that some families have brought their relatives here under the family-reunification

provisions in the law expressly for the purpose of gaining access to SSI. Thus it appears that the availability of welfare programs—programs that did not exist a century ago—has combined with the family-reunification provisions to create new incentives for immigration that complicate comparisons of the economics of immigration today with that in the nineteenth century.

But on balance, though today's low-skill immigrants may not contribute as 45 weightily to the economy as did their European counterparts a hundred years ago, and though some do indeed end up dependent on public assistance, as a group they make a positive economic contribution nevertheless. It is no accident that today's immigrants are concentrated in the richest states, among them California (home to fully one third of the country's immigrant population), just as those of the 1920s were. And just as in that earlier era, immigrants are not parasitic on the "native" economy but productive participants in it. The principal motivation for immigration remains what it was in the past: the search for productive employment. Most immigrants come in search of work, and most find it. Among working-age males, immigrant labor-force-participation rates and unemployment rates are statistically indistinguishable from those for native workers. The ancient wisdom still holds: *Ubi est pane, ibi est patria* ("Where there is bread, there is my country"). Not simply geography but also that powerful economic logic explains why Mexico is the principal contributor of immigrants to the United States today: the income gap between the United States and Mexico is the largest between any two contiguous countries in the world.

One study, by the Stanford economist Clark W. Reynolds, estimated the 46 future labor-market characteristics and prospects for economic growth in Mexico and the United States. For Mexico to absorb all the new potential entrants into its own labor markets, Reynolds concluded, its economy would have to grow at the improbably high rate of some seven percent a year. The United States, in contrast, if its economy is to grow at a rate of three percent a year, must find somewhere between five million and 15 million more workers than can be supplied by domestic sources. Reynolds's conclusion was obvious: Mexico and the United States need each other, the one to ease pressure on its employment markets, the other to find sufficient labor to sustain acceptable levels of economic growth. If Reynolds is right, the question with which I began—Can we still afford to be a nation of immigrants?—may be wrongly put. The proper question may be Can we afford *not* to be? (For another perspective on this question see this month's article by George J. Borjas.)

The Reconquista

But if economic necessity requires that the United States be a nation of im- 47 migrants into the indefinite future, as it has been for so much of its past, some important questions remain. Neither men nor societies live by bread alone, and present-day immigration raises historically unprecedented issues in the cultural and political realms.

48   Pluralism—the variety and dispersal of the immigrant stream—made it easier for millions of European immigrants to accommodate themselves to American society. Today, however, one large immigrant stream is flowing into a defined region from a single cultural, linguistic, religious, and national source: Mexico. Mexican immigration is concentrated heavily in the Southwest, particularly in the two largest and most economically and politically influential states—California and Texas. Hispanics, including Central and South Americans but predominantly Mexicans, today compose 28 percent of the population of Texas and about 31 percent of the population of California. More than a million Texans and more than three million Californians were born in Mexico. California alone holds nearly half of the Hispanic population, and well over half of the Mexican-origin population, of the entire country.

49   This Hispanicization of the American Southwest is sometimes called the Reconquista, a poetic reminder that the territory in question was, after all, incorporated into the United States in the first place by force of arms, in the Mexican War of the 1840s. There is a certain charm in this turn of the wheel of history, with its reminder that in the long term the drama of armed conquest may be less consequential than the prosaic effects of human migration and birth rates and wage differentials. But the sobering fact is that the United States has had no experience comparable to what is now taking shape in the Southwest.

50   Mexican-Americans will have open to them possibilities closed to previous immigrant groups. They will have sufficient coherence and critical mass in a defined region so that, if they choose, they can preserve their distinctive culture indefinitely. They could also eventually undertake to do what no previous immigrant group could have dreamed of doing: challenge the existing cultural, political, legal, commercial, and educational systems to change fundamentally not only the language but also the very institutions in which they do business. They could even precipitate a debate over a "special relationship" with Mexico that would make the controversy over the North American Free Trade Agreement look like a college bull session. In the process, Americans could be pitched into a soul-searching redefinition of fundamental ideas such as the meaning of citizenship and national identity.

51   All prognostications about these possibilities are complicated by another circumstance that has no precedent in American immigration history: the region of Mexican immigrant settlement in the southwestern United States is contiguous with Mexico itself. That proximity may continuously replenish the immigrant community, sustaining its distinctiveness and encouraging its as-

sertiveness. Alternatively, the nearness of Mexico may weaken the community's coherence and limit its political and cultural clout by chronically attenuating its members' permanence in the United States, as the accessibility of the mother country makes for a kind of perpetual repatriation process.

In any case, there is no precedent in American history for these possibilities. No previous immigrant group had the size and concentration and easy access to its original culture that the Mexican immigrant group in the Southwest has today. If we seek historical guidance, the closest example we have to hand is in the diagonally opposite corner of the North American continent, in Quebec. The possibility looms that in the next generation or so we will see a kind of Chicano Quebec take shape in the American Southwest, as a group emerges with strong cultural cohesiveness and sufficient economic and political strength to insist on changes in the overall society's ways of organizing itself and conducting its affairs. 52

Public debate over immigration has already registered this prospect, however faintly. How else to explain the drive in Congress, and in several states, to make English the "official" language for conducting civil business? In previous eras no such legislative muscle was thought necessary to expedite the process of immigrant acculturation, because alternatives to eventual acculturation were simply unimaginable. Less certain now that the traditional incentives are likely to do the work of assimilation, we seem bent on trying a *ukase*—a ham-handed and provocative device that may prove to be the opening chapter of a script for prolonged cultural warfare. Surely our goal should be to help our newest immigrants, those from Mexico especially, to become as well integrated in the larger American society as were those European "new" immigrants whom E. A. Ross scorned but whose children's patriotism George Patton could take for granted. To reach that goal we will have to be not only more clever than our ancestors were but also less confrontational, more generous, and more welcoming than our current anxieties sometimes incline us to be. 53

The present may echo the past, but will not replicate it. Yet the fact that events have moved us into *terra nova et incognita* does not mean that history is useless as a way of coming to grips with our situation. To the contrary, the only way we can know with certainty as we move along time's path that we have come to a genuinely new place is to know something of where we have been. "What's new in the starry sky, dear Argelander?" Kaiser Wilhelm I is said to have asked his state astronomer, to which Argelander replied, "And does Your Majesty already know the old?" Knowing the old is the project of historical scholarship, and only that knowledge can reliably point us toward the new. As Lincoln also said, "As our case is new, so we must think anew, and act anew. We must disenthrall ourselves, and then we shall save our country." 54

Patricia Kean

Blowing Up the Tracks

Patricia Kean is a writer whose works have appeared in _Lingua Franca,_ the _New York Times,_ and the _Washington Monthly,_ where this essay was first printed. She received her B.A. from Georgetown University, and an M.A. from the University of Wisconsin at Madison. She now writes on education issues for a variety of publications. In this essay, she focuses on the effects of "tracking" students into separate courses based on ability.

1   IT'S MORNING IN NEW YORK, and some seventh graders are more equal than others.

2   Class 7–16 files slowly into the room, prodded by hard-faced men whose walkie-talkies crackle with static. A pleasant looking woman shouts over the din, "What's rule number one?" No reply. She writes on the board. "Rule One: Sit down."

3   Rule number two seems to be an unwritten law: Speak slowly. Each of Mrs. H's syllables hangs in the air a second longer than necessary. In fact, the entire class seems to be conducted at 16 RPM. Books come out gradually. Kids wander about the room aimlessly. Twelve minutes into class, we settle down and begin to play "O. Henry Jeopardy," a game which requires students to supply one-word answers to questions like: "'O. Henry moved from North Carolina to what state—Andy? Find the word on the page."

4   The class takes out a vocabulary sheet. Some of the words they are expected to find difficult include: popular, ranch, suitcase, arrested, recipe, tricky, ordinary, humorous, and grand jury.

5   Thirty minutes pass. Bells ring, doors slam.

6   Class 7–1 marches in unescorted, mindful of rule number one. Paperbacks of Poe smack sharply on desks, notebooks rustle, and kids lean forward expectantly, waiting for Mrs. H. to fire the first question. What did we learn about the writer?

7   Hands shoot into the air. Though Edgar Allan Poe ends up sounding a lot like Jerry Lee Lewis—a booze-hound who married his 13-year-old cousin—these kids speak confidently, in paragraphs. Absolutely no looking at the book allowed.

8   We also have a vocabulary sheet, drawn from "The Tell-Tale Heart," containing words like: audacity, dissimulation, sagacity, stealthy, anxiety, derision, agony, and supposition.

9   As I sit in the back of the classroom watching these two very different groups of seventh graders, my previous life as an English teacher allows me to

make an educated guess and a chilling prediction. With the best of intentions, Mrs. H. is teaching the first group, otherwise known as the "slow kids," as though they are fourth graders, and the second, the honors group, as though they are high school freshmen. Given the odds of finding a word like "ordinary" on the SAT's, the children of 7–16 have a better chance of standing before a "grand jury" than making it to college.

Tracking, the practice of placing students in "ability groups" based on a   10 host of ill-defined criteria—everything from test scores to behavior to how much of a fuss a mother can be counted on to make—encourages even well-meaning teachers and administrators to turn out generation after generation of self-fulfilling prophecies. "These kids know they're no Einsteins," Mrs. H. said of her low-track class when we sat together in the teacher's lounge. "They know they don't read well. This way I can go really slowly with them."

With his grades, however, young Albert would probably be hanging right   11 here with the rest of lunch table 7–16. That's where I discover that while their school may think they're dumb, these kids are anything but stupid. "That teacher," sniffs a pretty girl wearing lots of purple lipstick. "She talks so slow. She thinks we're babies. She takes a year to do anything." "What about that other one?" a girl named Ingrid asks, referring to their once-a-week student teacher. "He comes in and goes like this: Rail (pauses) road. Rail (pauses) road. Like we don't know what railroad means!" The table breaks up laughing.

Outside the walls of schools across the country, it's slowly become an open   12 secret that enforced homogeneity benefits no one. The work of researchers like Jeannie Oakes of UCLA and Robert Slavin of Johns Hopkins has proven that tracking does not merely reflect differences—it causes them. Over time, slow kids get slower, while those in the middle and in the so-called "gifted and talented" top tracks fail to gain from isolation. Along the way, the practice re-segregates the nation's schools, dividing the middle from the lower classes, white from black and brown. As the evidence piles up, everyone from the Carnegie Corporation to the National Governors Association has called for change.

Though some fashionably progressive schools have begun to reform,   13 tracking persists. Parent groups, school boards, teachers, and administrators who hold the power within schools cling to the myths and wax apocalyptic about the horrors of heterogeneity. On their side is the most potent force known to man: bureaucratic inertia. Because tracking puts kids in boxes, keeps the lid on, and shifts responsibility for mediocrity and failure away from the schools themselves, there is little incentive to change a nearly-century old tradition. "Research is research," the principal told me that day, "This is practice."

Back Track

14   Tracking has been around since just after the turn of the century. It was then, as cities teemed with immigrants and industry, that education reformers like John Franklin Bobbitt began to argue that the school and the factory shared a common mission, to "work up the raw material into that finished product for which it was best adapted." By the twenties, the scientific principles that ruled the factory floor had been applied to the classroom. They believed the IQ test—which had just become popular—allowed pure science, not the whims of birth or class, to determine whether a child received the type of education appropriate for a future manager or a future laborer.

15   It hasn't quite worked out that way. Driven by standardized tests, the descendants of the old IQ tests, tracking has evolved into a kind of educational triage premised on the notion that only the least wounded can be saved. Yet when the classroom operates like a battleground, society's casualties mount, and the results begin to seem absurd: Kids who enter school needing more get less, while the already enriched get, well, enricher. Then, too, the low-track graduates of 70 years ago held a distinct advantage over their modern counterparts: If tracking prepared them for mindless jobs, at least those jobs existed.

16   The sifting and winnowing starts as early as pre-K. Three-year-old Ebony and her classmates have won the highly prized "gifted and talented" label after enduring a battery of IQ and psychological tests. There's nothing wrong with the "regular" class in this Harlem public school. But high expectations for Ebony and her new friends bring tangible rewards like a weekly field trip and music and computer lessons.

17   Meanwhile, regular kids move on to regular kindergartens where they too will be tested, and where it will be determined that some children need more help, perhaps a "pre-first grade" developmental year. So by the time they're ready for first grade reading groups, certain six-year-olds have already been marked as "sparrows"—the low performers in the class.

18   In the beginning, it doesn't seem to matter so much, because the other reading groups—the robins and the eagles—are just a few feet away and the class is together for most of the day. Trouble is, as they toil over basic drill sheets, the sparrows are slipping farther behind. The robins are gathering more challenging vocabulary words, and the eagles soaring on to critical thinking skills.

19   Though policies vary, by fourth grade many of these groups have flown into completely separate classrooms, turning an innocent three-tier reading system into three increasingly rigid academic tracks—honors, regular, and remedial—by middle school.

20   Unless middle school principals take heroic measures like buying expensive software or crafting daily schedules by hand, it often becomes a lot easier to sort everybody by reading scores. So kids who do well on reading tests can

land in the high track for math, science, social studies, even lunch, and move together as a self-contained unit all day. Friendships form, attitudes harden. Kids on top study together, kids in the middle console themselves by making fun of the "nerds" above and the "dummies" below, and kids on the bottom develop behavioral problems and get plenty of negative reinforcement.

By high school, many low-track students are locked out of what Jeannie   21 Oakes calls "gatekeeper courses," the science, math, and foreign language classes that hold the key to life after twelfth grade. Doors to college are slamming shut, though the kids themselves are often the last to know. When researcher Anne Wheelock interviewed students in Boston's public schools, they'd all insist they were going to become architects, teachers, and the like. What courses were they taking? "Oh, Keyboarding II, Earth Science, Consumer Math. This would be junior year and I'd ask, 'Are you taking Algebra?' and they'd say no."

Black Marks

A funny thing can happen to minority students on the way to being tracked.   22 Even when minority children score high, they often find themselves placed in lower tracks where counselors and principals assume they belong.

In Paula Hart's travels for The Achievement Council, a Los Angeles-based   23 educational advocacy group, she comes across district after district where black and Latino kids score in the 75th percentile for math, yet never quite make it into Algebra I, the classic gatekeeper course. A strange phenomenon occurs in inner city areas with large minority populations—high track classes shrink, and low track classes expand to fit humble expectations for the entire school population.

A few years ago, Dr. Norward Roussell's curiosity got the best of him. As   24 Selma, Alabama's first black school superintendent, he couldn't help but notice that "gifted and talented" tracks were nearly lily white in a district that was 70 percent black. When he looked for answers in the files of high school students, he discovered that a surprising number of low track minority kids had actually scored higher than their white top track counterparts.

Parents of gifted and talented students staged a full-scale revolt against   25 Roussell's subsequent efforts to establish logical standards for placement. In four days of public hearings, speaker after speaker said the same thing: We're going to lose a lot of our students to other schools. To Roussell, their meaning was clear: Put black kids in the high tracks and we pull white kids out of the system. More blacks and more low-income whites did make it to the top under the new criteria, but Roussell himself was left behind. The majority-white school board chose not to renew his contract, and he's now superintendent in Macon County, Alabama, a district that is overwhelmingly black.

26   Race and class divisions usually play themselves out in a more subtle fashion. Talk to teachers about how their high track kids differ from their low track kids and most speak not of intelligence, but of motivation and "family." It seems that being gifted and talented is hereditary after all, largely a matter of having parents who read to you, who take you to museums and concerts, and who know how to work the system. Placement is often a matter of who's connected. Jennifer P., a teacher in a Brooklyn elementary school saw a pattern in her class. "The principal put all the kids whose parents were in the PTA in the top tracks no matter what their scores were. He figures that if his PTA's happy, he's happy."

27   Once the offspring of the brightest and the best connected have been skimmed off in honors or regular tracks, low tracks begin to fill up with children whose parents are not likely to complain. These kids get less homework, spend less class time learning, and are often taught by the least experienced teachers, because avoiding them can become a reward for seniority in a profession where perks are few.

28   With the courts reluctant to get involved, even when tracking leads to racial segregation and at least the appearance of civil rights violations, changing the system becomes an arduous local battle fought school by school. Those who undertake the delicate process of untracking need nerves of steel and should be prepared to find resistance from every quarter, since, as Slavin notes, parents of high-achieving kids will fight this to the death. One-time guidance counselor Hart learned this lesson more than a decade ago when she and two colleagues struggled to introduce a now-thriving college curriculum program at Los Angeles' Banning High. Their efforts to open top-track classes to all students prompted death threats from an unlikely source—their fellow teachers.

Off Track Betting

29   Anne Wheelock's new book, *Crossing the Tracks*, tells the stories of schools that have successfully untracked or never tracked at all. Schools that make the transition often achieve dramatic results. True to its name, Pioneer Valley Regional school in Northfield, Massachusetts was one of the first in the nation to untrack. Since 1983, the number of Pioneer Valley seniors going on to higher education jumped from 37 to 80 percent. But, the author says, urban schools continue to lag behind. "We're talking about unequal distribution of reform," Wheelock declares. "Change is taking place in areas like Wellesley, Massachusetts and Jericho, Long Island. It's easier to untrack when kids are closer to one another to begin with."

30   It's also easier for educators to tinker with programs and make cosmetic adjustments than it is to ask them to do what bureaucrats hate most: give up

one method of doing things without having another to put in its place. Tracking is a system; untracking is a leap of faith. When difficult kids can no longer be dumped in low tracks, new ways must be found to deal with disruptive behavior: early intervention, intensive work with families, and lots of tutoring. Untracking may also entail new instructional techniques like cooperative group learning and peer tutoring, but what it really demands is flexibility and improvisation.

It also demands that schools—and the rest of us—admit that some kids will   31 be so disruptive or violent that a solution for dealing with them must be found *outside* of the regular public school system. New York City seems close to such a conclusion. Schools Chancellor Joseph Fernandez is moving forward with a voluntary "academy" program, planning separate schools designed to meet the needs of chronic troublemakers. One of them, the Wildcat Academy, run by a non-profit group of the same name, plans to enroll 150 students by the end of the year. Wildcat kids will attend classes from nine to five, wear uniforms, hold part-time jobs, and be matched with mentors from professional fields. Districts in Florida and California are conducting similar experiments.

Moving away from tracking is not about taking away from the gifted and   32 talented and giving to the poor. That, as Wheelock notes, is "political suicide." It's not even about placing more black and Latino kids in their midst, a kind of pre-K affirmative action. Rather, it's about raising expectations for everyone. Or, as Slavin puts it: "You can maintain your tracking system. Just put everyone into the top track."

That's not as quixotic as it sounds. In fact, it's long been standard practice   33 in the nation's Catholic schools, a system so backward it's actually progressive. When I taught in an untracked parochial high school, one size fit all—with the exception of the few we expelled for poor grades or behavior. My students, who differed widely in ability, interest, and background, nevertheless got Shakespeare, Thoreau, and Langston Hughes at the same pace, at the same time—and lived to tell the tale. Their survival came, in part, because my colleagues and I could decide if the cost of keeping a certain student around was too high and we had the option of sending him or her elsewhere if expulsion was warranted.

The result was that my honor students wrote elegant essays and made it to   34 Ivy League schools, right on schedule. And far from being held back by their "regular" and "irregular" counterparts, straight-A students were more likely to be challenged by questions they would never dream of asking. "Why are we studying this?" a big-haired girl snapping gum in the back of the room wondered aloud one day. Her question led to a discussion that turned into the best class I ever taught.

In four years, I never saw a single standardized test score. But time after   35 time I watched my students climb out of whatever mental category I had put them in. Tracking sees to it that they never get that chance. Flying directly in the face of Yogi Berra's rule Number One, it tells kids it's over before it's even begun. For ultimately, tracking stunts the opportunity for growth, the one area in which all children are naturally gifted.

Judith Ortiz Cofer

Advanced Biology

Born in 1952 in Puerto Rico, Judith Cofer moved to the U.S. with her family in 1956. Her poems and stories reflect her Hispanic heritage and her own struggle to live in two cultures. A collection of her personal essays and memoirs was published in 1990 as *Silent Dancing*, and the title essay was chosen for inclusion in *The Best American Essays of 1991*.

1   AS I LAY OUT CLOTHES FOR THE TRIP to Miami to do a reading from my recently published novel, then on to Puerto Rico to see my mother, I take a close look at my travel wardrobe—the tailored skirts in basic colors easily coordinated with my silk blouses—I have to smile to myself remembering what my mother had said about my conservative outfits when I visited her the last time—that I looked like the Jehovah's Witnesses who went from door to door in her pueblo trying to sell tickets to heaven to the die-hard Catholics. I would scare people she said. They would bolt their doors if they saw me approaching with my briefcase. As for her, she dresses in tropical colors—a red skirt and para-keet-yellow blouse look good on her tan skin, and she still has a good enough figure that she can wear a tight, black cocktail dress to go dancing at her favorite club, *El Palacio*, on Saturday nights. And, she emphasizes, still make it to the 10 o'clock mass on Sunday. Catholics can have fun and still be saved, she has often pointed out to me, but only if you pay your respects to God and all His Court with the necessary rituals. She has never accepted my gradual slipping out of the faith in which I was so strictly brought up.

2   As I pack my clothes into the suitcase, I recall our early days in Paterson, New Jersey, where we lived for most of my adolescence while my father was alive and stationed in Brooklyn Yard in New York. At that time, my mother's views on everything from clothing to (the forbidden subject) sex were ruled by the religious fervor that she had developed as a shield against the cold foreign city. These days we have traded places in a couple of areas since she has "gone

home" after my father's death, and "gone native." I chose to attend college in the United States and make a living as an English teacher and, lately, on the lecture circuit as a novelist and poet. But, though our lives are on the surface radically different, my mother and I have affected each other reciprocally over the past twenty years; she has managed to liberate herself from the rituals, mores, and traditions that "cramp" her style, while retaining her femininity and "Puertoricanness," while I struggle daily to consolidate my opposing cultural identities. In my adolescence, divided into my New Jersey years and my Georgia years, I received an education in the art of cultural compromise.

In Paterson in the 1960s I attended a public school in our neighborhood.   3
Still predominantly white and Jewish, it was rated very well academically in a city where the educational system was in chaos, deteriorating rapidly as the best teachers moved on to suburban schools following the black and Puerto Rican migration into, and the white exodus from, the city proper.

The Jewish community had too much at stake to make a fast retreat; many   4
of the small businesses and apartment buildings in the city's core were owned by Jewish families of the World War II generation. They had seen worse things happen than the influx of black and brown people that was scaring away the Italians and the Irish. But they too would gradually move their families out of the best apartments in their buildings and into houses in East Paterson, Fairlawn, and other places with *lawns*. It was how I saw the world then; either you lived without your square of grass or you bought a house to go with it. But for most of my adolescence, I lived among the Jewish people of Paterson. We rented an apartment owned by the Milsteins, proprietors also of the deli on the bottom floor. I went to school with their children. My father took his business to the Jewish establishments, perhaps because these men symbolized "dignified survival" to him. He was obsessed with privacy, and could not stand the personal turns conversations almost always took when two or more Puerto Ricans met casually over a store counter. The Jewish men talked too, but they concentrated on externals. They asked my father about his job, politics, his opinion on Vietnam, Lyndon Johnson. And my father, in his quiet voice, answered their questions knowledgeably. Sometimes before we entered a store, the cleaners, or a shoe-repair shop, he would tell me to look for the blue-inked numbers on the owner's left forearm. I would stare at these numbers, now usually faded enough to look like veins in the wrong place. I would try to make them out. They were a telegram from the past, I later decided, informing the future of the deaths of millions. My father discussed the Holocaust with me in the same hushed tones my mother used to talk about God's Mysterious Ways. I could not reconcile both in my mind. This conflict eventually led to my first serious clash with my mother over irreconcilable differences between the "real world" and religious doctrine.

5   It had to do with the Virgin Birth.

6   And it had to do with my best friend and study partner, Ira Nathan, the acknowledged scientific genius at school. In junior high school it was almost a requirement to be "in love" with an older boy. I was an eighth grader and Ira was in the ninth grade that year and preparing to be sent away to some prep school in New England. I chose him as my boyfriend (in the eyes of my classmates, if a girl spent time with a boy that meant they were "going together") because I needed tutoring in biology—one of his best subjects. I ended up having a crush on him after our first Saturday morning meeting at the library. Ira was my first exposure to the wonders of an analytical mind.

7   The problem was the subject. Biology is a dangerous topic for young teenagers who are themselves walking laboratories, experimenting with interesting combinations of chemicals every time they make a choice. In my basic biology class, we were looking at single-cell organisms under the microscope, and watching them reproduce in slow-motion films in a darkened classroom. Though the process was as unexciting as watching a little kid blow bubbles, we were aroused by the concept itself. Ira's advanced class was dissecting fetal pigs. He brought me a photograph of his project, inner organs labeled neatly on the paper the picture had been glued to. My eyes refused to budge from the line drawn from "genitals" to a part of the pig it pertained to. I felt a wave of heat rising from my chest to my scalp. Ira must have seen my discomfort, though I tried to keep my face behind the black curtain of my hair, but as the boy-scientist, he was relentless. He actually traced the line from label to pig with his pencil.

8   "All mammals reproduce sexually," he said in a teacherly monotone.

9   The librarian, far off on the other side of the room, looked up at us and frowned. Logically, it was not possible that she could have heard Ira's pronouncement, but I was convinced that the mention of sex enhanced the hearing capabilities of parents, teachers and librarians by one hundred percent. I blushed more intensely, and peeked through my hair at Ira.

10   He was holding the eraser of his pencil on the pig's blurry sexual parts and smiling at me. His features were distinctly Eastern European. I had recently seen the young singer Barbra Streisand on the Red Skelton show and had been amazed at how much similarity there was in their appearances. She could have been his sister. I was particularly attracted to the wide mouth and strong nose. No one that I knew in school thought that Ira was attractive, but his brains had long ago overshadowed his looks as his most impressive attribute. Like Ira, I was also a straight A student and also considered odd because I was one of the few Puerto Ricans on the honor roll. So it didn't surprise anyone that Ira and I had drifted toward each other. Though I could not have articulated it then, Ira was seducing me with his No. 2 pencil and the laboratory photograph of his fetal pig. The following Saturday, Ira brought in

his advanced biology book and showed me the transparencies of the human anatomy in full color that I was not meant to see for a couple more years. I was shocked. The cosmic jump between paramecium and the human body was almost too much for me to take in. These were the first grown people I had ever seen naked and they revealed too much.

"Human sexual reproduction can only take place when the male's sperm 11 is introduced into the female womb and fertilization of the egg takes place," Ira stated flatly.

The book was open to the page labeled "The Human Reproductive Sys- 12 tem." Feeling that my maturity was being tested, as well as my intelligence, I found my voice long enough to contradict Ira.

"There has been one exception to this, Ira." I was feeling a little smug 13 about knowing something that Ira obviously did not.

"Judith, there are no exceptions in biology, only mutations, and adapta- 14 tions through evolution." He was smiling in a superior way.

"The Virgin Mary had a baby without . . ." I couldn't say *having sex* in the 15 same breath as the name of the Mother of God. I was totally unprepared for the explosion of laughter that followed my timid statement. Ira had crumpled in his chair and was laughing so hard that his thin shoulders shook. I could hear the librarian approaching. Feeling humiliated, I started to put my books together. Ira grabbed my arm.

"Wait, don't go," he was still giggling uncontrollably, "I'm sorry. Let's talk 16 a little more. Wait, give me a chance to explain."

Reluctantly, I sat down again mainly because the librarian was already at 17 our table, hands on hips, whispering angrily: "If you *children* cannot behave in this *study area,* I will have to ask you to leave." Ira and I both apologized, though she gave him a nasty look because his mouth was still stretched from ear to ear in a hysterical grin.

"Listen, listen. I'm sorry that I laughed like that. I know you're Catholic 18 and you believe in the Virgin Birth (he bit his lower lip trying to regain his composure), but it's just not biologically possible to have a baby without . . . (he struggled for control) . . . losing your virginity."

I sank down on my hard chair. "Virginity." He had said another of the for- 19 bidden words. I glanced back at the librarian who was keeping her eye on us. I was both offended and excited by Ira's blasphemy. How could he deny a doc- trine that people had believed in for 2,000 years? It was part of my prayers every night. My mother talked about La Virgen as if she were our most im- portant relative.

Recovering from his fit of laughter, Ira kept his hand discreetly on my 20 elbow as he explained in the seductive language of the scientific laboratory how babies were made, and how it was impossible to violate certain natural laws.

21   "Unless God wills it," I argued feebly.

22   "There is no God," said Ira, and the last shred of my innocence fell away as I listened to his arguments backed up by irrefutable scientific evidence.

23   Our meetings continued all that year, becoming more exciting with every chapter in his biology book. My grades improved dramatically since one-celled organisms were no mystery to a student of advanced biology. Ira's warm, moist hand often brushed against mine under the table at the library, and walking home one bitter cold day, he asked me if I would wear his Beta Club pin. I nodded and when we stepped inside the hallway of my building where he removed his thick mittens which his mother had knitted, he pinned the blue enamel B to my collar. And to the hissing of the steam heaters, I received a serious kiss from Ira. We separated abruptly when we heard Mrs. Milstein's door open.

24   "Hello, Ira."

25   "Hello, Mrs. Milstein."

26   "And how is your mother? I haven't seen Fritzie all week. She's not sick, is she?"

27   "She's had a mild cold, Mrs. Milstein. But she is steadily improving." Ira's diction became extremely precise and formal when he was in the presence of adults. As an only child and a prodigy, he had to live up to very high standards.

28   "I'll call her today," Mrs. Milstein said, finally looking over at me. Her eyes fixed on the collar of my blouse which was, I later saw in our hall mirror, sticking straight up with Ira's pin attached crookedly to the edge.

29   "Good-bye, Mrs. Milstein."

30   "Nice to see you, Ira."

31   Ira waved awkwardly to me as he left. Mrs. Milstein stood in the humid hallway of her building watching me run up the stairs.

32   Our "romance" lasted only a week; long enough for Mrs. Milstein to call Ira's mother, and for Mrs. Nathan to call my mother. I was subjected to a lecture on moral behavior by my mother, who, carried away by her anger and embarrassed that I had been seen kissing a boy (understood: a boy who was not even Catholic), had begun a chain of metaphors for the loss of virtue that was on the verge of the tragi/comical:

33   "A *perdida*, a cheap item," she said trembling before me as I sat on the edge of my bed, facing her accusations, "a girl begins to look like one when she allows herself to be *handled* by men."

34   "Mother . . ." I wanted her to lower her voice so that my father, sitting at the kitchen table reading, would not hear. I had already promised her that I would confess my sin that Saturday and take communion with a sparkling clean soul. I had not been successful at keeping the sarcasm out of my voice. Her fury was fueled by her own bitter litany.

"A dirty joke, a burden to her family . . ." She was rolling with her Span- 35
ish now; soon the Holy Mother would enter into the picture for good measure. "It's not as if I had not taught you better. Don't you know that those people do not have the example of the Holy Virgin Mary and her Son to follow
and that is why they do things for the wrong reasons. Mrs. Nathan said she
did not want her son messing around with you—not because of the wrongness
of it—but because it would interfere with his studies!" She was yelling now.
"She's afraid that he will (she crossed herself at the horror of the thought)
make you pregnant!"

"We could say an angel came down and put a baby in my stomach, 36
Mother." She had succeeded in dragging me into her field of hysteria. She
grabbed my arm and pulled me to my feet.

"I do not want you associating any more than necessary with people who 37
do not have God, do you hear me?"

"They have a god!" I was screaming now too, trying to get away from her 38
suffocating grasp: "They have an intelligent god who doesn't ask you to believe
that a woman can get pregnant without having sex!" That's when she slapped
me. She looked horrified at what she had instinctively done.

"Nazi," I hissed, out of control by then too, "I bet you'd like to send Ira 39
and his family to a concentration camp!" At that time I thought that was the
harshest thing I could have said to anyone. I was certain that I had sentenced
my soul to eternal damnation the minute the words came out of my mouth;
but my cheek was burning from the slap and I wanted to hurt her. Father
walked into my room at that moment looking shocked at the sight of the two
of us entangled in mortal combat.

"Please, please," his voice sounded agonized. I ran to him and he held me 40
in his arms while I cried my heart out on his starched white shirt. My mother,
also weeping quietly, tried to walk past us, but he pulled her into the circle.
After a few moments, she put her trembling hand on my head.

"We are a family," my father said, "there is only the three of us against the 41
world. Please, please . . ." But he did not follow the "please" with any suggestions as to what we could do to make things right in a world that was as con-
fusing to my mother as it was to me.

I finished the eighth grade in Paterson, but Ira and I never got together to 42
study again. I sent his Beta club pin back to him via a mutual friend. Once in
a while I saw him in the hall or the playground. But he seemed to be in the
clouds, where he belonged. In the fall, I was enrolled at St. Joseph's Catholic
High School where everyone believed in the Virgin Birth, and I never had to
take a test on the human reproductive system. It was a chapter that was not
emphasized.

In 1968, the year Paterson, like many U.S. cities, exploded in racial vio- 43
lence, my father moved us to Augusta, Georgia, where two of his brothers had

retired from the army at Fort Gordon. They had convinced him that it was a healthier place to rear teenagers. For me it was a shock to the senses, like moving from one planet to another: where Paterson had concrete to walk on and gray skies, bitter winters, and a smorgasbord of an ethnic population, Georgia was red like Mars, and Augusta was green—exploding in colors in more gardens of azaleas and dogwood and magnolia trees—more vegetation than I imagined was possible anywhere not tropical like Puerto Rico. People seemed to come in two basic colors: black and blond. And I could barely understand my teachers when they talked in a slowed-down version of English like one of those old 78-speed recordings played at 33. But I was placed in all advanced classes and one of them was biology. This is where I got to see my first real fetal pig which my assigned lab partner had chosen. She picked it up gingerly by the ends of the plastic bag in which it was stored: "Ain't he cute?" she asked. I nodded, nearly fainting from the overwhelming combination of the smell of formaldehyde and my sudden flashback to my brief but intense romance with Ira Nathan.

44   "What you want to call him?" My partner unwrapped our specimen on the table, and I surprised myself by my instant recall of Ira's chart. I knew all the parts. In my mind's eye I saw the pencil lines, the labeled photograph. I had had an excellent teacher.

45   "Let's call him Ira."

46   "That's a funny name, but OK." My lab partner, a smart girl destined to become my mentor in things Southern, then gave me a conspiratorial wink and pulled out a little perfume atomizer from her purse. She sprayed Ira from snout to tail with it. I noticed this operation was taking place at other tables too. The teacher had conveniently left the room a few minutes before. I was once again stunned—almost literally knocked out by a fist of smell: "What is it?"

47   "*Intimate,*" my advanced biology partner replied smiling.

48   And by the time our instructor came back to the room, we were ready to delve into this mystery of muscle and bone; eager to discover the secrets that lie just beyond fear a little past loathing; of acknowledging the corruptibility of the flesh, and our own fascination with the subject.

49   As I finish packing, the telephone rings and it's my mother. She is reminding me to be ready to visit relatives, to go to a dance with her, and, of course, to attend a couple of the services at the church. It is the feast of the Black Virgin, revered patron saint of our home town in Puerto Rico. I agree to everything, and find myself anticipating the eclectic itinerary. Why not allow Evolution and Eve, Biology and the Virgin Birth? Why not take a vacation from logic? I will not be away for too long, I will not let myself be tempted to remain in the sealed garden of blind faith; I'll stay just long enough to rest myself from the exhausting enterprise of leading the examined life.

Student Essay

Benjamin James

Complaining Through College

Assigned to write an essay comparing two different periods in life, Benjamin took some inspiration from Judith Cofer's "Advanced Biology." However, unlike Cofer, Benjamin chose to show how his changing family situation affected his school life. The result is a simple but strong statement about the evolution of his own attitude toward his education.

ALL COLLEGE STUDENTS COMPLAIN: complaining is the unique feature that binds all of us through all of our many differences. As a college student, I complain too—but my complaints now take much different shape from the first time I went to college.

Then, I complained about homework, about how professors just didn't seem to understand that students are enrolled in four classes, that we couldn't center our lives around just one class. Professors would inevitably coordinate their assignments so I had a paper due in each of my classes on the same day. When you combine the pressures of a work study job, having a decent social life, and participating in the school newspaper, it's simply unreasonable to ask students to write four papers in a week.

I complained about my social life. All the best looking females were dating juniors and seniors, sometimes even graduate students. How's a freshman guy going to compete with that? Certainly there was no way the older women were going to give me the time of day. Parties were no place to meet people. Sure, you could dance and have fun with your friends, but no one would give a stranger a second look.

I complained about my job. I had the most boring job on campus—data entry in the Accounts Payable Department. Everyone who worked there was so bored by their job that they simply went through the motions. There was certainly no opportunity to do homework. The work was so boring that the boss made an unwritten rule that everyone could leave at 4:45 (even though we were paid to work until 5:00). Anyone who stayed even a few minutes late to finish up a task was branded a workaholic.

So I quit school.

Now, four years later, I'm back in school, but I'm married with a 6-month-old baby. My wife works during the day, so I'm taking care of the baby then. I go to night school while she feeds and bathes the baby and puts her to bed.

I'm still complaining, but my complaints are entirely different from when I was a single college student.

7   I don't complain about my homework—homework is the one thing in my life I have the most control over. It's amazing how much studying you can do in three hours a day—when you know that's the only three hours you'll get. I don't complain about my social life. What social life do you need when you're happily married with a beautiful baby, and family and friends constantly drop by to coo? I don't complain about my job. What work I do I enjoy—freelance typesetting for a local printer, while the baby naps.

8   So what do I complain about now? Well, the price of baby formula, for one. And how my baby just doesn't seem to understand that she shouldn't stay up all night crying when Daddy has a big exam the next day. I can't stand it when people aren't open-minded about our nonconventional lifestyle. I cringe when people suggest that I can't take care of a baby as well as her mother does. I seethe when they call me "Mr. Mom." In fact, the people who seem to understand my unusual life best of all are my fellow college students. They, like me, are juggling an entirely unreasonable assortment of seemingly incompatible responsibilities. They, like me, have a great, big, long, wonderful life ahead of them—if only they can first finish those two papers that are due next Friday!

5

Process Analysis

Process Analysis

1. **Know the process.** This guideline may seem obvious, but it's especially important when you're describing a procedure you expect others to follow. In that case, a good rule of thumb is never to write a procedure for a process you haven't performed yourself. Of course, you could analyze a process that people don't perform at all, such as the annual salmon run or the workings of an internal combustion engine. In such cases it still remains true that the clearer your understanding of the process, the better your process analysis is likely to be.

2. **Determine the type of analysis to write.** There are two major types of process analyses: *procedures* you expect someone to follow, and *descriptions* you offer simply to inform your readers. The distinction is critical: in a procedure, you need to give enough information for your readers to complete the process themselves; in an informative analysis, too much detail will likely only bore your audience.

3. **Break the process into steps.** Whether your goal is to instruct or to inform, to analyze a process you'll need to determine what the major steps of the process are. In many cases, the steps will follow a chronological sequence—as when building or repairing a physical object. Other processes—like the workings of a car engine—occur simultaneously, so you'll need to create your own divisions based on your opinion of what aspects of the process are most important. You can see this technique applied in "How to Write with Style": while the writing process is simply too complex to proceed in the same manner every time, Kurt Vonnegut makes the topic more approachable by breaking it into component parts. He doesn't suggest that the parts must always be followed in the same manner; they are simply guidelines to writing more effectively.

4. **Adjust the level of detail to match your audience.** Think about describing how a car engine works to an engineer, a mechanic, or a layperson. Naturally you'd adjust your description depending on your audience's level of expertise. Not only would the steps you describe be different, but so would the terms you use. You'd expect a mechanic to know the difference between a carburetor and a fuel pump, but you'd need to define these terms for a layperson.

Student Essay

Sarah Pennington Doud

Changing Kyle

This essay offers a very matter-of-fact description one of the realities of raising a child. You might be a bit shocked by the blunt, to-the-point, but completely accurate description of changing a diaper in this essay, but you shouldn't be—it's something everyone needs to know how to do.

FIRST, I HAVE TO CATCH HIM. Kyle runs with the discombobulated gait of a 1
paraplegic wearing artificial limbs for the first time. On the Rosslyn Children's Center playground, Kyle weaves between tricycles and hides in spaces
my left leg couldn't fit through, let alone my entire body. Our game of chase
is played out daily; providing primary day care for Kyle means changing his
dirty diapers even if I have to drag him off the Hippity Hop.

At twenty months of age, Kyle knows when he has had a bowel movement, 2
but he is not self-conscious about the portable toilet smell that wafts around
him like Pigpen's dust cloud. He would rather ride in the Cozy Coupe or go
down the Little Tikes slide—anything but have his diaper changed. When I
have him cornered, I scoop him up in my arms and promise I'll be as quick
as I can.

Changing Kyle's diaper can be more exciting than Monday night football 3
and a bag of chips: he is my "talker." Kyle started to speak in two-word phrases
at fourteen months and adds at least three new words to his vocabulary every
day. Once, upon hearing a caregiver remark that he'd been spoiled by my constant doting, Kyle responded, "I'm not spoiled. I'm *handsome.*" Kyle's delight-
fully healthy self-image results in part from the phenomenon Russell Baker
describes: "When you're the only pea in the pod, your parents are likely to get
you confused with the Hope Diamond."

Kyle's mother, Angela, a Dubliner, is genetically responsible for Kyle's red 4
hair and his Irish forehead (thin skin, thick skull). Angela blames her husband, Paul, a Polish-Italian, for Kyle's fiery temper. Kyle's temper tantrums on
the changing table are insufferable—a caregiver's version of Chinese water torture.

The diapering procedure at a licensed day care center has more steps than 5
the pre-flight check for the Space Shuttle. When fifteen children share the
same Formica changing table, every bacterial infection within fifty feet comes

looking for a host. A roll of changing paper rests at one end of the table, and pulling it down creates a protective layer between the table and Kyle's bottom. For huge bowel movements, "BMs," I wear two rubber gloves on each hand. I lay Kyle on the table, perpendicular to me, and give him something to hold in his hands. In my experience, boys *need* something to occupy their hands while I play with their favorite toy. During a blizzard last winter, I filled soda bottles with colored water, vegetable oil, and confetti, then glued the caps on. Now my staff stores the bottles in the changing room to keep their babies' idle hands busy. Toys are essential to the success of changing Kyle's diaper. He is *always* poopy.

6   I change Kyle's disposable diapers with wanton disregard for the environment. I use antibacterial wipes, three or four at a time, and when my gloves get dirty, I rip them off and put on new ones. Thank God for trash cans with step-on lids, and further thanks to the genius who left a window in the door to the changing room. When the smell becomes so bad I can't breathe, I put a hand on Kyle's stomach to keep him from rolling over and I lean out the window, sucking in fresh air.

7   Kyle's skin is so sensitive that sometimes I avoid using diaper wipes; instead, I moisten a handful of paper towels with warm water and use those to clean him. Kyle's blessed with a pharmacist father; Paul keeps his son's diaper shelf stocked with Nystatin, Desitin, A&D ointment, and sulfa oxide creams. Nystatin is our favorite—when Kyle's bottom bleeds with open sores and I still have to change him every hour, we spread the Nystatin over every inch of his rear end. Kyle understands that the "keem," as he calls it, is going to make his diaper rash "all better."

8   Kyle is a difficult child to change—in keeping with common European practice, Angela refused to let Kyle be circumcised, calling the surgery "barbaric" and "insensitive." I pull the foreskin back, exposing the tip of the penis, and wipe it clean. Bacteria thrive in unclean, uncircumcised penises. Regularly spraying the table with bleach solution reduces the risk of infection from Coxsackie (better known as hand, foot, and mouth disease), streptococcus, Fifth's Disease, and a host of other predatory viruses.

9   The rule for wiping is front to back for girls, back to front for boys. I pry open the folds of wrinkled pink skin over Kyle's testicles, his scrotum, which can trap stray flecks of excrement. I check his upper thighs, double-check his bottom, and apply diaper cream.

10   Putting the fresh diaper on is the easiest step: bottom up, diaper under, bottom down, the front of the diaper comes up and over his genitals and fastens to the back with adhesive tape. After changing sixty diapers a week for fourteen months, I can complete the process in less than two minutes. It's simple, if not easy. Difficult, but worth it. Like a red-haired toddler I know.

Kurt Vonnegut

How to Write with Style

Kurt Vonnegut's writing has often focused on the conundrum of a technological world—the profusion of technology that makes it so simple for government propaganda machines to inject their version of reality into society. Perhaps it is ironic that his work, especially after the publication and subsequent film of his novel *Slaughterhouse Five,* has acquired something of a cult following, particularly among the technological elite: there are more references to Vonnegut on the Internet than to any of the other writers appearing in this book. What has Vonnegut himself to say about all this? "The Internet stuff is spooky," Vonnegut commented after someone sent him a printed copy of the Alt.books.kurt-vonnegut FAQ World Wide Web page. "I am of course not on line. I do remember ham radio operators though, usually in attics or basements, pallid, unsociable, and obsessed, inhabiting a spirit world, and harmless." A writer could do worse than imitate Vonnegut's highly readable, impeccably precise style.

NEWSPAPER REPORTERS AND TECHNICAL WRITERS ARE TRAINED to reveal almost nothing about themselves in their writings. This makes them freaks in the world of writers, since almost all of the other ink-stained wretches in that world reveal a lot about themselves to readers. We call these revelations, accidental and intentional, elements of style.   1

These revelations tell us as readers what sort of person it is with whom we are spending time. Does the writer sound ignorant or informed, stupid or bright, crooked or honest, humorless or playful–? And on and on.   2

Why should you examine your writing style with the idea of improving it? Do so as a mark of respect for your readers, whatever you're writing. If you scribble your thoughts any which way, your readers will surely feel that you care nothing about them. They will mark you down as an egomaniac or a chowderhead—or worse, they will stop reading you.   3

The most damning revelation you can make about yourself is that you do not know what is interesting and what is not. Don't you yourself like or dislike writers mainly for what they choose to show you or make you think about? Did you ever admire an empty-headed writer for his or her mastery of the language? No.   4

So your own winning style must begin with ideas in your head.   5

1. Find a Subject You Care About

Find a subject you care about and which you in your heart feel others should care about. It is this genuine caring, and not your games with language, which will be the most compelling and seductive element in your style.   6

7   I am not urging you to write a novel, by the way—although I would not be sorry if you wrote one, provided you genuinely cared about something. A petition to the mayor about a pothole in front of your house or a love letter to the girl next door will do.

2. Do Not Ramble, Though

8   I won't ramble on about that.

3. Keep It Simple

9   As for your use of language: Remember that two great masters of language, William Shakespeare and James Joyce, wrote sentences which were almost childlike when their subjects were most profound. "To be or not to be?" asks Shakespeare's Hamlet. The longest word is three letters long. Joyce, when he was frisky, could put together a sentence as intricate and as glittering as a necklace for Cleopatra, but my favorite sentence in his short story "Eveline" is this one: "She was tired." At that point in the story, no other words could break the heart of a reader as those three words do.

10   Simplicity of language is not only reputable, but perhaps even sacred. The Bible opens with a sentence well within the writing skills of a lively fourteen-year-old: "In the beginning God created the heaven and the earth."

4. Have the Guts to Cut

11   It may be that you, too, are capable of making necklaces for Cleopatra, so to speak. But your eloquence should be the servant of the ideas in your head. Your rule might be this: If a sentence, no matter how excellent, does not illuminate your subject in some new and useful way, scratch it out.

5. Sound Like Yourself

12   The writing style which is most natural for you is bound to echo the speech you heard when a child. English was the novelist Joseph Conrad's third language, and much that seems piquant in his use of English was no doubt colored by his first language, which was Polish. And lucky indeed is the writer who has grown up in Ireland, for the English spoken there is so amusing and musical. I myself grew up in Indianapolis, where common speech sounds like a band saw cutting galvanized tin, and employs a vocabulary as unornamental as a monkey wrench.

13   In some of the more remote hollows of Appalachia, children still grow up hearing songs and locutions of Elizabethan times. Yes, and many Americans grow up hearing a language other than English, or an English dialect a majority of Americans cannot understand.

14   All these varieties of speech are beautiful, just as the varieties of butterflies are beautiful. No matter what your first language, you should treasure it all

your life. If it happens not to be standard English, and if it shows itself when you write standard English, the result is usually delightful, like a very pretty girl with one eye that is green and one that is blue.

I myself find that I trust my own writing most, and others seem to trust it 15 most, too, when I sound most like a person from Indianapolis, which is what I am. What alternatives do I have? The one most vehemently recommended by teachers has no doubt been pressed on you, as well: to write like cultivated Englishmen of a century or more ago.

6. Say What You Mean to Say

I used to be exasperated by such teachers, but am no more. I understand 16 now that all those antique essays and stories with which I was to compare my own work were not magnificent for their datedness or foreignness, but for saying precisely what their authors meant them to say. My teachers wished me to write accurately, always selecting the most effective words, and relating the words to one another unambiguously, rigidly, like parts of a machine. The teachers did not want to turn me into an Englishman after all. They hoped that I would become understandable—and therefore understood. And there went my dream of doing with words what Pablo Picasso did with paint or what any number of jazz idols did with music. If I broke all the rules of punctuation, had words mean whatever I wanted them to mean, and strung them together higgledy-piggledy, I would simply not be understood. So you, too, had better avoid Picasso-style or jazz-style writing, if you have something worth saying and wish to be understood.

Readers want our pages to look very much like pages they have seen be- 17 fore. Why? This is because they themselves have a tough job to do, and they need all the help they can get from us.

7. Pity the Readers

They have to identify thousands of little marks on paper, and make sense 18 of them immediately. They have to *read*, an art so difficult that most people don't really master it even after having studied it all through grade school and high school—twelve long years.

So this discussion must finally acknowledge that our stylistic options as 19 writers are neither numerous nor glamorous, since our readers are bound to be such imperfect artists. Our audience requires us to be sympathetic and patient teachers, even willing to simplify and clarify—whereas we would rather soar high above the crowd, singing like nightingales.

That is the bad news. The good news is that we Americans are governed 20 under a unique Constitution, which allows us to write whatever we please without fear of punishment. So the most meaningful aspect of our styles, which is what we choose to write about, is utterly unlimited.

8. For Really Detailed Advice

21   For a discussion of literary style in a narrower sense, in a more technical sense, I commend to your attention *The Elements of Style,* by William Strunk Jr., and E. B. White (Macmillan, 1979). E. B. White is, of course, one of the most admirable literary stylists this country has so far produced.

22   You should realize, too, that no one would care how well or badly Mr. White expressed himself, if he did not have perfectly enchanting things to say.

Peter Elbow

Desperation Writing

Peter Elbow has been teaching college writing since 1960 and has served as a consultant to several university writing centers. His books *Writing without Teachers* and *Writing with Power: Techniques of Mastering the Writing Process* are popular guides to clear, effective writing. He is a strong advocate of freewriting, stressing that editing should be done after the ideas are down on paper. His interest in writing came from his "own difficulties with it" and this has inspired him not only to write, but also to help others learn to write. He has written many articles about the teaching of writing and is an active contributor to the National Council of Teachers of English.

1   I KNOW I AM NOT ALONE in my recurring twinges of panic that I won't be able to write something when I need to, I won't be able to produce coherent speech or thought. And that lingering doubt is a great hindrance to writing. It's a constant fog or static that clouds the mind. I never got out of its clutches till I discovered that it was possible to write something—not something great or pleasing but at least something usable, workable—when my mind is out of commission. The trick is that you have to do all your cooking out on the table: Your mind is incapable of doing any inside. It means using symbols and pieces of paper not as a crutch but as a wheelchair.

2   The first thing is to admit your condition: Because of some mood or event or whatever, your mind is incapable of anything that could be called thought. It can put out a babbling kind of speech utterance, it can put a simple feeling, perception or sort-of-thought into understandable (though terrible) words. But it is incapable of considering anything in relation to anything else. The moment you try to hold that thought or feeling up against some other to see the relationship, you simply lose the picture—you get nothing but buzzing lines or waving colors.

So admit this. Avoid anything more than one feeling, perception, or thought. Simply write as much as possible. Try simply to steer your mind in the direction or general vicinity of the thing you are trying to write about and start writing and keep writing.

Just write and keep writing. (Probably best to write on only one side of the paper in case you should want to cut parts out with scissors—but you probably won't.) Just write and keep writing. It will probably come in waves. After a flurry, stop and take a brief rest. But don't stop too long. Don't think about what you are writing or what you have written or else you will overload the circuit again. Keep writing as though you are drugged or drunk. Keep doing this till you feel you have a lot of material that might be useful; or, if necessary, till you can't stand it any more—even if you doubt that there's anything useful there.

Then take a pad of little pieces of paper—or perhaps 3 × 5 cards—and simply start at the beginning of what you were writing, and as you read over what you wrote, every time you come to any thought, feeling, perception, or image that could be gathered up into one sentence or one assertion, do so and write it by itself on a little sheet of paper. In short, you are trying to turn, say, ten or twenty pages of wandering mush into twenty or thirty hard little crab apples. Sometimes there won't be many on a page. But if it seems to you that there are none on a page, you are making a serious error—the same serious error that put you in this comatose state to start with. You are mistaking lousy, stupid, second-rate, wrong, childish, foolish, worthless ideas for no ideas at all. Your job is not to pick out *good* ideas but to pick out ideas. As long as you were conscious, your words will be full of things that could be called feelings, utterances, ideas—things that can be squeezed into one simple sentence. This is your job. Don't ask for too much.

After you have done this, take those little slips or cards, read through them a number of times—not struggling with them, simply wandering and mulling through them; perhaps shifting them around and looking through in various sequences. In a sense these are cards you are playing solitaire with, and the rules of this particular game permit shuffling the unused pile.

The goal of this procedure with the cards is to get them to distribute themselves in two or three or ten or fifteen different piles on your desk. You can get them to do this almost by themselves if you simply keep reading through them in different orders; certain cards will begin to feel like they go with other cards. I emphasize this passive, thoughtless mode because I want to talk about desperation writing in its pure state. In practice, almost invariably at some point in the procedure, your sanity begins to return. It is often at this point. You actually are moved to have thoughts or—and the difference between active and passive is crucial here—to *exert* thought; to hold two cards together and *build* or *assert* a relationship. It is a matter of bringing energy to bear.

8   So you may start to be able to do something active with these cards, and begin actually to think. But if not, just allow the cards to find their own piles with each other by feel, by drift, by intuition, by mindlessness.

9   You have now engaged in the two main activities that will permit you to get something cooked out on the table rather than in your brain: writing out into messy words, summing up into single assertions, and even sensing relationships between assertions. You can simply continue to deploy these two activities.

10   If, for example, after the first round of writing, assertion-making, and pile-making, your piles feel as though they are useful and satisfactory for what you are writing—paragraphs or sections or trains of thought—then you can carry on from there. See if you can gather each pile up into a single assertion. When you can, then put the subsidiary assertions of that pile into their best order to fit with that single unifying one. If you *can't* get the pile into one assertion, then take the pile as the basis for doing some more writing out into words. In the course of this writing, you may produce for yourself the single unifying assertion you were looking for; or you may have to go through the cycle of turning the writing into assertions and piles and so forth. Perhaps more than once. The pile may turn out to want to be two or more piles itself; or it may want to become part of a pile you already have. This is natural. This kind of meshing into one configuration, then coming apart, then coming together and meshing into a different configuration— this is growing and cooking. It makes a terrible mess, but if you can't do it in your head, you have to put up with a cluttered desk and a lot of confusion.

11   If, on the other hand, all that writing *didn't* have useful material in it, it means that your writing wasn't loose, drifting, quirky, jerky, associative enough. This time try especially to let things simply remind you of things that are seemingly crazy or unrelated. Follow these odd associations. Make as many metaphors as you can—be as nutty as possible—and explore the metaphors themselves—open them out. You may have all your energy tied up in some area of your experience that you are leaving out. Don't refrain from writing about whatever else is on your mind: how you feel at the moment, what you are losing your mind over, randomness that intrudes itself on your consciousness, the pattern on the wallpaper, what those people you see out the window have on their minds—though keep coming back to the whateveritis you are supposed to be writing about. Treat it, in short, like ten-minute writing exercises. Your best perceptions and thoughts are always going to be tied up in whatever is really occupying you, and that is also where your energy is. You may end up writing a love poem—or a hate poem—in one of those little piles while the other piles will finally turn into a lab report on data processing or whatever you have to write about. But you couldn't, in

your present state of having your head shot off, have written that report without also writing the poem. And the report will have some of the juice of the poem in it and vice versa.

Jessica Mitford

Behind the Formaldehyde Curtain

Jessica Mitford's scathing exposé of the funeral industry in her 1963 book *The American Way of Death* was hardly her first act of protest against established morals and the staid way of life. The daughter of the proto-fascist Lord and Lady Redsdale, Mitford miffed her family by eloping with her left-wing activist second cousin (the nephew of Winston Churchill). They emigrated to the U.S. in 1939, but her husband, serving with the Royal Canadian Air Force, was killed in action over Germany in 1941. A political activist, Mitford joined the Communist party, and she and her second husband were active in the Civil Rights Congress. Her subsequent investigative books on the American prison system, obstetrics, and the trial of Dr. Spock fostered her reputation as "Queen of the Muckrakers." As a leader in investigative journalism, Mitford's writing set a standard that relied heavily on accurate process analysis, along with a good dose of her caustic wit.

Per her request, her memorial service was grand, with six black plumed horses pulling a carriage followed by a twelve-piece brass band. Her actual funeral, however, was a $475 cremation.

THE DRAMA BEGINS TO UNFOLD with the arrival of the corpse at the mortuary.   1

Alas, poor Yorick! How surprised he would be to see how his counterpart   2
of today is whisked off to a funeral parlor and is in short order sprayed, sliced, pierced, pickled, trussed, trimmed, creamed, waxed, painted, rouged and neatly dressed—transformed from a common corpse into a Beautiful Memory Picture. This process is known in the trade as embalming and restorative art, and is so universally employed in the United States and Canada that the funeral director does it routinely, without consulting corpse or kin. He regards as eccentric those few who are hardy enough to suggest that it might be dispensed with. Yet no law requires embalming, no religious doctrine commends it, nor is it dictated by considerations of health, sanitation, or even of personal daintiness. In no part of the world but in Northern America is it widely used. The purpose of embalming is to make the corpse presentable for viewing in a suitably costly container; and here too the funeral director routinely, without first consulting the family, prepares the body for public display.

Is all this legal? The processes to which a dead body may be subjected are   3
after all to some extent circumscribed by law. In most states, for instance, the

signature of next of kin must be obtained before an autopsy may be performed, before the deceased may be cremated, before the body may be turned over to a medical school for research purposes; or such provision must be made in the decedent's will. In the case of embalming, no such permission is required nor is it ever sought. A textbook, *The Principles and Practices of Embalming*, comments on this: "There is some question regarding the legality of much that is done within the preparation room." The author points out that it would be most unusual for a responsible member of a bereaved family to instruct the mortician, in so many words, to "embalm" the body of a deceased relative. The very term *embalming* is so seldom used that the mortician must rely upon custom in the matter. The author concludes that unless the family specifies otherwise, the act of entrusting the body to the care of a funeral establishment carries with it an implied permission to go ahead and embalm.

4   Embalming is indeed a most extraordinary procedure, and one must wonder at the docility of Americans who each year pay hundreds of millions of dollars for its perpetuation, blissfully ignorant of what it is all about, what is done, how it is done. Not one in ten thousand has any idea of what actually takes place. Books on the subject are extremely hard to come by. They are not to be found in most libraries or bookshops.

5   In an era when huge television audiences watch surgical operations in the comfort of their living rooms, when, thanks to the animated cartoon, the geography of the digestive system has become familiar territory even to the nursery school set, in a land where the satisfaction of curiosity about almost all matters is a national pastime, the secrecy surrounding embalming can, surely, hardly be attributed to the inherent gruesomeness of the subject. Custom in this regard has within this century suffered a complete reversal. In the early days of American embalming, when it was performed in the home of the deceased, it was almost mandatory for some relative to stay by the embalmer's side and witness the procedure. Today, family members who might wish to be in attendance would certainly be dissuaded by the funeral director. All others, except apprentices, are excluded by law from the preparation room.

6   A close look at what does actually take place may explain in large measure the undertaker's intractable reticence concerning a procedure that has become his major *raison d'être*. Is it possible he fears that public information about embalming might lead patrons to wonder if they really want this service? If the funeral men are loath to discuss the subject outside the trade, the reader may, understandably, be equally loath to go on reading at this point. For those who have the stomach for it, let us part the formaldehyde curtain. . . .

7   The body is first laid out in the undertaker's morgue—or rather, Mr. Jones is reposing in the preparation room—to be readied to bid the world farewell.

8   The preparation room in any of the better funeral establishments has the tiled and sterile look of a surgery, and indeed the embalmer–restorative artist

who does his chores there is beginning to adopt the term *dermasurgeon* (appropriately corrupted by some mortician-writers as "demi-surgeon") to describe his calling. His equipment, consisting of scalpels, scissors, augers, forceps, clamps, needles, pumps, tubes, bowls, and basins, is crudely imitative of the surgeon's, as is his technique, acquired in a nine- or twelve-month post-high school course in an embalming school. He is supplied by an advanced chemical industry with a bewildering array of fluids, sprays, pastes, oils, powders, creams, to fix or soften tissue, shrink or distend it as needed, dry it here, restore the moisture there. There are cosmetics, waxes, and paints to fill and cover features, even plaster of Paris to replace entire limbs. There are ingenious aids to prop and stabilize the cadaver: a Vari-Pose Head Rest, the Edwards Arm and Hand Positioner, the Repose Block (to support the shoulders during the embalming), and the Throop Foot Positioner, which resembles an old-fashioned stocks.

Mr. John H. Eckels, president of the Eckels College of Mortuary Science, thus describes the first part of the embalming procedure: "In the hands of a skilled practitioner, this work may be done in a comparatively short time and without mutilating the body other than by slight incision—so slight that it scarcely would cause serious inconvenience if made upon a living person. It is necessary to remove the blood, and doing this not only helps in the disinfecting, but removes the principal cause of disfigurements due to discoloration." 9

Another textbook discusses the all-important time element: "The earlier this is done, the better, for every hour that elapses between death and embalming will add to the problems and complications encountered. . . ." Just how soon should one get going on the embalming? The author tells us, "On the basis of such scanty information made available to this profession through its rudimentary and haphazard system of technical research, we must conclude that the best results are to be obtained if the subject is embalmed before life is completely extinct—that is, before cellular death has occurred. In the average case, this would mean within an hour after somatic death." For those who feel that there is something a little rudimentary, not to say haphazard, about this advice, a comforting thought is offered by another writer. Speaking of fears entertained in early days of premature burial, he points out, "One of the effects of embalming by chemical injection, however, has been to dispel fears of live burial." How true; once the blood is removed, chances of live burial are indeed remote. 10

To return to Mr. Jones, the blood is drained out through the veins and replaced by embalming fluid pumped in through the arteries. As noted in *The Principles and Practices of Embalming*, "every operator has a favorite injection and drainage point—a fact which becomes a handicap only if he fails or refuses to forsake his favorites when conditions demand it." Typical favorites are the 11 carotid artery, femoral artery, jugular vein, subclavian vein. There are various choices of embalming fluid. If Flextone is used, it will produce a "mild, flexible rigidity. The skin retains a velvety softness, the tissues are rubbery and pliable. Ideal for women and children." It may be blended with B. and G. Products Company's Lyf-Lyk tint, which is guaranteed to reproduce "nature's own skin texture . . . the velvety appearance of living tissue." Suntone comes in three separate tints: Suntan; Special Cosmetic Tint, a pink shade "especially indicated for female subjects"; and Regular Cosmetic Tint, moderately pink.

12   About three to six gallons of a dyed and perfumed solution of formaldehyde, glycerin, borax, phenol, alcohol; and water is soon circulating through Mr. Jones, whose mouth has been sewn together with a "needle directed upward between the upper lip and gum and brought out through the left nostril," with the corners raised slightly "for a more pleasant expression." If he should be bucktoothed, his teeth are cleaned with Bon Ami and coated with colorless nail polish. His eyes, meanwhile, are closed with flesh-tinted eye caps and eye cement.

13   The next step is to have at Mr. Jones with a thing called a trocar. This is a long, hollow needle attached to a tube. It is jabbed into the abdomen, poked around the entrails and chest cavity, the contents of which are pumped out and replaced with "cavity fluid." This done, and the hole in the abdomen sewn up, Mr. Jones's face is heavily creamed (to protect the skin from burns which may be caused by leakage of the chemicals), and he is covered with a sheet and left unmolested for a while. But not for long—there is more, much more, in store for him. He has been embalmed, but not yet restored, and the best time to start the restorative work is eight to ten hours after embalming, when the tissues have become firm and dry.

14   The object of all this attention to the corpse, it must be remembered, is to make it presentable for viewing in an attitude of healthy repose. "Our customs require the presentation of our dead in the semblance of normality . . . unmarred by the ravages of illness, disease, or mutilation," says Mr. J. Sheridan Mayer in his *Restorative Art*. This is rather a large order since few people die in the full bloom of health, unravaged by illness and unmarked by some disfigurement. The funeral industry is equal to the challenge: "In some cases the gruesome appearance of a mutilated or disease-ridden subject may be quite discouraging. The task of restoration may seem impossible and shake the confidence of the embalmer. This is the time for intestinal fortitude and determination. Once the formative work is begun and affected tissues are cleaned or removed, all doubts of success vanish. It is surprising and gratifying to discover the results which may be obtained."

15   The embalmer, having allowed an appropriate interval to elapse, returns to the attack, but now he brings into play the skill and equipment of sculptor and cosmetician. Is a hand missing? Casting one in plaster of Paris is a simple

matter. "For replacement purposes, only a cast of the back of the hand is necessary; this is within the ability of the average operator and is quite adequate." If a lip or two, a nose or an ear should be missing, the embalmer has at hand a variety of restorative waxes with which to model replacements. Pores and skin texture are simulated by stippling with a little brush, and over this cosmetics are laid on. Head off? Decapitation cases are rather routinely handled. Ragged edges are trimmed, and head joined to torso with a series of splints, wires, and sutures. It is a good idea to have a little something at the neck—a scarf or a high collar—when time for viewing comes. Swollen mouth? Cut out tissue as needed from inside the lips. If too much is removed, the surface contour can easily be restored by padding with cotton. Swollen necks and cheeks are reduced by removing tissue through vertical incisions made down each side of the neck. "When the deceased is casketed, the pillow will hide the suture incisions . . . as an extra precaution against leakage, the suture may be painted with liquid sealer."

The opposite condition is more likely to present itself—that of emaciation. His hypodermic syringe now loaded with massage cream, the embalmer seeks 16 out and fills the hollowed and sunken areas by injection. In this procedure the backs of the hands and fingers and the under-chin area should not be neglected.

Positioning the lips is a problem that recurrently challenges the ingenuity of the embalmer. Closed too tightly, they tend to give a stern, even disap- 17 proving expression. Ideally, embalmers feel, the lips should give the impression of being ever so slightly parted, the upper lip protruding slightly for a more youthful appearance. This takes some engineering, however, as the lips tend to drift apart. Lip drift can sometimes be remedied by pushing one or two straight pins through the inner margin of the lower lip and then inserting them between the two front upper teeth. If Mr. Jones happens to have no teeth, the pins can just as easily be anchored in his Armstrong Face Former and Denture Replacer. Another method to maintain lip closure is to dislocate the lower jaw, which is then held in its new position by a wire run through holes which have been drilled through the upper and lower jaws at the midline. As the French are fond of saying, *il faut souffrir pour être belle* (You have to suffer to be beautiful).

If Mr. Jones has died of jaundice, the embalming fluid will very likely turn him green. Does this deter the embalmer? Not if he has intestinal fortitude. 18 Masking pastes and cosmetics are heavily laid on, burial garments and casket interiors are color-correlated with particular care, and Jones is displayed beneath rose-colored lights. Friends will say "How *well* he looks." Death by carbon monoxide, on the other hand, can be rather a good thing from the embalmer's viewpoint: "One advantage is the fact that this type of discoloration is an exaggerated form of a natural pink coloration." This is nice because the healthy glow is already present and needs but little attention.

19   The patching and filling completed, Mr. Jones is now shaved, washed, and dressed. Cream-based cosmetic, available in pink, flesh, suntan, brunette, and blond, is applied to his hands and face, his hair is shampooed and combed (and, in the case of Mrs. Jones, set), his hands manicured. For the horny-handed son of toil special care must be taken; cream should be applied to remove ingrained grime, and the nails cleaned. "If he were not in the habit of having them manicured in life, trimming and shaping is advised for better appearance—never questioned by kin."

20   Jones is now ready for casketing (this is the present participle of the verb "to casket"). In this operation his right shoulder should be depressed slightly "to turn the body a bit to the right and soften the appearance of lying flat on the back." Positioning the hands is a matter of importance, and special rubber positioning blocks may be used. The hands should be cupped slightly for a more lifelike, relaxed appearance. Proper placement of the body requires a delicate sense of balance. It should lie as high as possible in the casket, yet not so high that the lid, when lowered, will hit the nose. On the other hand, we are cautioned, placing the body too low "creates the impression that the body is in a box."

21   Jones is next wheeled into the appointed slumber room where a few last touches may be added—his favorite pipe placed in his hand or, if he was a great reader, a book propped into position. (In the case of little Master Jones a Teddy bear may be clutched.) Here he will hold open house for a few days, visiting hours 10 A.M. to 9 P.M.

22   All now being in readiness, the funeral director calls a staff conference to make sure that each assistant knows his precise duties. Mr. Wilber Kriege writes: "This makes your staff feel that they are a part of the team, with a definite assignment that must be properly carried out if the whole plan is to succeed. You never heard of a football coach who failed to talk to his entire team before they go on the field. They have drilled on the plays they are to execute for hours and days, and yet the successful coach knows the importance of making even the bench-warming third-string substitute feel that he is important if the game is to be won." The winning of *this* game is predicated upon glass-smooth handling of the logistics. The funeral director has notified the pallbearers whose names were furnished by the family, has arranged for the presence of clergyman, organist, and soloist, has provided transportation for everybody, has organized and listed the flowers sent by friends. In *Psychology of Funeral Service* Mr. Edward A. Martin points out: "He may not always do as much as the family thinks he is doing, but it is his helpful guidance that they appreciate in knowing they are proceeding as they should. . . . The important thing is how well his services can be used to make the family believe they are giving unlimited expression to their own sentiment."

The religious service may be held in a church or in the chapel of the fu- 23
neral home; the funeral director vastly prefers the latter arrangement, for not
only is it more convenient for him but it affords him the opportunity to show
off his beautiful facilities to the gathered mourners. After the clergyman has
had his say, the mourners queue up to file past the casket for a last look at the
deceased. The family is *never* asked whether they want an open-casket cere-
mony; in the absence of their instruction to the contrary, this is taken for
granted. Consequently well over 90 percent of all American funerals feature
the open casket—a custom unknown in other parts of the world. Foreigners
are astonished by it. An English woman living in San Francisco described her
reaction in a letter to the writer:

> I myself have attended only one funeral here—that of an elderly fel- 24
> low worker of mine. After the service I could not understand why
> everyone was walking towards the coffin (sorry, I mean casket), but
> thought I had better follow the crowd. It shook me rigid to get there
> and find the casket open and poor old Oscar lying there in his brown
> tweed suit, wearing a suntan makeup and just the wrong shade of lip-
> stick. If I had not been extremely fond of the old boy, I have a horri-
> ble feeling that I might have giggled. Then and there I decided that I
> could never face another American funeral—even dead.

The casket (which has been resting throughout the service on a Classic 25
Beauty Ultra Metal Casket Bier) is now transferred by a hydraulically operated
device called Porto-Lift to a balloon-tired, Glide Easy casket carriage which
will wheel it to yet another conveyance, the Cadillac Funeral Coach. This may
be lavender, cream, light green—anything but black. Interiors, of course, are
color-correlated, "for the man who cannot stop short of perfection."

At graveside, the casket is lowered into the earth. This office, once the 26
prerogative of friends of the deceased, is now performed by a patented mechanical lowering device. A "Lifetime Green" artificial grass mat is at the
ready to conceal the sere earth, and overhead, to conceal the sky, is a portable
Steril Chapel Tent ("resists the intense heat and humidity of summer and the
terrific storms of winter . . . available in Silver Grey, Rose, or Evergreen").
Now is the time for the ritual scattering of earth over the coffin, as the
solemn words "earth to earth, ashes to ashes, dust to dust" are pronounced
by the officiating cleric. This can today be accomplished "with a mere flick
of the wrist with the Gordon Leak-Proof Earth Dispenser. No grasping of a
handful of dirt, no soiled fingers. Simple, dignified, beautiful, reverent! The
modern way!" The Gordon Earth Dispenser (at $5) is of nickel-plated brass
construction. It is not only "attractive to the eye and long wearing"; it is also
"one of the 'tools' for building better public relations" if presented as "an ap-

propriate non-commercial gift" to the clergyman. It is shaped something like a saltshaker.

27   Untouched by human hand, the coffin and the earth are now united.

28   It is in the function of directing the participants through this maze of gadgetry that the funeral director has assigned to himself his relatively new role of "grief therapist." He has relieved the family of every detail, he has revamped the corpse to look like a living doll, he has arranged for it to nap for a few days in a slumber room, he has put on a well-oiled performance in which the concept of *death* has played no part whatsoever—unless it was inconsiderately mentioned by the clergyman who conducted the religious service. He has done everything in his power to make the funeral a real pleasure for everybody concerned. He and his team have given their all to score an upset victory over death.

6

Classification

Writing Guidelines

Classification

1. **Develop a method of classification.** Classification is simply the organization of information into groups. You can classify using two methods: grouping similar items, such as types of poisonous snakes, and dividing parts of a larger item, such as components of a computer. In either case, you must decide how you'd like to classify the information: you could classify poisonous snakes according to their habitats, anatomical characteristics, or level of danger to humans. Depending on your audience, different methods will be more or less useful. Doctors (and campers) may be more interested in danger to humans, but biologists might prefer an arrangement according to habitat or anatomy.

2. **Make your classification consistent and complete.** While it's obvious that a classification of snakes that doesn't include rattlers wouldn't be very useful, some classification errors are subtler. It might seem unimportant to include the power cord in a classification of a computer, but if readers try to use your information to help buy the components for a computer, they won't have all the information they need. Consistency is also important. Don't start your discussion of pizza classifying by ingredients, then switch halfway through to an arrangement according to pizzeria locations.

3. **Use clear and specific examples.** Examples add life even to seemingly mundane topics. What's the most boring topic you can think of? Watching grass grow? Watching paint dry? In an essay classifying types of grass, examples make the difference between life and death (by boredom). Add a few examples—the neighbor whose Kentucky tall fescue grew so fast, he went through four lawnmower blades in a single summer; the obsessed gardener who was so driven to remove every blade of crabgrass from his lawn, he incinerated his front yard with a blowtorch—and suddenly even grass growing is exciting.

4. **Organize the essay to support your purpose.** Afraid your readers won't read past the first sentence in your grass-growing essay? Move the blowtorch example to the front. Want to leave your readers with a lasting final impression? Save your best category for last. You can organize your essay any way you want, as long as your readers are able to follow along. In order to hold readers' attention, classification essays need to make a point. Make sure your organization suits that purpose.

Judith Viorst

Friends, Good Friends—and Such Good Friends

Judith Viorst wanted to be a writer since she was a child; her first book was a collection of poems published in 1965. Her second collection, *It's Hard to Be Hip over Thirty and Other Tragedies of Married Life,* was published in 1968 and established Viorst as a best selling author of light verse. Her poems and also her children's books strike a chord with readers by shedding a humorous light on the little moments of everyday life—her inspiration frequently comes from her own marriage (to political reporter and journalist Milton Viorst) and her three children. Several of Viorst's articles in *Redbook* have won awards, and she won an Emmy in 1970 for her poetic monologues written for the CBS television special *Annie: The Women in the Life of a Man.* Although her writing has taken on deeper issues since she graduated from the Washington Psychoanalytic Institute, she still injects it with humor and compassion.

1   WOMEN ARE FRIENDS, I once would have said, when they totally love and support and trust each other, and bare to each other the secrets of their souls, and run—no questions asked—to help each other, and tell harsh truths to each other (no, you can't wear that dress unless you lose ten pounds first) when harsh truths must be told.

2   Women are friends, I once would have said, when they share the same affection for Ingmar Bergman, plus train rides, cats, warm rain, charades, Camus, and hate with equal ardor Newark and Brussels sprouts and Lawrence Welk and camping.

3   In other words, I once would have said that a friend is a friend all the way, but now I believe that's a narrow point of view. For the friendships I have and the friendships I see are conducted at many levels of intensity, serve many different functions, meet different needs and range from those as all-the-way as the friendship of the soul sisters mentioned above to that of the most nonchalant and casual playmates.

4   Consider these varieties of friendship:

5   1. Convenience friends. These are women with whom, if our paths weren't crossing all the time, we'd have no particular reason to be friends: a next-door neighbor, a woman in our car pool, the mother of one of our children's closest friends or maybe some mommy with whom we serve juice and cookies each week at the Glenwood Co-op Nursery.

6   Convenience friends are convenient indeed. They'll lend us their cups and silverware for a party. They'll drive our kids to soccer when we're sick. They'll take us to pick up our car when we need a lift to the garage. They'll even take our cats when we go on vacation. As we will for them.

7   But we don't, with convenience friends, ever come too close or tell too much; we maintain our public face and emotional distance. "Which means," says Elaine, "that I'll talk about being overweight but not about being depressed. Which means I'll admit being mad but not blind with rage. Which means that I might say that we're pinched this month but never that I'm worried sick over money."

8   But which doesn't mean that there isn't sufficient value to be found in these friendships of mutual aid, in convenience friends.

9   2. Special-interest friends. These friendships aren't intimate, and they needn't involve kids or silverware or cats. Their value lies in some interest jointly shared. And so we may have an office friend or a yoga friend or a tennis friend or a friend from the Women's Democratic Club.

10   "I've got one woman friend," says Joyce, "who likes, as I do, to take psychology courses. Which makes it nice for me—and nice for her. It's fun to go with someone you know and it's fun to discuss what you've learned, driving back from the classes." And for the most part, she says, that's all they discuss.

11   "I'd say that what we're doing is *doing* together, not being together," Suzanne says of her Tuesday-doubles friends. "It's mainly a tennis relationship, but we play together well. And I guess we all need to have a couple of playmates."

12   I agree.

13   My playmate is a shopping friend, a woman of marvelous taste, a woman who knows exactly *where* to buy *what*, and furthermore is a woman who always knows beyond a doubt what one ought to be buying. I don't have the time to keep up with what's new in eyeshadow, hemlines and shoes and whether the smock look is in or finished already. But since (oh, shame!) I care a lot about eyeshadow, hemlines and shoes, and since I don't *want* to wear smocks if the smock look is finished, I'm very glad to have a shopping friend.

14   3. Historical friends. We all have a friend who knew us when . . . maybe way back in Miss Meltzer's second grade, when our family lived in that three-room flat in Brooklyn, when our dad was out of work for seven months, when our brother Allie got in that fight where they had to call the police, when our sister married the endodontist from Yonkers and when, the morning after we lost our virginity, she was the first, the only, friend we told.

15   The years have gone by and we've gone separate ways and we've little in common now, but we're still an intimate part of each other's past. And so whenever we go to Detroit we always go to visit this friend of our girlhood. Who knows how we looked before our teeth were straightened. Who knows how we talked before our voice got un-Brooklyned. Who knows what we ate before we learned about artichokes. And who, by her presence, puts us in touch with an earlier part of ourself, a part of ourself it's important never to lose.

"What this friend means to me and what I mean to her," says Grace, "is 16 having a sister without sibling rivalry. We know the texture of each other's lives. She remembers my grandmother's cabbage soup. I remember the way her uncle played the piano. There's simply no other friend who remembers those things."

4. Crossroads friends. Like historical friends, our crossroads friends are 17 important for *what was*—for the friendship we shared at a crucial, now past, time of life. A time, perhaps, when we roomed in college together; or worked as eager young singles in the Big City together; or went together, as my friend Elizabeth and I did, through pregnancy, birth and that scary first year of new motherhood.

Crossroads friends forge powerful links, links strong enough to endure 18 with not much more contact than once-a-year letters at Christmas. And out of respect for those crossroads years, for those dramas and dreams we once shared, we will always be friends.

5. Cross-generational friends. Historical friends and crossroads friends 19 seem to maintain a special kind of intimacy—dormant but always ready to be revived—and though we may rarely meet, whenever we do connect, it's personal and intense. Another kind of intimacy exists in the friendships that form across generations in what one woman calls her daughter-mother and her mother-daughter relationships.

Evelyn's friend is her mother's age—"but I share so much more than I ever 20 could with my mother"—a woman she talks to of music, of books and of life. "What I get from her is the benefit of her experience. What she gets—and enjoys—from me is a youthful perspective. It's a pleasure for both of us."

I have in my own life a precious friend, a woman of 65 who has lived very 21 hard, who is wise, who listens well; who has been where I am and can help me understand it; and who represents not only an ultimate ideal mother to me but also the person I'd like to be when I grow up.

In our daughter role we tend to do more than our share of self-revelation; 22 in our mother role we tend to receive what's revealed. It's another kind of pleasure—playing wise mother to a questing younger person. It's another very lovely kind of friendship.

6. Part-of-a-couple friends. Some of the women we call our friends we 23 never see alone—we see them as part of a couple at couples' parties. And though we share interests in many things and respect each other's views, we aren't moved to deepen the relationship. Whatever the reason, a lack of time or—and this is more likely—a lack of chemistry, our friendship remains in the context of a group. But the fact that our feeling on seeing each other is always, "I'm *so* glad she's here" and the fact that we spend half the evening talking together says that this too, in its own way, counts as a friendship.

24   (Other part-of-a-couple friends are the friends that came with the marriage, and some of these are friends we could live without. But sometimes, alas, she married our husband's best friend; and sometimes, alas, she *is* our husband's best friend. And so we find ourself dealing with her, somewhat against our will, in a spirit of what I'll call *reluctant* friendship.)

25   7. Men who are friends. I wanted to write just of women friends, but the women I've talked to won't let me—they say I must mention man-woman friendships too. For these friendships can be just as close and as dear as those that we form with women. Listen to Lucy's description of one such friendship:

26   "We've found we have things to talk about that are different from what he talks about with my husband and different from what I talk about with his wife. So sometimes we call on the phone or meet for lunch. There are similar intellectual interests—we always pass on to each other the books that we love—but there's also something tender and caring too."

27   In a couple of crises, Lucy says, "he offered himself for talking and for helping. And when someone died in his family he wanted me there. The sexual, flirty part of our friendship is very small, but *some*—just enough to make it fun and different." She thinks—and I agree—that the sexual part, though small, is always *some*, is always there when a man and a woman are friends.

28   It's only in the past few years that I've made friends with men, in the sense of a friendship that's *mine*, not just part of two couples. And achieving with them the ease and the trust I've found with women friends has value indeed. Under the dryer at home last week, putting on mascara and rouge, I comfortably sat and talked with a fellow named Peter. Peter, I finally decided, could handle the shock of me minus mascara under the dryer. Because we care for each other. Because we're friends.

29   8. There are medium friends, and pretty good friends, and very good friends indeed, and these friendships are defined by their level of intimacy. And what we'll reveal at each of these levels of intimacy is calibrated with care. We might tell a medium friend, for example, that yesterday we had a fight with our husband. And we might tell a pretty good friend that this fight with our husband made us so mad that we slept on the couch. And we might tell a very good friend that the reason we got so mad in that fight that we slept on the couch had something to do with that girl who works in his office. But it's only to our very best friends that we're willing to tell all, to tell what's going on with that girl in his office.

30   The best of friends, I still believe, totally love and support and trust each other, and bare to each other the secrets of their souls, and run—no questions asked—to help each other, and tell harsh truths to each other when they must be told.

But we needn't agree about everything (only 12-year-old girl friends agree   31
about *everything*) to tolerate each other's point of view. To accept without
judgment. To give and to take without ever keeping score. And to *be* there,
as I am for them and as they are for me, to comfort our sorrows, to celebrate
our joys.

William Zinsser

College Pressures

William Zinsser's knowledge of writing comes firsthand and started with his first job working at the *New York Herald Tribune* from 1946 to 1959. His experience with college pressures comes from not only his own schooling at Princeton University, but also from his nine years of teaching English at Yale University. It was his popular writing course that inspired his book *On Writing Well: An Informal Guide to Writing Nonfiction*, which has become a classic guide to writing. He has also written books about his other passions: baseball, jazz, and traveling.

Dear Carlos: I desperately need a dean's excuse for my chem midterm which will   1
begin in about 1 hour. All I can say is that I totally blew it this week. I've fallen
incredibly, inconceivably behind.

Carlos: Help! I'm anxious to hear from you. I'll be in my room and won't leave it   2
until I hear from you. Tomorrow is the last day for . . .

Carlos: I left town because I started bugging out again. I stayed up all night to fin-   3
ish a take-home make-up exam & am typing it to hand in on the 10th. It was due
on the 5th. P.S. I'm going to the dentist. Pain is pretty bad.

Carlos: Probably by Friday I'll be able to get back to my studies. Right now I'm   4
going to take a long walk. This whole thing has taken a lot out of me.

Carlos: I'm really up the proverbial creek. The problem is I really bombed the his-   5
tory final. Since I need that course for my major I . . .

Carlos: Here follows a tale of woe. I went home this weekend, had to help my   6
Mom, & caught a fever so didn't have much time to study. My professor . . .

7   *Carlos: Aargh! Trouble. Nothing original but everything's piling up at once. To be brief, my job interview . . .*

8   *Hey Carlos, good news! I've got mononucleosis.*

9   Who are these wretched supplicants, scribbling notes so laden with anxiety, seeking such miracles of postponement and balm? They are men and women who belong to Branford College, one of the twelve residential colleges at Yale University, and the messages are just a few of the hundreds that they left for their dean, Carlos Hortas—often slipped under his door at 4 A.M.—last year.

10   But students like the ones who wrote those notes can also be found on campuses from coast to coast—especially in New England and at many other private colleges across the country that have high academic standards and highly motivated students. Nobody could doubt that the notes are real. In their urgency and their gallows humor they are authentic voices of a generation that is panicky to succeed.

11   My own connection with the message writers is that I am master of Branford College. I live in its Gothic quadrangle and know the students well. (We have 485 of them.) I am privy to their hopes and fears—and also to their stereo music and their piercing cries in the dead of the night ("Does anybody ca-a-are?"). If they went to Carlos to ask how to get through tomorrow, they come to me to ask how to get through the rest of their lives.

12   Mainly I try to remind them that the road ahead is a long one and that it will have more unexpected turns than they think. There will be plenty of time to change jobs, change careers, change whole attitudes and approaches. They don't want to hear such liberating news. They want a map—right now—that they can follow unswervingly to career security, financial security, Social Security and, presumably, a prepaid grave.

13   What I wish for all students is some release from the clammy grip of the future. I wish them a chance to savor each segment of their education as an experience in itself and not as a grim preparation for the next step. I wish them the right to experiment, to trip and fall, to learn that defeat is as instructive as victory and is not the end of the world.

14   My wish, of course, is naïve. One of the few rights that America does not proclaim is the right to fail. Achievement is the national god, venerated in our media—the million-dollar athlete, the wealthy executive—and glorified in our praise of possessions. In the presence of such a potent state religion, the young are growing up old.

15   I see four kinds of pressure working on college students today: economic pressure, parental pressure, peer pressure, and self-induced pressure. It is easy to look around for villains—to blame the colleges for charging too much money,

the professors for assigning too much work, the parents for pushing their children too far, the students for driving themselves too hard. But there are no villains; only victims.

"In the late 1960s," one dean told me, "the typical question that I got from   16
students was 'Why is there so much suffering in the world?' or 'How can I make a contribution?' Today it's 'Do you think it would look better for getting into law school if I did a double major in history and political science, or just majored in one of them?'" Many other deans confirmed this pattern. One said: "They're trying to find an edge—the intangible something that will look better on paper if two students are about equal."

Note the emphasis on looking better. The transcript has become a sacred   17
document, the passport to security. How one appears on paper is more important than how one appears in person. A is for Admirable and B is for Borderline, even though, in Yale's official system of grading, A means "excellent" and B means "very good." Today, looking very good is no longer good enough, especially for students who hope to go on to law school or medical school. They know that entrance into the better schools will be an entrance into the better law firms and better medical practices where they will make a lot of money. They also know that the odds are harsh. Yale Law School, for instance, matriculates 170 students from an applicant pool of 3,700; Harvard enrolls 550 from a pool of 7,000.

It's all very well for those of us who write letters of recommendation for   18
our students to stress the qualities of humanity that will make them good lawyers or doctors. And it's nice to think that admission officers are really reading our letters and looking for the extra dimension of commitment or concern. Still, it would be hard for a student not to visualize these officers shuffling so many transcripts studded with As that they regard a B as positively shameful.

The pressure is almost as heavy on students who just want to graduate and   19
get a job. Long gone are the days of the "gentleman's C," when students journeyed through college with a certain relaxation, sampling a wide variety of courses—music, art, philosophy, classics, anthropology, poetry, religion—that would send them out as liberally educated men and women. If I were an employer I would rather employ graduates who have this range and curiosity than those who narrowly pursued safe subjects and high grades. I know countless students whose inquiring minds exhilarate me. I like to hear the play of their ideas. I don't know if they are getting As or Cs, and I don't care. I also like them as people. The country needs them, and they will find satisfying jobs. I tell them to relax. They can't.

Nor can I blame them. They live in a brutal economy. Tuition, room, and   20
board at most private colleges now comes to at least $7,000 [in 1979], not

counting books and fees. This might seem to suggest that the colleges are getting rich. But they are equally battered by inflation. Tuition covers only 60 percent of what it costs to educate a student, and ordinarily the remainder comes from what colleges receive in endowments, grants, and gifts. Now the remainder keeps being swallowed by the cruel costs—higher every year—of just opening the doors. Heating oil is up. Insurance is up. Postage is up. Health-premium costs are up. Everything is up. Deficits are up. We are witnessing in America the creation of a brotherhood of paupers—colleges, parents, and students, joined by the common bond of debt.

21   Today it is not unusual for a student, even if he works part time at college and full time during the summer, to accrue $5,000 in loans after four years—loans that he must start to repay within one year after graduation. Exhorted at commencement to go forth into the world, he is already behind as he goes forth. How could he not feel under pressure throughout college to prepare for this day of reckoning? I have used "he," incidentally, only for brevity. Women at Yale are under no less pressure to justify their expensive education to themselves, their parents, and society. In fact, they are probably under more pressure. For although they leave college superbly equipped to bring fresh leadership to traditionally male jobs, society hasn't yet caught up with this fact.

22   Along with economic pressure goes parental pressure. Inevitably, the two are deeply intertwined.

23   I see many students taking pre-medical courses with joyless tenacity. They go off to their labs as if they were going to the dentist. It saddens me because I know them in other corners of their life as cheerful people.

24   "Do you want to go to medical school?" I ask them.

25   "I guess so," they say, without conviction, or "Not really."

26   "Then why are you going?"

27   "Well, my parents want me to be a doctor. They're paying all this money and . . ."

28   Poor students, poor parents. They are caught in one of the oldest webs of love and duty and guilt. The parents mean well; they are trying to steer their sons and daughters toward a secure future. But the sons and daughters want to major in history or classics or philosophy—subjects with no "practical" value. Where's the payoff on the humanities? It's not easy to persuade such loving parents that the humanities do indeed pay off. The intellectual faculties developed by studying subjects like history and classics—an ability to synthesize and relate, to weigh cause and effect, to see events in perspective—are just the faculties that make creative leaders in business or almost any general field. Still, many fathers would rather put their money on courses that point toward a specific profession—courses that are pre-law, pre-medical, pre-business, or, as I sometimes heard it put, "pre-rich."

But the pressure on students is severe. They are truly torn. One part of them feels obligated to fulfill their parents' expectations; after all, their parents are older and presumably wiser. Another part tells them that the expectations that are right for their parents are not right for them. 29

I know a student who wants to be an artist. She is very obviously an artist and will be a good one—she has already had several modest local exhibits. Meanwhile she is growing as a well-rounded person and taking humanistic subjects that will enrich the inner resources out of which her art will grow. But her father is strongly opposed. He thinks that an artist is a "dumb" thing to be. The student vacillates and tries to please everybody. She keeps up with her art somewhat furtively and takes some of the "dumb" courses her father wants her to take—at least they are dumb courses for her. She is a free spirit on a campus of tense students—no small achievement in itself—and she deserves to follow her muse. 30

Peer pressure and self-induced pressure are also intertwined, and they begin almost at the beginning of freshman year. 31

"I had a freshman student I'll call Linda," one dean told me, "who came in and said she was under terrible pressure because her roommate, Barbara, was much brighter and studied all the time. I couldn't tell her that Barbara had come in two hours earlier to say the same thing about Linda." 32

The story is almost funny—except that it's not. It's symptomatic of all the pressures put together. When every student thinks every other student is working harder and doing better, the only solution is to study harder still. I see students going off to the library every night after dinner and coming back when it closes at midnight. I wish they would sometimes forget about their peers and go to a movie. I hear the clacking of typewriters in the hours before dawn. I see the tension in their eyes when exams are approaching and papers are due: *Will I get everything done?* 33

Probably they won't. They will get sick. They will get "blocked." They will sleep. They will oversleep. They will bug out. *Hey, Carlos, help!* 34

Part of the problem is that they do more than they are expected to do. A professor will assign five-page papers. Several students will start writing ten-page papers to impress him. Then more students will write ten-page papers, and a few will raise the ante to fifteen. Pity the poor student who is still just doing the assignment. 35

"Once you have twenty or thirty percent of the student population deliberately overexerting," one dean points out, "it's bad for everybody. When a teacher gets more and more effort from his class, the student who is doing normal work can be perceived as not doing well. The tactic works, psychologically." 36

Why can't the professor just cut back and not accept longer papers? He can, and he probably will. But by then the term will be half over and the dam- 37 age done. Grade fever is highly contagious and not easily reversed. Besides, the professor's main concern is with his course. He knows his students only in relation to the course and doesn't know that they are also overexerting in their other courses. Nor is it really his business. He didn't sign up for dealing with the student as a whole person and with all the emotional baggage the student brought along from home. That's what deans, masters, chaplains, and psychiatrists are for.

38   To some extent this is nothing new: a certain number of professors have always been self-contained islands of scholarship and shyness, more comfortable with books than with people. But the new pauperism has widened the gap still further, for professors who actually like to spend time with students don't have as much time to spend. They are also overexerting. If they are young, they are busy trying to publish in order not to perish, hanging by their fingernails onto a shrinking profession. If they are old and tenured, they are buried under the duties of administering departments—as departmental chairmen or members of committees—that have been thinned out by the budgetary axe.

39   Ultimately it will be the students' own business to break the circles in which they are trapped. They are too young to be prisoners of their parents' dreams and their classmates' fears. They must be jolted into believing in themselves as unique men and women who have the power to shape their own future.

40   "Violence is being done to the undergraduate experience," says Carlos Hortas. "College should be open-ended: at the end it should open many, many roads. Instead, students are choosing their goal in advance, and their choices narrow as they go along. It's almost as if they think that the country has been codified in the type of jobs that exist—that they've got to fit into certain slots. Therefore, fit into the best-paying slot.

41   "They ought to take chances. Not taking chances will lead to a life of colorless mediocrity. They'll be comfortable. But something in the spirit will be missing."

42   I have painted too drab a portrait of today's students, making them seem a solemn lot. That is only half of their story; if they were so dreary I wouldn't so thoroughly enjoy their company. The other half is that they are easy to like. They are quick to laugh and to offer friendship. They are not introverts. They are unusually kind and are more considerate of one another than any student generation I have known.

43   Nor are they so obsessed with their studies that they avoid sports and extracurricular activities. On the contrary, they juggle their crowded hours to play on a variety of teams, perform with musical and dramatic groups, and write for campus publications. But this in turn is one more cause of anxiety. There are too many choices. Academically, they have 1,300 courses to select

from; outside class they have to decide how much spare time they can spare and how to spend it.

This means that they engage in fewer extracurricular pursuits than their 44 predecessors did. If they want to row on the crew and play in the symphony they will eliminate one; in the '60s they would have done both. They also tend to choose activities that are self-limiting. Drama, for instance, is flourishing in all twelve of Yale's residential colleges as it never has before. Students hurl themselves into these productions—as actors, directors, carpenters, and technicians—with a dedication to create the best possible play, knowing that the day will come when the run will end and they can get back to their studies.

They also can't afford to be the willing slave of organizations like the *Yale* 45 *Daily News*. Last spring at the one-hundredth anniversary banquet of that paper—whose past chairmen include such once and future kings as Potter Stewart, Kingman Brewster, and William F. Buckley, Jr.—much was made of the fact that the editorial staff used to be small and totally committed and that "newsies" routinely worked fifty hours a week. In effect they belonged to a club; Newsies is how they defined themselves at Yale. Today's student will write one or two articles a week, when he can, and he defines himself as a student. I've never heard the word Newsie except at the banquet.

If I have described the modern undergraduate primarily as a driven crea- 46 ture who is largely ignoring the blithe spirit inside who keeps trying to come out and play, it's because that's where the crunch is, not only at Yale but throughout American education. It's why I think we should all be worried about the values that are nurturing a generation so fearful of risk and so goal-obsessed at such an early age.

I tell students that there is no one "right" way to get ahead—that each of them 47 is a different person, starting from a different point and bound for a different destination. I tell them that change is a tonic and that all the slots are not codified nor the frontiers closed. One of my ways of telling them is to invite men and women who have achieved success outside the academic world to come and talk informally with my students during the year. They are heads of companies or ad agencies, editors of magazines, politicians, public officials, television magnates, labor leaders, business executives, Broadway producers, artists, writers, economists, photographers, scientists, historians—a mixed bag of achievers.

I ask them to say a few words about how they got started. The students as- 48 sume that they started in their present profession and knew all along that it was what they wanted to do. Luckily for me, most of them got into their field by a circuitous route, to their surprise, after many detours. The students are startled. They can hardly conceive of a career that was not pre-planned. They can hardly imagine allowing the hand of God or chance to nudge them down some unforeseen trail.

Mary Austin

Water Trails of the Ceriso

Though her books sometimes barely covered their own expenses, Mary Austin's fame in the West was made secure by her intense personality and her association with the literary and cultural elite of the region: she had ties with Jack London, Bret Harte, Ansel Adams, and Willa Cather, to name a few. Her many books, including *Land of Little Rain, Earth Horizon*, and *Taos Pueblo*, were recognized as great works by the literary community of the time. Yet her work has only recently begun to be accepted into the larger "canon" of American literature. In "Water Trails of the Ceriso," which originally appeared in *Land of Little Rain*, Mary Austin (1868–1934) offers a unique perspective on the lives of the inhabitants of the desert.

1   BY THE END OF THE DRY SEASON the water trails of the Ceriso are worn to a white ribbon in the leaning grass, spread out faint and fanwise toward the homes of gopher and ground rat and squirrel. But however faint to man-sight, they are sufficiently plain to the furred and feathered folk who travel them. Getting down to the eye level of rat and squirrel kind, one perceives what might easily be wide and winding roads to us if they occurred in thick plantations of trees three times the height of a man. It needs but a slender thread of barrenness to make a mouse trail in the forest of the sod. To the little people the water trails are as country roads, with scents as signboards.

2   It seems that man-height is the least fortunate of all heights from which to study trails. It is better to go up the front of some tall hill, say the spur of Black Mountain, looking back and down across the hollow of the Ceriso. Strange how long the soil keeps the impression of any continuous treading, even after grass has overgrown it. Twenty years since, a brief heyday of mining at Black Mountain made a stage road across the Ceriso, yet the parallel lines that are the wheel traces show from the height dark and well defined. Afoot in the Ceriso one looks in vain for any sign of it. So all the paths that wild creatures use going down to the Lone Tree Spring are mapped out whitely from this level, which is also the level of the hawks.

3   There is little water in the Ceriso at the best of times, and that little brackish and smelling vilely, but by a lone juniper where the rim of the Ceriso breaks away to the lower country, there is a perpetual rill of fresh sweet drink in the midst of lush grass and watercress. In the dry season there is no water else for a man's long journey of a day. East to the foot of the Black Mountain, and north and south without counting, are the burrows of small rodents, rat and squirrel kind. Under the sage are the shallow forms of the jack-rabbits,

and in the dry banks of washes, and among the strewn fragments of black rock, lairs of bobcat, fox, and coyote.

The coyote is your true water-witch, one who snuffs and paws, snuffs and 4 paws again at the smallest spot of moisture-scented earth until he has freed the blind water from the soil. Many water-holes are no more than this detected by the lean hobo of the hills in localities where not even an Indian would look for it.

It is the opinion of many wise and busy people that the hill-folk pass the 5 ten-month interval between the end and renewal of winter rains, with no drink; but your true idler, with days and nights to spend beside the water trails, will not subscribe to it. The trails begin, as I said, very far back in the Ceriso, faintly, and converge in one span broad, white, hard-trodden way in the gully of the spring. And why trails if there are no travelers in that direction?

I have yet to find the land not scarred by the thin, far roadways of rabbits 6 and what not of furry folks that run in them. Venture to look for some seldom-touched water-hole, and so long as the trails run with your general direction make sure you are right, but if they begin to cross yours at never so slight an angle, to converge toward a point left or right of your objective, no matter what the maps say, or your memory, trust them; they *know*.

It is very still in the Ceriso by day, so that were it not for the evidence of 7 those white beaten ways, it might be the desert it looks. The sun is hot in the dry season, and the days are filled with the glare of it. Now and again some unseen coyote signals his pack in a long-drawn, dolorous whine that comes from no determinate point, but nothing stirs much before mid-afternoon. It is a sign when there begin to be hawks skimming above the sage that the little people are going about their business.

We have fallen on a very careless usage, speaking of wild creatures as if 8 they were bound by some such limitation as hampers clockwork. When we say of one and another, they are night prowlers, it is perhaps true only as the things they feed upon are more easily come by in the dark, and they know well how to adjust themselves to conditions wherein food is more plentiful by day. And their accustomed performance is very much a matter of keen eye, keener scent, quick ear, and a better memory of sights and sounds than man dares boast. Watch a coyote come out of his lair and cast about in his mind where he will go for his daily killing. You cannot very well tell what decides him, but very easily that he has decided. He trots or breaks into short gallops, with very perceptible pauses to look up and about at landmarks, alters his tack a little, looking forward and back to steer his proper course. I am persuaded that the coyotes in my valley, which is narrow and beset with steep, sharp hills, in long passages steer by the pinnacles of the sky-line, going with head cocked to one side to keep to the left or right of such and such a promontory.

I have trailed a coyote often, going across country, perhaps to where some 9 slant-winged scavenger hanging in the air signaled prospect of a dinner, and found his track such as a man, a very intelligent man accustomed to a hill country, and a little cautious, would make to the same point. Here a detour to avoid a stretch of too little cover, there a pause on the rim of gully to pick the better way,—and it is usually the best way,—and making his point with the greatest economy of effort. Since the time of Seyavi the deer have shifted their feeding ground across the valley at the beginning of deep snows, by way of the Black Rock, fording the river at Charley's Butte, and making straight for the mouth of the cañon that is the easiest going to the winter pastures on Waban. So they still cross, though whatever trail they had has been long broken by ploughed ground; but from the mouth of Tinpah Creek, where the deer come out of the Sierras, it is easily seen that the creek, the point of Black Rock, and Charley's Butte are in line with the wide bulk of shade that is the foot of Waban Pass. And along with this the deer have learned that Charley's Butte is almost the only possible ford, and all the shortest crossing of the valley. It seems that the wild creatures have learned all that is important to their way of life except the changes of the moon. I have seen some prowling fox or coyote, surprised by its sudden rising from behind the mountain wall, slink in its increasing glow, watch it furtively from the cover of near-by brush, unprepared and half uncertain of its identity until it rode clear of the peaks, and finally make off with all the air of one caught napping by an ancient joke. The moon in its wanderings must be a sort of exasperation to cunning beasts, likely to spoil by untimely risings some fore-planned mischief.

10   But to take the trail again; the coyotes that are astir in the Ceriso of late afternoons, harrying the rabbits from their shallow forms, and the hawks that sweep and swing above them, are not there from any mechanical promptings of instinct, but because they know of old experience that the small fry are about to take to seed gathering and the water trails. The rabbits begin it, taking the trail with long, light leaps, one eye and ear cocked to the hills from whence a coyote might descend upon them at any moment. Rabbits are a foolish people. They do not fight except with their own kind, nor use their paws except for feet, and appear to have no reason for existence but to furnish meals for meat-eaters. In flight they seem to rebound from the earth of their own elasticity, but keep a sober pace going to the spring. It is the young watercress that tempts them and the pleasures of society, for they seldom drink. Even in localities where there are flowing streams they seem to prefer the moisture that collects on herbage, and after rains may be seen rising on their haunches to drink delicately the clear drops caught in the tops of the young sage. But drink they must, as I have often seen them mornings and evenings at the rill that goes by my door. Wait long enough at the Lone Tree Spring and sooner or later they will all come in. But here their matings are accomplished, and though they are fearful of so little as a cloud shadow or blown

leaf, they contrive to have some playful hours. At the spring the bobcat drops down upon them from the black rock, and the red fox picks them up returning in the dark. By day the hawk and eagle overshadow them, and the coyote has all times and seasons for his own.

Cattle, when there are any in the Ceriso, drink morning and evening, 11 spending the night on the warm last lighted slopes of neighboring hills, stirring with the peep o' day. In these half wild spotted steers the habits of an earlier lineage persist. It must be long since they have made beds for themselves, but before lying down they turn themselves round and round as dogs do. They choose bare and stony ground, exposed fronts of westward facing hills, and lie down in companies. Usually by the end of the summer the cattle have been driven or gone of their own choosing to the mountain meadows. One year a maverick yearling, strayed or overlooked by the vaqueros, kept on until the season's end, and so betrayed another visitor to the spring that else I might have missed. On a certain morning the half-eaten carcass lay at the foot of the black rock, and in moist earth by the rill of the spring, the foot-pads of a cougar, puma, mountain lion, or whatever the beast is rightly called. The kill must have been made early in the evening, for it appeared that the cougar had been twice to the spring; and since the meat-eater drinks little until he has eaten, he must have fed and drunk, and after an interval of lying up in the black rock, had eaten and drunk again. There was no knowing how far he had come, but if he came again the second night he found that the coyotes had left him very little of his kill.

Nobody ventures to say how infrequently and at what hour the small fry 12 visit the spring. There are such numbers of them that if each came once between the last of spring and the first of winter rains, there would still be water trails. I have seen badgers drinking about the hour when the light takes on the yellow tinge it has from coming slantwise through the hills. They find out shallow places, and are loath to wet their feet. Rats and chipmunks have been observed visiting the spring as late as nine o'clock mornings. The larger spermophiles that live near the spring and keep awake to work all day, come and go at no particular hour, drinking sparingly. At long intervals on half-lighted days, meadow and field mice steal delicately along the trail. These visitors are all too small to be watched carefully at night, but for evidence of their frequent coming there are the trails that may be traced miles out among the crisping grasses. On rare nights, in the places where no grass grows between the shrubs, and the sand silvers whitely to the moon, one sees them whisking to and fro on innumerable errands of seed gathering, but the chief witnesses of their presence near the spring are the elf owls. Those burrow-haunting, speckled fluffs of greediness begin a twilight flitting toward the spring, feeding as they go on grasshoppers, lizards, and small, swift creatures, diving into burrows to catch field mice asleep, battling with chipmunks at their own doors, and getting down in great numbers toward the lone juniper. Now owls do not love water greatly on its own account. Not to my knowledge have I caught one drinking or bathing, though on night wanderings across the mesa they flit up from under the horse's feet along stream borders. Their presence near the spring in great numbers would indicate the presence of the things they feed upon. All night the rustle and soft hooting keeps on in the neighborhood of the spring, with seldom small shrieks of mortal agony. It is clear day before they have all gotten back to their particular hummocks, and if one follows cautiously, not to frighten them into some near-by burrow, it is possible to trail them far up the slope.

13   The crested quail that troop in the Ceriso are the happiest frequenters of the water trails. There is no furtiveness about their morning drink. About the time the burrowers and all that feed upon them are addressing themselves to sleep, great flocks pour down the trails with that peculiar melting motion of moving quail, twittering, shoving, and shouldering. They splatter into the shallows, drink daintily, shake out small showers over their perfect coats, and melt away again into the scrub, preening and pranking, with soft contented noises.

14   After the quail, sparrows and ground-inhabiting birds bathe with the utmost frankness and a great deal of splutter; and here in the heart of noon hawks resort, sitting panting, with wings aslant, and a truce to all hostilities because of the heat. One summer there came a road-runner up from the lower valley, peeking and prying, and he had never any patience with the water baths of the sparrows. His own ablutions were performed in the clean, hopeful dust of the chaparral; and whenever he happened on their morning splatterings, he would depress his glossy crest, slant his shining tail to the level of his body, until he looked most like some bright venomous snake, daunting them with shrill abuse and feint of battle. Then suddenly he would go tilting and balancing down the gully in fine disdain, only to return in a day or two to make sure the foolish bodies were still at it.

15   Out on the Ceriso about five miles, and wholly out of sight of it, near where the immemorial foot trail goes up from Saline Flat toward Black Mountain, is a water sign worth turning out of the trail to see. It is a laid circle of stones large enough not to be disturbed by any ordinary hap, with an opening flanked by two parallel rows of similar stones, between which were an arrow placed, touching the opposite rim of the circle, it would point as the crow flies to the spring. It is the old, indubitable water mark of the Shoshones. One still finds it in the desert ranges in Salt Wells and Mesquite valleys, and along the slopes of Waban. On the other side of Ceriso, where the black rock begins, about a mile from the spring, is the work of an older, forgotten people. The rock hereabout is all volcanic, fracturing with a crystalline whitish surface, but weathered outside to furnace blackness. Around the spring, where must have

been a gathering place of the tribes, it is scored over with strange pictures and symbols that have no meaning to the Indians of the present day; but out where the rock begins, there is carved into the white heart of it a pointing arrow over the symbol for distance and a circle full of wavy lines reading thus: "In this direction three [units of measurement unknown] is a spring of sweet water; look for it."

Student Essay

Diana Peck

The Shellfish of Arey's Pond

The quintessential *bad* essay topic is "What I did during my summer vacation." It has acquired such a negative reputation that few students are even assigned it anymore, leaving elementary school teachers across the nation struggling to come up with adequate lesson plans for the first day of school. Yet even topics like this one can be turned into great essays if the recollections are described with a fond realism and the whole piece makes a good point. Diana Peck does precisely that in this essay, progressing in a careful manner from descriptions of the most common shellfish of her pond to the most coveted. A simple description becomes a quest, and in the end becomes a comment on the relationship of humanity and nature.

THE ATLANTIC OCEAN POUNDING THE CAPE COD SHORELINE finds a break in   1
the dunes just north of Monomoy Point. Here, it can enter the calm, shallow waters of Pleasant Bay, separated from the ocean's surf by the outsized sand dune named Nauset. Continuing a tidal journey, some ocean water finds its way to the northern reaches of the bay and sidetracks into a small channel called Namequoit. Twice a day, every day, ocean water completes its journey down this channel and fills Arey's Pond, one of the many ponds that terminate similar channels. Nursed by this fresh supply of nutrient-rich waters, Arey's Pond, small though it is, has until recently provided the spawning grounds for a rich variety of marine fauna. When I was a child, many a summer day's activities revolved around the shellfish life of the pond.

The periwinkle was both the most common and the most useless shellfish   2
in the pond. Hundreds of these small black snails, the size of lima beans, littered our tiny beach at low tide. As we stepped on them, unable to avoid them, they squashed into the wet sand, emerging undaunted a moment later. Although edible, they were useless as food since it would have taken a dozen

of their soft black insides to produce a thimbleful of escargots. Adults ignored periwinkles, and even children quickly tired of picking them up, waiting for them to stick their bodies out of the shells, then poking them to watch them disappear inside their shells. Sometimes, picking up these shells, we were surprised to find the tiniest fiddler crab had made an empty shell its home. Struggling to pull its right claw, equal in size to the rest of its body, inside the borrowed shell, the crab entertained us for a few moments. We enjoyed it far more, however, when an adult fiddler crab, accidentally shell-less, would run frantically around the beach, terrorized by its vulnerability.

3   Less common were the horseshoe crabs which the tide brought to our beach. Often they were paired, the male glued to the back of the female, and it thrilled us to pick up one spiny tail and lift up the two helpless, heavy bodies, their dozens of small underlegs thrashing in the air. The dark brown armored semicircles of their bodies, often about ten inches in width, were too heavy for us to hold for long, and so they would usually be freed within a half-minute. Meatless, they had only one use: sometimes my father split a female horseshoe crab with one blow of his axe, put each of her halves in an eel pot, and attracted eels for miles around with her roe.

4   An animal which was not particularly common but could be found accidentally was the blue crab. The big brother of the Maryland soft-shell crab, this species offered little meat and was therefore usually ignored except at a clambake where the joy of cracking open the shells excused the meager store of meat. The only aggressive variety of shellfish we encountered, this type of crab would endlessly surprise us, pinching our toes as we waded in the water, gripping our drop lines as we pulled up what we thought was a flounder, staring at us through the wires as we hauled up our eel pots.

5   But hiding in the mud of the pond were the rare bivalves with edible meat, especially sought-after by adults who, aided by curious children, spent whole afternoons searching for them, spurred on by my father's enthusiasm. The most common of the bivalves were clams, called soft-shell clams by the tourists but just plain clams by Cape Codders. My father led the expeditions at dead-low tide, armed with a shovel and a bucket. In the sand near the water, he looked for telltale air holes, then dug a shovelful of mud and dumped it out on the beach. The children, responsible for combing the mud with their fingers to find the smooth, oval bodies of the clams, usually squeezed each clam, watching it squirt a last stream of water through its long, thick neck, then tossed it unceremoniously into the waiting bucket. We worked our way down the shoreline until, as the tide started in, we stood in a few inches of water. Over and over, my father dug into the muck, sending swirls of black grit into the water, raising the pungent smell of disturbed compost, dumping shovelfuls of oozing mud into the shallow water for us to search. Over and over we gushed the mud through our fingers, plucked out the clams, and moved on

to the next shovelful, often stepping into the soft warm muck up to our ankles, hearing the "pop" of the suction as we pulled out our feet. The clams, hard-won from the mud, would provide a feast of steamers for all the relatives, as well as bait for the next day's fishing.

More difficult to find were the quahogs, and not until we were older did my father teach us, one by one, how to find them. Adults considered them more of a delicacy than the clams and either ate the meat raw or ground it for chowder. A hard-shelled clam, quahogs have no necks and keep their mantles inside their tightly closed shells. They, too, burrow in the mud, but they keep a ridge of shell just above the surface. To find quahogs, my father, in goggles and bathing suit, floated face down along the shoreline where the water was about a foot deep. The water being too murky to see through, he pulled himself along, feeling the mud with his hands for the telltale ridge. When he found one, he loosened the surrounding mud with his fingers and pulled the quahog out of its hiding place. This was a slow, arduous process, demanding too much patience for most of us children. But my father was motivated by his love for the result of his labors, especially enjoying the sweet flavor of the small quahogs' meat, called cherrystones, as he swallowed them raw. 6

Even more treasured than quahogs and more difficult to find were the jewels of Arey's Pond: the oysters. Even my father, experienced shellfisherman as he was, had a special smile as he emerged from the water with an oyster. Hiding in their sharp, blotchy, irregularly shaped shells amidst the roots of the eel grass at the shore's edge, oysters were impossible to see. Feeling for them was difficult, because the edges of the eel grass felt similar to the layered edges of the oyster's shell. The grass eventually yielded to pressure, while the oyster remained firm, but anyone pressing hard enough to distinguish the difference was sure to cut his fingers on the reedy edge of the grass or the sharp edge of a shell. Wearing gloves made the hands too clumsy to detect the difference. For my father it was a labor of love. The scores of tiny cuts on his fingers were small payment for the joy of eating a raw oyster, captured only minutes before. Children were never offered oysters, and those adults fortunate enough to be present when my father caught some usually mirrored his sublime expression as they swallowed the fresh meat. Even the oyster's shell had value, serving as bureau-top catch-alls, ash trays, or a decorative border for the garden. 7

We still visit Arey's Pond whenever we can, my father still digging for clams and searching for quahogs. But some years ago, the channel to the bay was deepened to provide access for pleasure boats. The shellfish never recovered. After two or three years some of the clams came back and a few quahogs can still be found, but the oysters are gone and none of the crabs can negotiate the channel. Only the periwinkles remain in abundance to remind us of how it once was. 8

7

Cause & Effect

Guidelines for

Cause & Effect

1. **Understand the problem.** Cause and effect analysis requires an in-depth understanding of a process or event. It's an analysis often applied by historians, engineers and anyone interested in how or why something happens. Historians typically immerse themselves in information— letters, newspaper reports, census data—before attempting to assess a historical event. Your professors may ask you to do a cause and effect analysis in an essay exam for a different reason—to make sure *you* understand the material.

2. **Be careful in attributing causes.** Although timing of events is essential to causal analysis, just because one event precedes another doesn't mean it caused it. As a rule, the more remote the possible cause, the less likely it was to have precipitated a given effect. More immediate causes are easier to prove, but they often reveal only trivial insights: "He was caught speeding because he pressed too hard on the accelerator," is not as relevant as "He was caught speeding because he didn't notice he was in a school zone," or better still, "He didn't notice he was in a school zone because he was talking on his cell phone."

3. **Support your analysis with evidence.** In cause-effect analysis, because causes are often so difficult to pinpoint, evidence becomes very important. Well-selected evidence can make the difference between an insightful essay and speculative garbage. Even Barbara Carton's humorous story on quotation marks still makes its point by offering many examples, offering several different perspectives on the issue. Cathy Young makes her point about the causes of sexism by citing examples both from the United States and her native Soviet Union.

4. **Organize your analysis to make your point.** The most obvious strategy for organizing a cause-effect essay is chronological. However, unless you're writing a humorous essay like Suzanne Scarbek's "Monkey See, Monkey Do," this strategy is often ineffective—the improbable chain of events depicted in Suzanne's essay may make you laugh, but it probably doesn't convince that there's a single cause of bad writing. More effective organization strategies place the most convincing cause last, or lead the reader through the logic of a complex cause and effect.

Chief Seattle

Address

Chief Seattle (1786?–1866) was chief of the Duwamish and other tribes when the United States took possession of what are now the states of Washington and Oregon. His tribes' situation when he made this speech was
similar to what had already been the fate of hundreds of tribes across America: faced with the overwhelming
might and numbers of Americans, they were forced into signing disadvantageous treaties—eventually losing
almost everything they had. Seattle's speech was made in response to Governor Isaac Stevens' offer to pur-
chase two million acres of Duwampo territory. As Seattle's speech implies, his tribe in fact had little choice in
the matter. There has been speculation in recent years that the text of this speech was largely fabricated, that
Seattle's words were appropriated by white men after the fact. Nonetheless, whatever the source of these words,
they remain a profound statement of Native American philosophy, which has been used by whites and Indians
alike to better understand the Indian world.

THE GOVERNOR MADE A FINE SPEECH, but he was outranged and outclassed   1
that day. Chief Seattle, who answered on behalf of the Indians, towered a foot
above the Governor. He wore his blanket like the toga of a Roman senator,
and he did not have to strain his famous voice, which everyone agreed was au-
dible and distinct at a distance of half a mile. Seattle's oration was in
Duwamish. Doctor Smith, who had learned the language, wrote it down; under the flowery garlands of his translation the speech rolls like an articulate
iron engine, grim with meanings that outlasted his generation and may out-
last all the generations of men. As the amiable follies of the white race become
less amiable, the iron rumble of old Seattle's speech sounds louder and more
ominous. Standing in front of Doctor Maynard's office in the stumpy clearing, with his hand on the little Governor's head, the white invaders about him
and his people before him, Chief Seattle said:

"Yonder sky that has wept tears of compassion upon my people for cen-   2
turies untold, and which to us appears changeless and eternal, may change.
Today is fair. Tomorrow may be overcast with clouds. My words are like the stars
that never change. Whatever Seattle says the great chief at Washington can rely
upon with as much certainty as he can upon the return of the sun or the seasons. The White Chief says that Big Chief at Washington sends us greetings of
friendship and goodwill. That is kind of him for we know he has little need of
our friendship in return. His people are many. They are like the grass that covers vast prairies. My people are few. They resemble the scattering trees of a
storm-swept plain. The great, and—I presume—good, White Chief sends us word
that he wishes to buy our lands but is willing to allow us enough to live com-

fortably. This indeed appears just, even generous, for the Red Man no longer has rights that he need respect, and the offer may be wise also, as we are no longer in need of an extensive country. . . . I will not dwell on, nor mourn over, our untimely decay, nor reproach our paleface brothers with hastening it, as we too may have been somewhat to blame.

3   "Youth is impulsive. When our young men grow angry at some real or imaginary wrong, and disfigure their faces with black paint, it denotes that their hearts are black, and then they are often cruel and relentless, and our old men and old women are unable to restrain them. Thus it has ever been. Thus it was when the white men first began to push our forefathers further westward. But let us hope that the hostilities between us may never return. We would have everything to lose and nothing to gain. Revenge by young men is considered gain, even at the cost of their own lives, but old men who stay at home in times of war, and mothers who have sons to lose, know better.

4   "Our good father at Washington—for I presume he is now our father as well as yours, since King George has moved his boundaries further north—our great good father, I say, sends us word that if we do as he desires he will protect us. His brave warriors will be to us a bristling wall of strength, and his wonderful ships of war will fill our harbors so that our ancient enemies far to the northward—the Hydas and Tsimpsians—will cease to frighten our women, children, and old men. Then in reality will he be our father and we his children. But can that ever be? Your God is not our God! Your God loves your people and hates mine. He folds his strong and protecting arms lovingly about the paleface and leads him by the hand as a father leads his infant son—but He has forsaken His red children—if they really are his. Our God, the Great Spirit, seems also to have forsaken us. Your God makes your people wax strong every day. Soon they will fill the land. Our people are ebbing away like a rapidly receding tide that will never return. The white man's God cannot love our people or He would protect them. They seem to be orphans who can look nowhere for help. How then can we be brothers? How can your God become our God and renew our prosperity and awaken in us dreams of returning greatness? If we have a common heavenly father He must be partial—for He came to his paleface children. We never saw Him. He gave you laws but He had no word for His red children whose teeming multitudes once filled this vast continent as stars fill the firmament. No; we are two distinct races with separate origins and separate destinies. There is little in common between us.

5   "To us the ashes of our ancestors are sacred and their resting place is hallowed ground. You wander far from the graves of your ancestors and seemingly without regret. Your religion was written upon tables of stone by the iron finger of your God so that you could not forget. The Red Man could never comprehend nor remember it. Our religion is the traditions of our ancestors—the dreams of

our old men, given them in solemn hours of night by the Great Spirit; and the visions of our sachems; and it is written in the hearts of our people.

"Your dead cease to love you and the land of their nativity as soon as they 6 pass the portals of the tomb and wander way beyond the stars. They are soon forgotten and never return. Our dead never forget the beautiful world that gave them being.

"Day and night cannot dwell together. The Red Man has ever fled the ap- 7 proach of the White Man, as the morning mist flees before the morning sun. However, your proposition seems fair and I think that my people will accept it and will retire to the reservation you offer them. Then we will dwell apart in peace, for the words of the Great White Chief seem to be the words of nature speaking to my people out of dense darkness.

"It matters little where we pass the remnant of our days. They will not be 8 many. A few more moons; a few more winters—and not one of the descendants of the mighty hosts that once moved over this broad land or lived in happy homes, protected by the Great Spirit, will remain to mourn over the graves of a people once more powerful and hopeful than yours. But why should I mourn at the untimely fate of my people? Tribe follows tribe, and nation follows nation, like the waves of the sea. It is the order of nature, and regret is useless. Your time of decay may be distant, but it will surely come, for even the White Man whose God walked and talked with him as friend with friend, cannot be exempt from the common destiny. We may be brothers after all. We will see.

"We will ponder your proposition, and when we decide we will let you 9 know. But should we accept it, I here and now make this condition that we will not be denied the privilege without molestation of visiting at any time the tombs of our ancestors, friends and children. Every part of this soil is sacred in the estimation of my people. Every hillside, every valley, every plain and grove, has been hallowed by some sad or happy event in days long vanished. . . . The very dust upon which you now stand responds more lovingly to their footsteps than to yours, because it is rich with the blood of our ancestors and our bare feet are conscious of the sympathetic touch. . . . Even the little children who lived here and rejoiced here for a brief season will love these somber solitudes and at eventide they greet shadowy returning spirits. And when the last Red Man shall have perished, and the memory of my tribe shall have become a myth among the White Men, these shores will swarm with the invisible dead of my tribe, and when your children's children think themselves alone in the field, the store, the shop, upon the highway, or in the silence of the pathless woods, they will not be alone. . . . At night when the streets of your cities and villages are silent and you think them deserted, they will throng with the returning hosts that once filled and still love this beautiful land. The White Man will never be alone.

"Let him be just and deal kindly with my people, for the dead are not powerless." 10

W. E. B. DuBois

The Souls of White Folk

William Edgar Burghardt DuBois was a descendant of a French Huguenot and an African slave. He received B.A. degrees from both Fisk and Harvard Universities and a Ph.D. from the University of Berlin. He taught, at various times, at Wilberforce, the University of Pennsylvania, and Atlanta University, holding professorships in Greek, Latin, Sociology, Economics, and History. In addition, he edited many publications, including *Crisis*, the journal of the National Association for the Advancement of Colored People, from 1910 to 1934. One of his most famous works was *The Souls of Black Folk*—both a fine piece of English prose and a plea for greater understanding of blacks by whites. Seven years later, in 1910, he wrote this essay as a plea to whites to understand themselves.

1   HIGH IN THE TOWER WHERE I SIT beside the loud complaining of the human sea I know many souls that toss and whirl and pass, but none there are that puzzle me more than the Souls of White Folk. Not, mind you, the souls of them that are white, but souls of them that have become painfully conscious of their whiteness; those in whose minds the paleness of their bodily skins is fraught with tremendous and eternal significance.

2   Forgetting (as I can at times forget) the meaning of this singular obsession to me and my folk, I become the more acutely sensitive to the marvelous part this thought is playing today, and to the way it is developing the Souls of White Folk, and I wonder what the end will be.

3   The discovery of personal whiteness among the world's people is a very modern thing—a nineteenth- and twentieth-century matter, indeed. The ancient world would have laughed at such a distinction. The Middle Ages regarded it with mild curiosity, and even up into the eighteenth century we were hammering our national manikins into one great Universal Man with fine frenzy, which ignored color and race as well as birth. Today we have changed all that, and the world, in sudden emotional conversation, has discovered that it is white, and, by that token, wonderful.

4   When I seek to explain this, to me, inexplicable phenomenon, there always creeps first to my mind the analogy of the child and his candy. To every child there comes a time when the toothsomeness of his sweets is strangely enhanced by the thought that his playmate has none. Further than this, however, the analogy fails, for with one accord the mother world seeks to teach this child the third new joy of sharing. Any thought, however, of sharing their color is to white folk not simply unthinkable, but its mention is liable to lead to violent explosions of anger and vituperation. Not only is there this unre-

buked and vociferously applauded greediness, but something that sounds like: "I shall keep my candy and you shall not have yours." Or, in other words, it is not the obvious proposition: "I am white and you are black," but the astonishing declaration, "I am white and you are nothing."

This assumption that of all the hues of God, whiteness alone is candy to   5 the world child—is inherently and obviously better than brownness or tan— leads to curious acts; even the sweeter souls of the dominant world, as they discourse with me on weather, weal and woe, are continually playing above their actual words an obligato of turn and tone, saying:

"My poor unwhite thing! Weep not nor rage. I know, too well, that the   6 curse of God lies heavy on you. Why? That is not for me to say; but be brave! Do your work in your lowly sphere, praying the good Lord that into heaven above, where all is love, you may one day, be born—white!"

At such times I have an unholy desire to laugh, and to ask with seemingly   7 irrelevance and certain irreverence: "But what on earth is whiteness, that one should so desire it?"

Then always somehow, some way, silently but clearly, I am given to un-   8 derstand that whiteness is the ownership of the earth, forever and ever, Amen!

Now, what is the effect on a man or a nation when it comes passionately to   9 believe such an extraordinary dictum as this? That nations are coming to believe it is manifest daily. Wave on wave, each with increasing virulence, is dashing this new religion of whiteness on the shores of our time. Its first effects are funny; the strut of the Southerner, the arrogance of the Englishman amuck, the whoop of the hoodlum who vicariously leads your mob. Next it appears dampening generous enthusiasm in what we once counted glorious: To free the slave is discovered to be tolerable only insofar as it freed his master. Do we sense somnolent writhings in black Africa, or angry groans in India, or triumphant "banzais" in Japan? "To your tents, O Israel!" These nations are not white. Build warships and heft the Big Stick.

After the more comic manifestations and chilling of generous enthusiasm,   10 come subtler, darker deeds. Everything considered, the title to the universe claimed by white folk is faulty. It ought at least to look plausible. How easy, then, by emphasis and omission, to make every child believe that every great soul the world ever saw was a white man's soul; that every great thought the world ever knew was a white man's thought; that every great deed the world ever did was a white man's deed; that every great dream the world ever sang was a white man's dream. In fine, that if from the world were dropped everything that could not fairly be attributed to white folk the world would, if anything, be even greater, truer, better than now. And if all this be a lie, is it not a lie in a great cause?

Here it is that the comedy verges to tragedy. The first minor note is struck   11 all unconsciously by those worthy souls in whom consciousness of high descent brings burning desire to spread the gift abroad—the obligation of nobility to the ignoble. Such sense of duty assumes two things: A real possession of the heritage and its frank appreciation by the humbly born. So long, then, as humble black folk, voluble with thanks, receive barrels of old clothes from lordly and generous whites, there is much mental peace and moral satisfaction. But when the black man begins to dispute the white man's title to certain alleged bequests of the Father's in wage and position, authority and training; and when his attitude toward charity is sullen anger rather than humble jollity; when he insists on his human rights to swagger and swear and waste—then the spell is suddenly broken and the philanthropist is apt to be ready to believe that Negroes are impudent, that the South is right, and that Japan wants to fight us.

12   Mentally the blight has fallen on American science. The race problem is not insoluble if the correct answer is sought. It is insoluble if the wrong answer is insisted upon as it has been insisted upon for thrice a hundred years. A very moderate brain can show that two and two is four. But no human ingenuity can make that sum three or five. This American science has long attempted to do. It has made itself the handmaid of a miserable prejudice. In its attempt to justify the treatment of black folk it has repeatedly suppressed evidence, misquoted authority, distorted fact and deliberately lied. It is wonderful that in the very lines of social study, where America should shine, it has done nothing.

13   Worse than this is our moral and religious plight. We profess a religion of high ethical advancement, a spiritual faith, of respect for truth, despising of personal riches, a reverence for humility, and not simply justice to our fellows, but personal sacrifice of our good for theirs. It is a high aim, so high that we ought not utterly to be condemned for not reaching it, so long as we strive bravely toward it. Do we, as a people? On the contrary, we have injected into our creed a gospel of human hatred and prejudice, a despising of our less fortunate fellows, not to speak of our reverence for wealth, which flatly contradicts the Christian ideal. Granting all that American Christianity has done to educate and uplift black men, it must be frankly admitted that there is absolutely no logical method by which the treatment of black folk by white folk in this land can be squared with any reasonable statement or practice of the Christian ideal.

14   What is the result? It is either the abandonment of the Christian ideal or hypocrisy. Some frankly abandon Christianity when it comes to the race problem and say: Religion does not enter here. They then retire to some more primitive paganism and live there, enlightened by such prejudices as they adopt or inherit. This is retrogression toward barbarism, but it is at least honest. It is infinitely better than its widely accepted alternative, which attempts to reconcile color caste and Christianity, and sees or affects to see no incongruity. What ails the religion of a land when its strongholds of orthodoxy are to be found in those regions where race prejudice is most uncompromising, vindictive, and cruel; where human brotherhood is a lie?

The one great moral issue of America upon which the Church of Christ   15
comes nearest being dumb is the question as to the application of the golden
rule between white and black folk.

All this I see and hear up in my tower above the thunder of the seven seas.   16
From my narrowed windows I stare into the night that looms beneath the
cloud-swept stars. Eastward and westward storms are brewing great, ugly whirl-
winds of hatred and blood and cruelty. I will not believe them inevitable. I
will not believe that all that was must be—that all the shameful drama of the
past must be done again today before the sunlight sweeps the silver seas.

If I cry amid this roar of elemental forces, must my cry be vain because it   17
is but a cry—a small and human cry amid Promethean gloom?

Back beyond the world and swept by these wild white faces of the awful   18
dead, why will this Soul of the White Folk, this modern Prometheus, hang
bound by his own binding, tethered by a labor of the past? I hear his mighty cry
reverberating through the world, "I am white!" Well and good, O Prometheus,
divine thief! The world is wide enough for two colors, two little shinings of the
sun; why then devour your own vitals when I answer, "I am black"?

Student Essay

Susan Scarbek

Monkey See, Monkey Do

Though this essay seems mostly to complain about writing instructors, it also has a good point to make about writing: there is no one way to write well. Sometimes "I am going bananas" is just the right sentence for the situation.

DURING A RECENT WORKSHOP ON GRAMMAR, a sentence—"I am going ba-   1
nanas"—was introduced for comment. A short poll of this class has rendered
some suggestions about the kinds of responses a teacher would give if a student dared to write such a sentence.

"I am going bananas." The teacher will write "Slang. Please rewrite" in the   2
margin. The student will obviously know what's slangy about the sentence, so no
further comment is needed. This approach avoids the sticky question of verbs altogether and especially avoids discussion of intransitive, transitive, and linking
verbs.

The teacher will probably get "I am going crazy" as the rewritten sentence.   3

If this does indeed occur, the teacher can choose between two attacks: (1) Ignore it and go on, or (2) Mark "Too colloquial for Standard English models. Please rewrite." The latter is the more common, and certainly the preferred teacher response, since it affords her the opportunity to explain what colloquialisms are and why Standard English is *so* much better. After she has explained how "crazy" can be improved upon, she'll probably get the following rewrite: "I am losing my mind."

4   This sentence will really allow the teacher to deliver the *coup de grace* to the student! She'll simply write "Idiom" next to the sentence. After all, everyone knows you don't *really* lose your mind unless you have a particularly leaky cranium. If people really could lose their minds, others of us would find them lying around, wouldn't we? The student, of course, will believe this to be another error, and take one of two courses. He'll either give up, or produce an unsolicited rewrite.

5   The result might look like this: "As a response to certain unfavorable stimuli in an increasingly complex and hostile environment, this subject is developing a labile personality and is rapidly approaching an irrational state of mind." This, fellow writers, is a teacher's gold mine. She might begin with wordiness and jargon, but the majority of students polled (99.9%) felt that the following teacher comment would be most fitting and would help the student understand the intricacies of the English language more fully: "Jargon. Be concise and clear. Why don't you just write, 'I'm going bananas'?"

Barbara Carton

Why Does "Everybody" Now Put "Everything" in Quotation Marks?

Because it Moves Merchandise and Lends That Bit of Stress That the Occasion Calls For

Though she is a staff reporter for the *Wall Street Journal,* Barbara Carton's stories focus on the whimsical side of life. Writing about ordinary topics like turkey stuffing, Carton injects much-needed humor into the staid business newspaper. In this selection, which appeared in 1999, Carton comments on the random quotation marks that seem to be popping up almost everywhere.

OUR 'GOAL' IS TO HELP OUR CUSTOMERS CONSERVE ENERGY.   1
　　　　　　　　　　　　　—Letter from Atlas Oil Co., Westwood, Mass.   2
Thank you for . . . keeping your 'health' club as clean as possible.   3
　　　　　　　　　　　—Locker-room sign, World Trade Center, New York   4
Call it overzealous marketing. Or pretentiousness. Maybe it's the work of   5
those who might charitably be called 'challenged, punctuationwise.'

Whatever the reason, an 'epidemic' of runaway 'quotation marks' is rag-   6
ing in the world of words.

'I've seen it in letters I get from my brother,' says Michael Pemberton, an   7
assistant professor of English at the University of Illinois. 'Quotation marks
around words that seem so amazingly commonplace I can't understand why
he's doing it.'

'I've seen it a lot in Yellow Pages advertising,' adds Richard Dowis, presi-   8
dent of the Society for the Preservation of English Language and Literature,
in Waleska, Ga. He has also noticed signs such as the ones in diners that say,
'Please pay the 'cashier.'' They will have cashier in quotation marks as if to
suggest the person behind the counter isn't really up to snuff.

The 'Doonesbury' cartoon that ran Friday in the *New York Daily News*,   9
among other newspapers, contained this bit of conversation:

'You think he'll be 'impressed' by quotation marks?'   10
'Sure—he's a college boy.'   11

Tom McArthur, who edits the Oxford Companion to the English Lan-   12
guage in Cambridge, England, sees errant quotes popping up throughout
Britain. 'I have a colleague on a committee here who is a structural engineer,'
he says. 'His writing is peppered with this kind of quotation.'

As any of our academic experts could explain, the rightful job of quotation   13
marks is to denote words first uttered elsewhere, or titles of books and other
works. They are also used to enclose nicknames or unfamiliar terms.

In its proper place, the quotation mark keeps company with timeless and   14
noble utterances. Misplaced, as it is with growing frequency, it surrounds commonly understood words. But why?

Modern-day stress is one reason.   15

A lot of these quotation marks are stress-related. Marvin Owen, general   16
manager of Automated Church Systems Inc. of Florence, S.C., says his six
staff writers employ quotes for added punch. 'If something's really important,'
Mr. Owen says, 'you've got to do whatever you can to get it in front of them.'
Really important, following this precept, is the Sunday-offerings tally that the
software firm compiles for churches across the country. Parishioners at these
churches receive their 'Record of Contributions' in quotes.

At the Fitness Co., New York-area manager Bonnie Patrick had irony as   17
well as stress in mind when she wrote the World Trade Center sign thanking
members for keeping the health club clean. 'Our point was, if you leave your

sneakers out, as everybody does, on top of the lockers, they smell and it's an unhealthy situation and we belong to a health club,' says Ms. Patrick. 'We were trying to do a play on words and, at the same time, get the point across.'

18   For some reason, stores (among other users of English) find quotation marks irresistible when the word 'all' comes up. According to a sign at the Souper Salad deli in downtown Boston, 'One hot lid fits 'all' size coffee cups.' Super Stop & Shop grocery stores in the same city advertise ''All Natural' Jumbo Sea Scallops.' Similarly, the Appalachian Mountain Club lists various services in a letter to members, noting that membership entitles them to discounts on 'all of the above.'

19   Mary N. Bruder of Pittsburgh, a former English teacher who operates the 'Grammar Lady' Web site, has noticed people using the apostrophe to form plurals, 'tomato's,' for example, and figures it's part of the same trend affecting quotation marks.

20   It would seem to be. Indeed, the 'trend' appears to have had its 'origins' long ago. Witness this bit from a 1985 Dave Barry column:

21   'Dear Mr. Language Person: What is the purpose of the apostrophe?

22   'The apostrophe is used mainly in hand-lettered small-business signs to alert the reader that an 'S' is coming up at the end of a word, as in: WE DO NOT ACCEPT PERSONAL CHECK'S. Another important grammar concept to bear in mind when creating hand-lettered small-business signs is that you should put quotation marks around random words for decoration, as in 'TRY' OUR HOT DOG'S, or even TRY 'OUR' HOT DOG'S.

23   John Broderick, author of 'The Able Writer: A Rhetoric and Handbook,' suspects that many people have a 'vague feeling' about quotation marks, but 'are not literate enough—literally, widely and well-read enough—fully to have grasped the subtleties involved.'

24   Consider this sign placed on three stores in the Boston area: 'Join Our Team. Economy Hardware. 'Hiring.''

25   'The writer seems to try to disassociate himself or herself from taking full responsibility for the word,' says Prof. Broderick, who teaches English at Old Dominion University in Norfolk, Va. 'Maybe they're only 'hiring' until the job is filled.' Similarly, in the case of the Atlas letter about conservation, 'Maybe the oil company doesn't want to be forced actually to achieve their 'goal.''

26   Dr. Broderick adds: 'I'm trying to be kind in finding interpretations.'

27   Rob Renaud, general manager of the hardware stores that are 'hiring,' blames the sign company. 'It wasn't our idea to put the quotation marks there,' he says. 'We just wanted to stress hiring, and maybe that's their style of stressing something. We wanted a sign that stood out, not a regular old help-wanted sign.'

Sign painter Rick Hammar, of Pelham, N.H., installed the quotation   28
marks for Mr. Renaud, but he usually prefers stars. 'Like, we did some
bumper stickers and on the very top line we had a star, then it said, 'Think
Women' and then another star, and then in big bold letters, it said, 'Think
Republican.''

In any case, Mr. Hammar says, sign painters don't call these kinds of punc-   29
tuation 'quotation marks'—they call them 'slashes.' Besides, he says, 'We have
a license in art to do what we want.'

Cathy Young

Keeping Women Weak

Born in the Soviet Union in 1963, Cathy Young emigrated to the United States in 1980. After graduating from
Rutgers University, she began a successful career as a writer, publishing several books including the autobio-
graphical *Growing up in Moscow*. Building on her unique perspective, Young's works on racism, feminism, and
Generation X have appeared in the *American Spectator*, the *Detroit Free Press*, and the *Wall Street Journal*.

NOT LONG AGO, I attended a conference on women's research and activism in   1
the nineties, attended by dozens of feminist academics, writers, and public figures. At the wrap-up session, a middle-aged history professor from the Mid-
west introduced a discordant note into the spirit of celebration. "The fact,"
she said, "is that young women just aren't interested in feminism or feminist
ideas, even though they are leading feminist lives—planning to become
lawyers, doctors, professionals. What is it about feminism, and about our approach, that puts young women off?"

In response, some blamed "the backlash," others "homophobia." One   2
woman protested that there *were* young feminists out there, citing sexual harassment lawsuits filed by high-school girls—apparently a greater accomplishment
than merely preparing for a career. Another declared that what feminist educators needed to give their students was "an understanding of the power dynamic,"
not "quote-unquote objectivity." (Could it be something about comments like
these that turns female students off?) Missing from this picture was any serious
discussion of what modern feminism has to offer modern young women.

Feminism meant a great deal to me when I came to the United States thir-   3
teen years ago, after a childhood spent in the Soviet Union. Indeed, one of
the things that elated me the most about America was women's liberation.

4   The society in which I had grown up was one that officially proclaimed sexual equality and made it a point of great pride yet stereotyped men and women in ways reminiscent of the American fifties. At school, we had mandatory home economics for girls and shop for boys, a practice no one thought of challenging. At the music school for the gifted where my mother taught piano, to say that someone played "like a girl"—pleasantly, neatly, and without substance—was a commonly used putdown; in literary reviews, the highest compliment to be paid a woman writer or poet was that she wrote like a man.

5   As I approached college age, I learned that there was tacit but widely known discrimination against women in the college-entrance exams, on the assumption that a less-capable male would in the end be a more valuable asset than a bright female, who would have boys and makeup and marriage on her mind. And all too many smart, ambitious girls seemed to accept this injustice as inevitable, assuming simply that they had to be twice as good as the boys to prove themselves.

6   It was just as unquestioningly accepted that housework, including the arduous task of Soviet shopping, was women's work; when the problem of women's excessive double burden at home and on the job was mentioned at all, the proposed solution was always for men to be paid more and for women to spend more time at home, not for men to pitch in with domestic chores. And although my parents' relationship was an uncommonly equal one, my father still quoted to me the dictum (coming from Karl Marx, a thinker he generally did not regard as much of an authority) that "woman's greatest strength is her weakness."

7   My discovery of America was also a discovery of feminism—not only Ms. magazine and The Feminine Mystique but also the open and straightforward manner of young American women I met. This was in stark contrast to the style that so many Russian women reverently equated with "femininity"—a more-or-less affected air of capriciousness and frailty, a flirtatious deference to men. I admired the easy camaraderie between boys and girls on American college campuses, the independence and self-confidence of young women who invited guys on dates and picked up the tab, drove when they were out with male companions, and wouldn't let anyone treat them like frail, helpless little things.

8   Those early impressions may have been too optimistic, perhaps somewhat superficial, perhaps incomplete. But I don't think they were wrong.

9   Becoming an American as a teenager in 1980, I joined the first generation of American women who had grown up assuming not only that they would work most of their lives but also that they were the equals of men and that they could be anything they wanted to be (except maybe a full-time homemaker). This was also the first generation, really, to have grown up after the sexual revolution—at a time when, at least among the educated, the nice-girls-

don't sexual standard vanished almost completely. In a somewhat dizzying reversal of traditional norms, many girls felt embarrassed telling their first lovers that they were virgins (at least that's how I felt).

Of course new choices meant new pressures. I never thought a world of 10 sexual equality would be a utopia of peace and harmony. I did believe that our generation of women, and men, was on its way to achieving a world in which people were judged as individuals and not on the basis of their gender; a world in which men and women worked and loved in equal partnership—even if, inevitably, they continued every so often to make each other miserable and furious.

And then something funny happened on the way to that feminist future. 11 We were told that we were victims, with little control over our lives and our choices; we were told that we needed to be protected.

When the right said that women were victimized by career opportunities 12 and sexual freedom, it didn't matter much—at least to the middle-class, college-educated women who were the main beneficiaries of these new opportunities. Who, in those social circles, was going to listen to people who said that wives should obey their husbands and stick to the kitchen and nursery—to Phyllis Schlafly or Jerry Falwell, notorious reactionaries with little impact on mass culture?

But the message of victimhood also came from the feminist left. Every- 13 where around us, we were told, was a backlash seeking to snatch from us the freedoms we had gained. We were told that we were the targets of a hidden war and had better start acting like one, searching for subtle signs of enemy forays everywhere. If we believed that we had never experienced gender-based injustice and had never felt particularly restricted by our gender, we were not just naive but dangerous: we were turning our backs on feminism and fostering the myth that its major battles had been won.

Whenever a campus study has shown that young people of both sexes in- 14 creasingly share the same values and aspirations and that most college women are quite confident of their ability to succeed in the workplace and to combine family and career, older feminists seem far from pleased. Their warnings—oh, just wait until these young women get a taste of the real world and find that they still face prejudice and discrimination—can sound almost gleeful.

Older feminists talk a good line about empowering young women and let- 15 ting them speak in their own voices; but that goes only as long as these voices say all the approved things. At a university workshop on peer sexual harassment in schools I attended in the spring of 1993, some of the panelists complained that many girls didn't seem to understand what sexual harassment was; when boys made passes or teased them sexually they just shrugged it off, or they thought it was funny and actually liked it. "They need to be educated," one speaker said earnestly, "that the boys aren't just joking around with you, that it's harassment."

16   Ignored in all this discussion was intriguing evidence of the assertive, even aggressive sexuality of many of today's teenage girls, who apparently do a bit of harassing of their own. If girls seemed to revel in sexual attention, that could only be a sign of "low self-esteem" or inability to say no.

17   Judging by all those complaints about the unraised consciousness of the young, the preoccupation with the sexual and other victimization of high-school and college females is not coming, by and large, from young women themselves. Most of them, I believe, tend to regard all the extreme rhetoric as a sort of background noise; if they think about feminism at all, they often decide that they want no part of it—even if they're all for equal rights. The kind of feminists they usually see in their midst may further contribute to this alienation.

18   When I was still in college, I began to notice, alongside the spirited, independent, ambitious young women I admired, a different product of the feminist age: the ever-vigilant watchdog on the alert for signs of sexism. Occasionally, she made a good point; when our environmental science professor blamed overpopulation in part on Third World women "choosing" to have lots of babies, a student spoke up to note that for most Third World women, childbearing was hardly a matter of choice.

19   More typical, alas, was the young woman in my human sexuality class who was constantly pouncing on the professor for saying something like "People who suffer from premature ejaculation . . ." ("Are you implying that only men are people?"). When he had the audacity to cite data indicating that some rapists were motivated primarily by hatred of women and the desire to dominate them but others were driven primarily by sexual impulses, she went ballistic: "The ONLY thing that causes rape is men wanting to control and terrorize women, and you're trying to make it SEXY!" Later, this person bragged about having caused the poor prof "a lot of trouble" by filing a complaint with the dean.

20   Paranoid is a red-flag word to many feminists—understandably so, since it has been used all too often to dismiss women's rightful concerns about sexism. But what other word can come to mind when a woman claims that her writing instructor's selection of a sample of bad writing—a conservative Christian screed linking pornography and communism—was a personal insult directed at her, since she had sometimes worn a Women Against Pornography button in school?

21   And what can one expect when Naomi Wolf, a writer hailed as a trailblazer of a new "Third Wave" of feminism for the younger generation, urges women to undertake—and men, to gracefully (and gratefully) second—"the arduous, often boring, nonnegotiable *daily chore of calling attention to sexism*" (em-

phasis mine)? In the essay "Radical Heterosexuality, or, How to Love a Man and Save Your Feminist Soul" (published in the twentieth-anniversary issue of *Ms.*), Wolf describes how even well-intentioned men tend to be blind to the horrific things women have to put up with:

> *Recently, I walked down a New York City avenue with a woman friend, X,*   22
> *and a man friend, Y. I pointed out to Y the leers, hisses, and invitations to sit*
> *on faces. Each woman saw clearly what the other woman saw, but Y was baf-*
> *fled. . . . A passerby makes kissy-noises with his tongue while Y is scrutinizing*
> *the menu of the nearest bistro. "There, there! Look! Listen!" we cried. "What?*
> *Where? Who?" wailed poor Y, valiantly, uselessly spinning.*

Like poor Y, I am baffled. God knows, I've been taking walks in Manhat-   23
tan at least once or twice a week for nearly thirteen years now, and not a single invitation to sit on a face, not even a single hiss as far as I recall—nothing
more dramatic than the occasional "You look gorgeous today" or "That's a
pretty outfit," and certainly nothing like the constant barrage Wolf describes.
Even the time I wore a new dress that exposed much more cleavage than I realized, all it cost me was one fairly tame remark (as I was stepping into a subway car, a man who was stepping off stared at my bosom and muttered, "Very
nice"). Applied to everyday life and interpersonal relations, "eternal vigilance
is the price of liberty" strikes me as a rather disastrous motto to adopt.

Like all would-be revolutionaries, the radical feminists seek to subordinate   24
private life to ideology—an endeavor that I find, quite simply, frightening. You
don't have to spend part of your life under a totalitarian system (though
maybe it helps) to realize that social and political movements that subordinate
life to ideology have a nasty way of turning coercive, whether it's the mass violence of communism or the neo-Puritan controls of "P.C."

This is not to say that there is no room for rethinking traditional attitudes,   25
on things ranging from who picks up the check in the restaurant to who takes
care of the baby. Millions of women and men are grappling with these issues
at home and in the workplace, some more successfully than others. But that
doesn't mean they have to walk around with their eyes glued to a microscope.

Eternal vigilance is a tempting trap for post-baby-boomer feminists. It has   26
been often remarked that women of earlier generations had to struggle against
visible and overt barriers, such as being denied admission to law school, or told
that only men need apply for certain jobs or that married women shouldn't
work. It seemed that once such barriers dropped, equality would come
quickly. It didn't quite turn out that way; there were other, more insidious
roadblocks, from a working mother's guilt over taking a business trip to a professor's unconscious tendency to call on the boys in the class. The problem,
however, is that subtle sexism is an elusive target, with plenty of room for error

and misinterpretation. If you complain to your professor that you find the course work too difficult and he says, "Well, I've always thought girls didn't belong in this class anyway," there's not a shadow of a doubt that he's a sexist pig. But suppose he says, "Hey, start working harder or drop the class, but don't come whining to me." Is he being insensitive to you as a woman? (An incident of this sort figured in a recent sex-discrimination suit at the University of Minnesota.) Or is he simply a blunt fellow who believes people should stand on their own two feet and who would have treated a male student exactly the same? And if he had been tough on a man but sensitive and solicitous toward a woman student, wouldn't that have been exactly the kind of paternalism feminists used to oppose?

27   But then, certain aspects of cutting-edge feminism do smack of a very old-fashioned paternalism, a sort of chivalry without the charm. At some campus meetings, it is considered P.C. for men who are first in line for the microphone to cede their place to a woman in order to ensure that female speakers—apparently too timid to just get up and get in line—get a proper hearing. Ladies first?

28   Definitions of "hostile environment" sexual harassment often seem like a throwback to prefeminist, if not positively Victorian, standards of how to treat a lady: no off-color jokes, no sexual remarks, no swearing and, God forbid, no improper advances. Surveys purporting to gauge the prevalence of harassment lump together sexual blackmail—demands for sex as a condition of promotion, good grades, or other rewards—with noncoercive advances from coworkers or fellow students, with sexual jokes or innuendo, "improper staring" or "winking."

29   Well, guess what: women too make off-color jokes and risqué comments, and even sexual advances. Sure, many women at one time or another also have to deal with obnoxious, lecherous, and/or sexist jerks. But in most cases, especially if the man is not a superior, they're perfectly capable of putting a jerk back in his place. Of course, radical feminists such as Catharine MacKinnon tell us that there is *always* an imbalance of power between a man and a woman: even if you're studying for an MBA and have a prestigious job lined up, you're still powerless. Now there's a message guaranteed to build up self-confidence and self-esteem.

30   A video on sexual harassment, broadcast on public television twice in January 1993 and available free through an 800 number, includes a segment on a university experiment in which unwitting male students are assigned to supervise the computer work of an attractive girl. Before leaving them alone, the male research assistant pretends to take small liberties with the young woman (putting a hand on her shoulder, bending closely over her) while explaining the work process, and in most cases the male student proceeds to imitate this behavior or even push it a little further.

Then, the young woman—who, of course, has known what's been going on   31
the whole time—talks on camera about how the experience has helped her understand what it's like to feel powerless. But doesn't this powerlessness have at
least something to do with the fact that she was undoubtedly instructed not
to show displeasure? Is it such a good idea to teach young women that, short
of legal intervention, they have no way of dealing with such annoyances?

I don't believe that our views or our allegiances are determined solely or   32
primarily by age. Still, one might have expected our generation to articulate a
feminism rooted in the experience of women who have never felt subordi-
nated to men, have never felt that their options were limited by gender in any
significant way or that being treated as sexual beings diminished their per-
sonhood. This is not, of course, the experience of all young women; but it is
the experience of many, and an experience that should be taken as a model.
Perhaps those of us who have this positive view of our lives and our relationships with men have not lived up to our responsibility to translate that view
into a new feminist vision.

In an *Esquire* article about sexual politics and romantic love on campus in   33
the nineties, Janet Viggiani, then–assistant dean for coeducation at Harvard,
was quoted as saying, "I think young women now are very confused. . . . They
don't have many models for how to be strong females and feminine. Many of
their models are victim models—passive, weak, endangered." In recent years,
feminist activism has focused almost entirely on negatives, from eating disorders to sexual violence and abuse. Sadly, these problems are all too real, and
they certainly should be confronted; what they should not be is the central
metaphor for the female condition or for relations between women and men,
or for feminism. What does it mean when the only time young women and
girls think of feminism is not when they think of achievement but when they
think of victimization?

The emphasis on victimhood has had an especially dramatic effect on at-   34
titudes toward sexuality. We didn't revel in our sexual freedom for too long;
as if the shadow of AIDS weren't bad enough, sex was suddenly fraught with
danger and violence as much as possibilities of pleasure, or even more so. A
cartoon in the *Nation* shows a girl grooming herself before a mirror, with the
caption, "Preparing for a date"—and in the next frame, a boy doing the same,
with the caption, "Preparing for a date rape." Pamphlets on sexual assault
warn that one out of every five dates ends in a rape, and that up to 25 percent
of college women become victims: "Since you can't tell who has the potential
for rape by simply looking, be on your guard with every man."

If these numbers are true, women would be well advised either to forswear   35
dating altogether or to carry a can of Mace on every date. But what about
these numbers? When one looks at how they are obtained, and how rape is
defined, it becomes clear that the acquaintance-rape hysteria not only gives

young women an exaggerated picture of the dangers they face in the company of men but essentially demeans women, absolving or stripping them of all responsibility for their behavior.

36   The question is not whether a woman's provocative dress, flirtatious behavior, or drinking justifies sexual assault; that attitude is now on the wane, for which the women's movement certainly deserves credit. It's not even a question of whether a woman should have to fight back and risk injury to prove that she did not consent to sex. The latest crusade makes a woman a victim of rape if she did not rebuff a man's sexual advances because she was too shy or didn't want to hurt his feelings, or if she had sex while drunk (not passed out, just sufficiently intoxicated so that her inhibitions were loosened) and felt bad about it afterwards. In a typical scenario, a couple is making out and then the woman pulls back and says, "I really think we shouldn't," and the man draws her back toward him, *nonforcibly*, and continues to fondle her, or says, "Oh come on, you know you want it," and eventually they end up having sex. If the woman feels that the intercourse was "unwanted," she can—according to the anti-date-rape activists—claim to be a victim, no different from the woman who's attacked at knifepoint in a dark, empty parking lot.

37   A few years ago, I was at the apartment of an ex-boyfriend with whom I was still on friendly terms; after a couple of beers, we started kissing. When his hand crept under my skirt, I suddenly sobered up and thought of several good reasons why I should not go to bed with the guy. I wriggled out of his arms, got up, and said, "That's enough." Undaunted, he came up from behind and squeezed my breasts. I rammed my elbow into his chest, forcefully enough to make the point, and snapped, "Didn't you hear me? I said, enough."

38   Some people might say that I overreacted (my ex-boyfriend felt that way), but the logic of modern-day radical feminists suggests the opposite: that I displayed a heroism that cannot be required of any woman in a situation like that because she could expect the guy to beat her up, to maim her, even if he hadn't made any threats or shown any violent tendencies. A "reasonable" woman would have passively submitted and then cried rape.

39   Even "no means no" is no longer enough; some activists want to say that yes means no, or at least the absence of an explicit yes means no. Feminist legal theorist MacKinnon suggests that much of what our society regards as consensual sex hardly differs from rape and that, given women's oppression, it is doubtful "whether consent is a meaningful concept" at all. Which is to say that, like underage children and the mentally retarded, women are to be presumed incapable of valid consent. MacKinnon's frequent ally, polemicist Andrea Dworkin, states bluntly that all intercourse is rape.

40   This reasoning is still very far from mainstream acceptance. Even MacKinnon only expresses such views when addressing fairly narrow and con-

verted audiences, not when she's interviewed on TV. Yet a 1992 report by the Harvard Date Rape Task Force recommended that university guidelines define rape as "any act of sexual intercourse that occurs without the expressed consent of the person." What does this mean—that a consent form must be signed before a date? Or that, as a couple moves toward the bed after passionate and mutual heavy petting, the man should ask the woman if she's quite sure she wants to? (A friend who just graduated from college tells me that some men are actually beginning to act that way.) And perhaps he has to keep asking every time: the couple's prior sexual relationship, the advocates say, makes no difference whatsoever.

Clearly, this vision leaves no room for spontaneity, for ambiguity, for pas- 41
sionate, wordless, animal sex. What's more, it is, in the end, deeply belittling to women, who apparently cannot be expected to convey their wishes clearly or to show a minimum of assertiveness. It also perpetuates a view of woman as the passive and reticent partner who may or may not want sex and man as the pursuer who is naturally presumed to want it: *she* is not required to ask for *his* consent (even though, given some current definitions, plenty of women must have committed rape at least a few times in their lives; I'm sure I have). Sex is something men impose on women. We're back full circle to fragile, chaste, nineteenth-century womanhood.

And some people think that's good. Recently, I got into a discussion with 42
a conservative Catholic male who vehemently argued that the campaign against date rape was nothing more than a distorted expression of women's legitimate rejection of sexual freedom, a thing so contrary to their chaste natures. Casual sex, he said, makes women (but not men) feel cheap and used, and what they're doing now is using the extreme language of rape to describe this exploitation; things were really better under the much-maligned double standard, when women were expected to say no to sex, and thus accorded more protection from male lust. To some conservatives, the outcry about sexual harassment confirms what conservatives have known all along: women want to be put on a pedestal and treated like ladies; they find sexual advances insulting because they are chaster than men.

I don't think that's true. Most young women have no wish to return to the 43
days when they were branded as sluts if they said yes. It may be, however, that this generation's confusion over sexual boundaries has to do with the pains of transition from one set of morals to another, of contradictory cultural messages: the traditional ones of chastity as the basis of female self-respect and reputation and the new ones of sexual liberation and female desire. Sometimes, we may not think we're "cheap" if we go to bed with a man we just met—at least, we're no worse than the guy is for going to bed with a woman he just met—yet when we wake up the next morning we may find that *he* thinks less of us but not of himself. And we may find, to our chagrin, that feminine coy-

ness is not quite as extinct as we might like to think. The other day, a very liberated fortysomething friend of mine breezily said, "Oh, of course no modern woman says no when she means yes." Alas, recent studies (done by feminist researchers) show that *by their own admission*, about half of college women sometimes do.

44   But there may be another reason, too, for this generation's susceptibility to the victim mentality: overconfidence in the perfectibility of life. The sexual-liberation rhetoric itself overlooked the complexity of human emotions and fostered the belief that sexual relationships could be free of all manipulation or unfair pressure. More generally, there is the idealistic arrogance of middle-class boys and girls who have grown up in a sheltered, affluent environment, accustomed to the notion that getting one's way is a basic right. The old cliché "Life isn't fair" is not only unpopular nowadays but profoundly suspect, seen as a smokescreen designed by the oppressors to keep the oppressed—women and minorities, in particular—in their place. Yes, it has been used for such purposes often enough. But often it happens to be true, and to disregard that is to invite disastrous consequences—like the belief that anyone, male or female, is entitled to an annoyance-free life.

45   The danger in the new radical feminism is not only that it legitimizes what is, deep down, an extremely retrograde view of women; it also seeks to regulate personal relationships to a degree unprecedented since the Puritans roamed the earth. If you feel that a man has enticed or pressured you into having unwanted sex, you don't confront him and call him a manipulative creep; you run to a campus grievance committee and demand redress. If you don't like the way a coworker has been putting his hand on your shoulder, you don't have to tell him to stop it—you can go and file a lawsuit instead. Courts and law-enforcement authorities are being asked to step into situations where, short of installing hidden cameras in every bedroom and every office hallway, they have no way of finding out on whose side the truth is. Of course, many millions of women and men remain relatively unaffected by this relentless politicization of the personal. Still, the damage is being done.

46   Again, it may be my Soviet background that makes me especially sensitive to the perils of this aggressive, paternalistic interventionism. In the Soviet *ancien régime*, it was not uncommon to report one's unfaithful spouse to the Communist party bureau at his (or, less commonly, her) workplace, and conflicts between husband and wife—particularly if both were party members—were often settled at public meetings that satisfied both the voyeuristic and the viciously moralistic impulses of the other comrades.

47   What are we going to be, then? Assertive, strong women (and sometimes, surely, also needy and vulnerable, because we *are* human), seeing ourselves as no better or worse than men; aware of but not obsessed with sexism; interested in loving and equal relationships but with enough confidence in our-

selves, and enough understanding of human foibles, to know better than to scrutinize every move we or our partners make for political incorrectness? Or full-time agents of the gender-crimes police?

Women's liberation is not yet a completed task. Sexism still lingers and in- 48 justice toward women still exists, particularly in the distribution of domestic tasks. We are still working on new standards and values to guide a new, equal relationship between men and women. But "Third Wave" feminism, which tries to fight gender bias by defining people almost entirely in terms of gender, is not the way to go.

We need a "Third Way" feminism that rejects the excesses of the gender 49 fanatics *and* the sentimental traditionalism of the Phyllis Schlaflys; one that does not seek special protections for women and does not view us as too socially disadvantaged to take care of ourselves. Because on the path that feminism has taken in the past few years, we are allowing ourselves to be treated as frail, helpless little things—by our would-be liberators.

8

Analogy

Analogy

1. **Use analogy to clarify your main point.** An analogy is simply a comparison of two apparently different things. In "High Tide in Tucson," for example, Barbara Kingsolver compares her own life to that of a hermit crab she accidentally brought home from a vacation in the Caribbean. One of her points in the essay is that she has carried habits from her previous life in Kentucky to her new life in Arizona. By describing the dramatic shift in the crab's life—removal from the tropical beach to an arid desert—she illustrates how much her own life has changed. If Kingsolver had simply started by describing her move to Arizona, the point may still have been made, but it would have been neither as clear nor as powerful.

2. **Make sure your analogy is appropriate.** Writing a useful analogy requires care. If the connection between the subject of your analogy and your main point is either too close or too remote, the analogy will usually be ineffective. If Kingsolver had compared moving to Arizona with moving to New Mexico, it would have been difficult to understand how significant the move was in her life. Similarly, if she had compared moving to a bowl of fruit, the analogy would be nonsensical. You should also take care not to offend with your analogies—comparing nuns to Nazis, for example, is generally a bad idea.

3. **Support your analogy with details.** Careful use of detail can help your analogy come alive. Kingsolver describes the hermit crab for many pages before she makes the connection to her own life. John Muir, in "A Wind-Storm in the Forest," paints a vivid picture of windswept treetops roiling like a raging sea.

4. **Remember that analogy does not constitute proof.** An analogy can clarify your point, but it cannot prove it. In his essay "Modern Day Mobsters," when Maurice Johnson compares banks to gangsters, his point relies on the fact that we've all had bad experiences with banks. If his point wasn't supported by both a general belief and the actual evidence he gives to support the idea that banks use predatory practices, using an analogy wouldn't be enough to save it.

Barbara Kingsolver

High Tide in Tucson

Barbara Kingsolver's novels and poems reflect her own transition from the Kentucky of her childhood to the American Southwest where she now resides. Kingsolver's narrative is given depth by her background as a biologist (with a Master's Degree from the University of Arizona) and compassion by her unflinching belief in human rights and political activism. Her writing is often a curious blend of the southern accents of her youth and the Hispanic and Native American influences of her adopted home in the Southwest. She has won awards from the American Library Association and the United Nations National Council of Women, as well as the Edward Abbey Ecofiction Award. In this title selection from her first collection of essays, Kingsolver uses the metaphor of the natural world to muse on her common themes of family, community, and human nature.

A HERMIT CRAB LIVES IN MY HOUSE. Here in the desert he's hiding out from   1
local animal ordinances, at minimum, and maybe even the international laws
of native-species transport. For sure, he's an outlaw against nature. So be it.

He arrived as a stowaway two Octobers ago. I had spent a week in the Ba-   2
hamas, and while I was there, wishing my daughter could see those sparkling
blue bays and sandy covers, I did exactly what she would have done: I collected
shells. Spiky murexes, smooth purple moon shells, ancient-looking whelks
sand-blasted by the tide—I tucked them in the pockets of my shirt and shorts
until my lumpy, suspect hemlines gave me away, like a refugee smuggling the
family fortune. When it was time to go home, I rinsed my loot in the sink and
packed it carefully into a plastic carton, then nested it deep in my suitcase for
the journey to Arizona.

I got home in the middle of the night, but couldn't wait till morning   3
to show my hand. I set the carton on the coffee table for my daughter to
open. In the dark living room her face glowed, in the way of antique stories about children and treasure. With perfect delicacy she laid the shells
out on the table, counting, sorting, designating scientific categories like
yellow-striped pinky, Barnacle Bill's pocketbook . . . Yeek! She let loose a
sudden yelp, dropped her booty, and ran to the far end of the room. The
largest, knottiest whelk had begun to move around. First it extended one
long red talon of a leg, tap-tap-tapping like a blind man's cane. Then came
half a dozen more red legs, plus a pair of eyes on stalks, and a purple claw
that snapped open and shut in a way that could not mean We come in
Friendship.

Who could blame this creature? It had fallen asleep to the sound of the   4
Caribbean tide and awakened on a coffee table in Tucson, Arizona, where the

nearest standing water source of any real account was the municipal sewage-treatment plant.

5   With red stiletto legs splayed in all directions, it lunged and jerked its huge shell this way and that, reminding me of the scene I make whenever I'm moved to rearrange the living-room sofa by myself. Then, while we watched in stunned reverence, the strange beast found its bearings and began to reveal a determined, crabby grace. It felt its way to the edge of the table and eased itself over, not falling bang to the floor but hanging suspended underneath within the long grasp of its ice-tong legs, lifting any two or three at a time while many others still held in place. In this remarkable fashion it scrambled around the underside of the table's rim, swift and sure and fearless like a rock climber's dream.

6   If you ask me, when something extraordinary shows up in your life in the middle of the night, you give it a name and make it the best home you can.

7   The business of naming involved a grasp of hermit-crab gender that was way out of our league. But our household had a deficit of males, so my daughter and I chose Buster, for balance. We gave him a terrarium with clean gravel and a small cactus plant dug out of the yard and a big cockleshell full of tap water. All this seemed to suit him fine. To my astonishment our local pet store carried a product called Vitaminized Hermit Crab Cakes. Tempting enough (till you read the ingredients) but we passed, since our household leans more toward the recycling ethic. We give him leftovers. Buster's rapture is the day I drag the unidentifiable things in cottage cheese containers out of the back of the fridge.

8   We've also learned to give him a continually changing assortment of seashells, which he tries on and casts off like Cinderella's stepsisters preening for the ball. He'll sometimes try to squeeze into ludicrous outfits too small to contain him (who can't relate?). In other moods, he will disappear into a conch the size of my two fists and sit for a day, immobilized by the weight of upward mobility. He is in every way the perfect housemate: quiet, entertaining, and willing to eat up the trash. He went to school for first-grade show-and-tell, and was such a hit the principal called up to congratulate me (I think) for being a broad-minded mother.

9   It was a long time, though, before we began to understand the content of Buster's character. He required more patient observation than we were in the habit of giving to a small, cold-blooded life. As months went by, we would periodically notice with great disappointment that Buster seemed to be dead. Or not entirely dead, but ill, or maybe suffering the crab equivalent of the blues. He would burrow into a gravelly corner, shrink deep into his shell, and not move, for days and days. We'd take him out to play, dunk him in water, offer him a new frock—nothing. He wanted to be still.

10   Life being what it is, we'd eventually quit prodding our sick friend to cheer

up, and would move on to the next stage of a difficult friendship: neglect. We'd ignore him wholesale, only to realize at some point later on that he'd lapsed into hyperactivity. We'd find him ceaselessly patrolling the four corners of his world, turning over rocks, rooting out and dragging around truly disgusting pork-chop bones, digging up his cactus and replanting it on its head. At night when the household fell silent I would lie in bed listening to his methodical pebbly racket from the opposite end of the house. Buster was manic-depressive.

I wondered if he might be responding to the moon. I'm partial to lunar cy- 11
cles, ever since I learned as a teenager that human females in their natural state—which is to say, sleeping outdoors—arrive at menses in synchrony and ovulate with the full moon. My imagination remains captive to that primordial village: the comradely grumpiness of new-moon days, when the entire world at once would go on PMS alert. And the compensation that would turn up two weeks later on a wild wind, under that great round headlamp, driving both men and women to distraction with the overt prospect of conception. The surface of the land literally rises and falls—as much as fifty centimeters!—as the moon passes over, and we clayfooted mortals fall like dominoes before the swell. It's no surprise at all if a full moon inspires lyricists to corny love songs, or inmates to slamming themselves against barred windows. A hermit crab hardly seems this impetuous, but animals are notoriously responsive to the full moon: wolves howl; roosters announce daybreak all night. Luna moths, Arctic loons, and lunatics have a sole inspiration in common. Buster's insomniac restlessness seemed likely to be a part of the worldwide full-moon fellowship.

But it wasn't, exactly. The full moon didn't shine on either end of his 12
cycle, the high or the low. We tried to keep track, but it soon became clear: Buster marched to his own drum. The cyclic force that moved him remained as mysterious to us as his true gender and the workings of his crustacean soul.

Buster's aquarium occupies a spot on our kitchen counter right next to the 13
coffeepot, and so it became my habit to begin mornings with chin in hands, pondering the oceanic mysteries while awaiting percolation. Finally, I remembered something. Years ago when I was a graduate student of animal behavior, I passed my days reading about the likes of animals' internal clocks. Temperature, photoperiod, the rise and fall of hormones—all these influences have been teased apart like so many threads from the rope that pulls every creature to its regulated destiny. But one story takes the cake. F. A. Brown, a researcher who is more or less the grandfather of the biological clock, set about in 1954 to track the cycles of intertidal oysters. He scooped his subjects from the clammy coast of Connecticut and moved them into the basement of a laboratory in landlocked Illinois. For the first fifteen days in their new aquariums, the oysters kept right up with their normal intertidal behavior: they spent time shut away in their shells, and time with their mouths wide

open, siphoning their briny bath for the plankton that sustained them, as the tides ebbed and flowed on the distant Connecticut shore. In the next two weeks, they made a mystifying shift. They still carried out their cycles in unison, and were regular as the tides, but their high-tide behavior didn't coincide with high tide in Connecticut, or for that matter California, or any other tidal charts known to science. It dawned on the researchers after some calculations that the oysters were responding to high tide in Chicago. Never mind that the gentle mollusks lived in glass boxes in the basement of a steel-and-cement building. Nor that Chicago has no ocean. In the circumstances, the oysters were doing their best.

14   When Buster is running around for all he's worth, I can only presume it's high tide in Tucson. With or without evidence, I'm romantic enough to believe it. This is the lesson of Buster, the poetry that camps outside the halls of science: Jump for joy, hallelujah. Even a desert has tides.

15   When I was twenty-two, I donned the shell of a tiny yellow Renault and drove with all I owned from Kentucky to Tucson. I was a typical young American, striking out. I had no earthly notion that I was bringing on myself a calamity of the magnitude of the one that befell poor Buster. I am the commonest kind of North American refugee: I believe I like it here, far-flung from my original home. I've come to love the desert that bristles and breathes and sleeps outside my windows. In the course of seventeen years I've embedded myself in a family here—neighbors, colleagues, friends I can't foresee living without, and a child who is native to this ground, with loves of her own. I'm here for good, it seems.

16   And yet I never cease to long in my bones for what I left behind. I open my eyes on every new day expecting that a creek will run through my backyard under broad-leafed maples, and that my mother will be whistling in the kitchen. Behind the howl of coyotes, I'm listening for meadowlarks, I sometimes ache to be rocked in the bosom of the blood relations and busybodies of my childhood. Particularly in my years as a mother without a mate, I have deeply missed the safety net of extended family.

17   In a city of half a million I still really look at every face, anticipating recognition, because I grew up in a town where every face meant something to me. I have trouble remembering to lock the doors. Wariness of strangers I learned the hard way. When I was new to the city, I let a man into my house one hot afternoon because he seemed in dire need of a drink of water; when I turned from the kitchen sink I found sharpened steel shoved against my belly. And so I know, I know. But I cultivate suspicion with as much difficulty as I force tomatoes to grow in the drought-stricken hardpan of my strange backyard. No creek runs here, but I'm still listening to secret tides, living as if I belonged to an earlier place: not Kentucky, necessarily, but a welcoming earth and a human family. A forest. A species.

In my life I've had frightening losses and unfathomable gifts: A knife in [18] my stomach. The death of an unborn child. Sunrise in a rain forest. A stupendous column of blue butterflies rising from a Greek monastery. A car that spontaneously caught fire while I was driving it. The end of a marriage, followed by a year in which I could barely understand how to keep living. The discovery, just weeks ago when I rose from my desk and walked into the kitchen, of three strangers industriously relieving my house of its contents.

I persuaded the strangers to put down the things they were holding (what [19] a bizarre tableau of anti-Magi they made, these three unwise men, bearing a camera, an electric guitar, and a Singer sewing machine), and to leave my home, pronto. My daughter asked excitedly when she got home from school, "Mom, did you say bad words?" (I told her this was the very occasion that bad words exist for.) The police said, variously, that I was lucky, foolhardy, and "a brave lady." But it's not good luck to be invaded, and neither foolish nor brave to stand your ground. It's only the way life goes, and I did it, just as years ago I fought off the knife; mourned the lost child; bore witness to the rain forest; claimed the blue butterflies as Holy Spirit in my private pantheon; got out of the burning car; survived the divorce by putting one foot in front of the other and taking good care of my child. On most important occasions, I cannot think how to respond, I simply do. What does it mean, anyway, to be an animal in human clothing? We carry around these big brains of ours like the crown jewels, but mostly I find that millions of years of evolution have prepared me for one thing only: to follow internal rhythms. To walk upright, to protect my loved ones, to cooperate with my family group—however broadly I care to define it—to do whatever will help us thrive. Obviously, some habits that saw us through the millennia are proving hazardous in a modern context: for example, the yen to consume carbohydrates and fat whenever they cross our path, or the proclivity for unchecked reproduction. But it's surely worth forgiving ourselves these tendencies a little, in light of the fact that they are what got us here. Like Buster, we are creatures of inexplicable cravings. Thinking isn't everything. The way I stock my refrigerator would amuse a level-headed interplanetary observer, who would see I'm responding not to real necessity but to the dread of famine honed in the African savannah. I can laugh at my Rhodesian Ridgeback as she furtively sniffs the houseplants for a place to bury bones, and circles to beat down the grass before lying on my kitchen floor. But she and I are exactly the same kind of hairpin.

We humans have to grant the presence of some past adaptations, even in [20] their unforgivable extremes, if only to admit they are permanent rocks in the steam we're obliged to navigate. It's easy to speculate and hard to prove, ever, that genes control our behaviors. Yet we are persistently, excruciatingly adept at many things that seem no more useful to modern life than the tracking of tides in a desert. At recognizing insider/outsider status, for example, starting with white vs. black and grading straight into distinctions so fine as to baffle the bystander—Serb and Bosnian, Hutu and Tutsi, Crip and Blood. We hold that children learn discrimination from their parents, but they learn if fiercely and well, world without end. Recite it by rote like a multiplication table. Take it to heart, though it's neither helpful nor appropriate, anymore than it is to hire the taller of two men applying for a position as bank clerk, though statistically we're likely to do that too. Deference to the physical superlative, a preference for the scent of our own clan: a thousand anachronisms dance down the strands of our DNA from a hidebound tribal past, guiding us toward the glories of survival, and some vainglories as well. If we resent being bound by these ropes, the best hope is to seize them out like snakes, by the throat, look them in the eye and own up to their venom.

21   But we rarely do, silly egghead of a species that we are. We invent the most outlandish intellectual grounds to justify discrimination. We tap our toes to chaste love songs about the silvery moon without recognizing them as hymns to copulation. We can dress up our drives, put them in three-piece suits or ballet slippers, but still they drive us. The wonder of it is that our culture attaches almost unequivocal shame to our animal nature, believing brute urges must be hurtful, violent things. But it's no less an animal instinct that leads us to marry (species that benefit from monogamy tend to practice it); to organize a neighborhood cleanup campaign (rare and doomed is the creature that fouls its nest); to improvise and enforce morality (many primates socialize their young to be cooperative and ostracize adults who won't share food).

22   It's starting to look as if the most shameful tradition of Western civilization is our need to deny we are animals. In just a few centuries of setting ourselves apart as landlords of the Garden of Eden, exempt from the natural order and entitled to hold dominion, we have managed to behave like so-called animals anyway, and on top of it to wreck most of what took three billion years to assemble. Air, water, earth, and fire—so much of our own element so vastly contaminated, we endanger our own future. Apparently we never owned the place after all. Like every other animal, we're locked into our niche: the mercury in the ocean, the pesticides on the soybean fields, all comes home to our breastfed babies. In the silent spring we are learning it's easier to escape from a chain gang than a food chain. Possibly we will have the sense to begin a new century by renewing our membership in the Animal Kingdom.

23   Not long ago I went backpacking in the Eagle Tail Mountains. This range is a trackless wilderness in western Arizona that most people would call God-forsaken, taking for granted God's preference for loamy topsoil and regular precipitation. Whoever created the Eagle Tails had dry heat on the agenda, and a thing for volcanic rock. Also cactus, twisted mesquites, and five-alarm sunsets. The hiker's program in a desert like this is dire and blunt: carry in enough water to keep you alive till you can find a water source; then fill your

bottles and head for the next one, or straight back out. Experts warn adventurers in this region, without irony, to drink their water while they're still alive, as it won't help later.

Several canyons looked promising for springs on our topographical map, but turned up dry. Finally, at the top of a narrow, overgrown gorge we found a blessed tinaja, a deep, shaded hollow in the rock about the size of four or five claw-foot tubs, holding water. After we drank our fill, my friends struck out again, but I opted to stay and spend the day in the hospitable place that had slaked our thirst. On either side of the natural water tank, two shallow caves in the canyon wall faced each other, only a few dozen steps apart. By crossing from one to the other at noon, a person could spend the whole day here in shady comfort—or in colder weather, follow the winter sun. Anticipating a morning of reading, I pulled *Angle of Repose* out of my pack and looked for a place to settle on the flat, dusty floor of the west-facing shelter. Instead, my eyes were startled by a smooth corn-grinding stone. It sat in the exact center of its rock bowl, as if the Hohokam woman or man who used this mortar and pestle had walked off and left them there an hour ago. The Hohokam disappeared from the earth in A.D. 1450. It was inconceivable to me that no one had been here since then, but that may have been the case—that is the point of trackless wilderness. I picked up the grinding stone. The size and weight and smooth, balanced perfection of it in my hand filled me at once with a longing to possess it. In its time, this excellent stone was the most treasured thing in a life, a family, maybe the whole neighborhood. To whom it still belonged. I replaced it in the rock depression, which also felt smooth to my touch. Because my eyes now understood how to look at it, the ground under my feet came alive with worked flint chips and pottery shards. I walked across to the other cave and found its floor just as lively with historic debris. Hidden under brittlebush and catclaw I found another grinding stone, this one some distance from the depression in the cave floor that once answered its pressure daily, for the grinding of corn or mesquite beans.

For a whole day I marveled at this place, running my fingers over the knife edges of dark flint chips, trying to fit together thick red pieces of shattered clay jars, biting my lower lip like a child concentrating on a puzzle. I tried to guess the size of whole pots from the curve of the broken pieces: some seemed as small as my two cupped hands, and some maybe as big as a bucket. The sun scorched my neck, reminding me to follow the shade across to the other shelter. Bees hummed at the edge of the water hole, nosing up to the water, their abdomens pulsing like tiny hydraulic pumps; by late afternoon they rimmed the pool completely, a collar of busy lace. Off and on, the lazy hand of a hot breeze shuffled the white leaves of the brittlebush. Once I looked up to see a screaming pair of red-tailed hawks mating in midair, and once a clatter of hooves warned me to hold still. A bighorn ram emerged through the brush, his head bent low under his hefty cornice, and ambled by me with nothing on his mind so much as a cool drink.

26   How long can a pestle stone lie still in the center of its mortar? That long ago—that recently—people lived here. *Here*, exactly, and not one valley over, or two, or twelve, because this place had all a person needs: shelter, food, and permanent water. They organized their lives around a catchment basin in a granite boulder, conforming their desires to the earth's charities; they never expected the opposite. The stories I grew up with lauded Moses for striking the rock and bringing forth the bubbling stream. But the stories of the Hohokam—oh, how they must have praised that good rock.

27   At dusk my friends returned with wonderful tales of the ground they had covered. We camped for the night, refilled our canteens, and hiked back to the land of plumbing and a fair guarantee of longevity. But I treasure my memory of the day I lingered near water and covered no ground. I can't think of a day in my life in which I've had such a clear fix on what it means to be human.

28   *Want is* a thing that unfurls unbidden like fungus, opening large upon itself, stopless, filling the sky. But *needs*, from one day to the next, are few enough to fit in a bucket, with room enough left to rattle like brittlebush in a dry wind.

29   For each of us—furred, feathered, or skinned alive—the whole earth balances on the single precarious point of our own survival. In the best of times, I hold in mind the need to care for things beyond the self: poetry, humanity, grace. In other times, when it seems difficult merely to survive and be happy about it, the condition of my thought tastes as simple as this: let me be a good animal today. I've spent months at a stretch, even years, with that taste in my mouth, and have found that it serves.

30   But it seems a wide gulf to cross, from the raw, green passion for survival to the dispassionate, considered state of human grace. How does the animal mind construct a poetry for the modern artifice in which we now reside? Often I feel as disoriented as poor Buster, unprepared for the life that zooms headlong past my line of sight. This clutter of human paraphernalia and counterfeit necessities—what does it have to do with the genuine business of life on earth? It feels strange to me to be living in a box, hiding from the steadying influence of the moon; wearing the hide of a cow, which is supposed to be dyed to match God-knows-what, on my feet; making promises over the telephone about things I will do at a precise hour next *year*. (I always feel the urge to add, as my grandmother does, "Lord willing and the creeks don't rise!") I find it impossible to think, with a straight face, about what colors ought not to be worn after Labor Day. I can become hysterical over the fact that someone, somewhere, invented a thing called the mushroom scrubber, and that many other people undoubtedly feel they *need* to possess one. It's completely usual for me to get up in the morning, take a look around, and laugh out loud.

Strangest of all, I am carrying on with all of this in a desert, two thousand 31 miles from my verdant childhood home. I am disembodied. No one here remembers how I was before I grew to my present height. I'm called upon to reinvent my own childhood time and again; in the process, I wonder how I can ever know the truth about who I am. If someone had told me what I was headed for in that little Renault—that I was stowing away in a shell, bound to wake up to an alien life on a persistently foreign shore—I surely would not have done it. But no one warned me. My culture, as I understand it, values independence above all things—in part to ensure a mobile labor force, grease for the machine of a capitalist economy. Our fairy table commands: Little Pig, go out and seek your fortune! So I did.

Many years ago I read that the Tohono O'odham, who dwell in the deserts 32 near here, traditionally bury the umbilicus of a newborn son or daughter somewhere close to home and plant a tree over it, to hold the child in place. In a sentimental frame of mind, I did the same when my own baby's cord fell off. I'm staring at the tree right now, as I write—a lovely thing grown huge outside my window, home to woodpeckers, its boughs overarching the house, as dissimilar from the sapling I planted seven years ago as my present life is from the tidy future I'd mapped out for us all when my baby was born. She will roam light-years from the base of that tree. I have no doubt of it. I can only hope she's growing as the tree is, absorbing strength and rhythms and a trust in the seasons, so she will always be able to listen for home.

I feel remorse about Buster's monumental relocation; it's a weighty re- 33 sponsibility to have thrown someone else's life into permanent chaos. But as for my own, I can't be sorry I made the trip. Most of what I learned in the old place seems to suffice for the new: if the seasons like Chicago tides come at ridiculous times and I have to plant in September instead of May, and if I have to make up family from scratch, what matters is that I do have sisters and tomato plants, the essential things. Like Buster, I'm inclined to see the material backdrop of my life as mostly immaterial, compared with what moves inside of me. I hold on to my adopted shore, chanting private vows: wherever I am, let me never forget to distinguish *want* from *need*. Let me be a good animal today. Let me dance in the waves of my private tide, the habits of survival and love.

Every one of us is called upon, probably many times, to start a new life. A 34 frightening diagnosis, a marriage, a move, loss of a job or a limb or a loved one, a graduation, bringing a new baby home: it's impossible to think at first how this all will be possible. Eventually, what moves it all forward is the subterranean ebb and flow of being alive among the living.

In my own worst seasons I've come back from the colorless world of de- 35 spair by forcing myself to look hard, for a long time, at a single glorious thing: a flame of red geranium outside my bedroom window. And then another: my daughter in a yellow dress. And another: the perfect outline of a full, dark sphere behind the crescent moon. Until I learned to be in love with my life again. Like a stroke victim retraining new parts of the brain to grasp lost skills, I have taught myself joy, over and over again.

36   It's not such a wide gulf to cross, then, from survival to poetry. We hold fast to the old passions of endurance that buckle and creak beneath us, dovetailed, tight as a good wooden boat to carry us onward. And onward full tilt we go, pitched and wrecked and absurdly resolute, driven in spite of everything to make good on a new shore. To be hopeful, to embrace one possibility after another—that is surely the basic instinct. Baser even than hate, the thing with teeth, which can be stilled with a tone of voice or stunned by beauty. If the whole world of the living has to turn on the single point of remaining alive, that pointed endurance is the poetry of hope. The thing with feathers.

37   What a stroke of luck. What a singular brute feat of outrageous fortune: to be born to citizenship in the Animal Kingdom. We love and we lose, go back to the start and do it right over again. For every heavy forebrain solemnly cataloging the facts of a harsh landscape, there's a rush of intuition behind it crying out: High tide! Time to move out into the glorious debris. Time to take this life for what it is.

John Muir

A Wind-Storm in the Forests

John Muir (1838–1914) has had so many mountains, trails, creeks, and lakes named for him that the U.S. Geological Survey has said it would refuse to approve naming any more landmarks after Muir, to avoid confusion on maps. In his zeal to see the great natural sites of North America, he has been burned by sulfur vents on Mt. Shasta (to avoid being frozen in a blizzard), lived on a crust of bread while hiking through the Alaskan wilderness (so as to see more, while traveling lightly), and survived bouts of malaria and typhoid fever in the swamps of Florida. A founder of the Sierra Club, which has been credited with preserving much of California's wilderness, Muir later in life began to write about some of the spectacular wild lands he so loved—the better for the rest of us to appreciate it. Though we may never experience a severe windstorm in an expansive forest, Muir can relate that experience from his own unconventional viewpoint, painting a picture so vivid that we almost feel like we *are* there, experiencing the storm with Muir.

1   THE MOUNTAIN WINDS, LIKE THE DEW AND RAIN, sunshine and snow, are measured and bestowed with love on the forests to develop their strength and beauty. However restricted the scope of other forest influences, that of the

winds is universal. The snow bends and trims the upper forests every winter, the lightning strikes a single tree here and there, while avalanches mow down thousands at a swoop as a gardener trims out a bed of flowers. But the winds go to every tree, fingering every leaf and branch and furrowed bole; not one is forgotten; the Mountain Pine towering with outstretched arms on the rugged buttresses of the icy peaks, the lowliest and most retiring tenant of the dells; they seek and find them all, caressing them tenderly, bending them in lusty exercise, stimulating their growth, plucking off a leaf or limb as required, or removing an entire tree or grove, now whispering and cooing through the branches like a sleepy child, now roaring like the ocean; the winds blessing the forests, the forests the winds, with ineffable beauty and harmony as the sure result.

After one has seen pines six feet in diameter bending like grasses before a mountain gale, and ever and anon some giant falling with a crash that shakes the hills, it seems astonishing that any, save the lowest thickset trees, could ever have found a period sufficiently stormless to establish themselves; or, once established, that they should not, sooner or later, have been blown down. But when the storm is over, and we behold the same forests tranquil again, towering fresh and unscathed in erect majesty, and consider what centuries of storms have fallen upon them since they were first planted,—hail, to break the tender seedlings; lightning, to scorch and shatter; snow, winds, and avalanches, to crush and overwhelm,—while the manifest result of all this wild storm-culture is the glorious perfection we behold; then faith in Nature's forestry is established, and we cease to deplore the violence of her most destructive gales, or of any other storm-implement whatsoever. 2

There are two trees in the Sierra forests that are never blown down, so long as they continue in sound health. These are the Juniper and the Dwarf Pine of the summit peaks. Their stiff, crooked roots grip the storm-beaten ledges like eagles' claws, while their lithe, cord-like branches bend round compliantly, offering but slight holds for winds, however violent. The other alpine conifers—the Needle Pine, Mountain Pine, Two-leaved Pine, and Hemlock Spruce—are never thinned out by this agent to any destructive extent, on account of their admirable toughness and the closeness of their growth. In general the same is true of the giants of the lower zones. The kingly Sugar Pine, towering aloft to a height of more than 200 feet, offers a fine mark to storm-winds; but it is not densely foliaged, and its long, horizontal arms swing round compliantly in the blast, like tresses of green, fluent algae in a brook; while the Silver Firs in most places keep their ranks well together in united strength. The Yellow or Silver Pine is more frequently overturned than any other tree on the Sierra, because its leaves and branches form a larger mass in proportion to its height, while in many places it is planted sparsely, leaving open 3 lanes through which storms may enter with full force. Furthermore, because it is distributed along the lower portion of the range, which was the first to be left bare on the breaking up of the ice-sheet at the close of the glacial winter, the soil it is growing upon has been longer exposed to post-glacial weathering, and consequently is in a more crumbling, decayed condition than the fresher soils farther up the range, and therefore offers a less secure anchorage for the roots.

4   While exploring the forest zones of Mount Shasta, I discovered the path of a hurricane strewn with thousands of pines of this species. Great and small had been uprooted or wrenched off by sheer force, making a clean gap, like that made by a snow avalanche. But hurricanes capable of doing this class of work are rare in the Sierra, and when we have explored the forests from one extremity of the range to the other, we are compelled to believe that they are the most beautiful on the face of the earth, however we may regard the agents that have made them so.

5   There is always something deeply exciting, not only in the sounds of winds in the woods, which exert more or less influence over every mind, but in their varied waterlike flow as manifested by the movements of the trees, especially those of the conifers. By no other trees are they rendered so extensively and impressively visible, not even by the lordly tropic palms or tree-ferns responsive to the gentlest breeze. The waving of a forest of the giant Sequoias is indescribably impressive and sublime, but the pines seem to me the best interpreters of winds. They are mighty waving goldenrods, ever in tune, singing and writing wind-music all their long century lives. Little, however, of this noble tree-waving and tree-music will you see or hear in the strictly alpine portion of the forests. The burly Juniper, whose girth sometimes more than equals its height, is about as rigid as the rocks on which it grows. The slender lash-like sprays of the Dwarf Pine stream out in wavering ripples, but the tallest and slenderest are far too unyielding to wave even in the heaviest gales. They only shake in quick, short vibrations. The Hemlock Spruce, however, and the Mountain Pine, and some of the tallest thickets of the Two-leaved species bow in storms with considerable scope and gracefulness. But it is only in the lower and middle zones that the meeting of winds and woods is to be seen in all its grandeur.

6   One of the most beautiful and exhilarating storms I ever enjoyed in the Sierra occurred in December, 1874, when I happened to be exploring one of the tributary valleys of the Yuba River. The sky and the ground and the trees had been thoroughly rain-washed and were dry again. The day was intensely pure, one of those incomparable bits of California winter, warm and balmy and full of white sparkling sunshine, redolent of all the purest influences of the spring, and at the same time enlivened with one of the most bracing wind-storms conceivable. Instead of camping out, as I usually do, I then chanced to be stopping

at the house of a friend. But when the storm began to sound, I lost no time in pushing out into the woods to enjoy it. For on such occasions Nature has always something rare to show us, and the danger to life and limb is hardly greater than one would experience crouching deprecatingly beneath a roof.

It was still early morning when I found myself fairly adrift. Delicious sunshine came pouring over the hills, lighting the tops of the pines, and setting free a steam of summery fragrance that contrasted strangely with the wild tones of the storm. The air was mottled with pine-tassels and bright green plumes, that went flashing past in the sunlight like birds pursued. But there was not the slightest dustiness, nothing less pure than leaves, and ripe pollen, and flecks of withered bracken and moss. I heard trees falling for hours at the rate of one every two or three minutes; some uprooted, partly on account of the loose, water-soaked condition of the ground; others broken straight across, where some weakness caused by fire had determined the spot. The gestures of the various trees made a delightful study. Young Sugar Pines, light and feathery as squirrel-tails, were bowing almost to the ground; while the grand old patriarchs, whose massive boles had been tried in a hundred storms, waved solemnly above them, their long, arching branches streaming fluently on the gale, and every needle thrilling and ringing and shedding off keen lances of light like a diamond. The Douglas Spruces, with long sprays drawn out in level tresses, and needles massed in a gray, shimmering glow, presented a most striking appearance as they stood in bold relief along the hilltops. The madroños in the dells, with their red bark and large glossy leaves tilted every way, reflected the sunshine in throbbing spangles like those one so often sees on the rippled surface of a glacier lake. But the Silver Pines were now the most impressively beautiful of all. Colossal spires 200 feet in height waved like supple goldenrods chanting and bowing low as if in worship, while the whole mass of their long, tremulous foliage was kindled into one continuous blaze of white sun-fire. The force of the gale was such that the most steadfast monarch of them all rocked down to its roots with a motion plainly perceptible when one leaned against it. Nature was holding high festival, and every fiber of the most rigid giants thrilled with glad excitement.

I drifted on through the midst of this passionate music and motion, across many a glen, from ridge to ridge; often halting in the lee of a rock for shelter, or to gaze and listen. Even when the grand anthem had swelled to its highest pitch, I could distinctly hear the varying tones of individual trees;—Spruce, and Fir, and Pine, and leafless Oak,—and even the infinitely gentle rustle of the withered grasses at my feet. Each was expressing itself in its own way,—singing its own song, and making its own peculiar gestures,—manifesting a richness of variety to be found in no other forest I have yet seen. The coniferous woods of Canada, and the Carolinas, and Florida, are made up of trees that resemble one another about as nearly as blades of grass, and grow close together in much the same way. Coniferous trees, in general, seldom possess individual character, such as is manifest among Oaks and Elms. But the California forests are made up of a greater number of distinct species than any other in the world. And in them we find, not only a marked differentiation into special groups, but also a marked individuality in almost every tree, giving rise to storm effects indescribably glorious.

9   Toward midday, after a long, tingling scramble through copses of hazel and ceanothus, I gained the summit of the highest ridge in the neighborhood; and then it occurred to me that it would be a fine thing to climb one of the trees to obtain a wider outlook and get my ear close to the Æolian music of its topmost needles. But under the circumstances the choice of a tree was a serious matter. One whose instep was not very strong seemed in danger of being blown down, or of being struck by others in case they should fall; another was branchless to a considerable height above the ground, and at the same time too large to be grasped with arms and legs in climbing; while others were not favorably situated for clear views. After cautiously casting about, I made choice of the tallest of a group of Douglas Spruces that were growing close together like a tuft of grass, no one of which seemed likely to fall unless all the rest fell with it. Though comparatively young, they were about 100 feet high, and their lithe, brushy tops were rocking and swirling in wild ecstasy. Being accustomed to climb trees in making botanical studies, I experienced no difficulty in reaching the top of this one, and never before did I enjoy so noble an exhilaration of motion. The slender tops fairly flapped and swished in the passionate torrent, bending and swirling backward and forward, round and round, tracing indescribable combinations of vertical and horizontal curves, while I clung with muscles firm braced, like a bobolink on a reed.

10   In its widest sweeps my tree-top described an arc of from twenty to thirty degrees, but I felt sure of its elastic temper, having seen others of the same species still more severely tried—bent almost to the ground indeed, in heavy snows—without breaking a fiber. I was therefore safe, and free to take the wind into my pulses and enjoy the excited forest from my superb outlook. The view from here must be extremely beautiful in any weather. Now my eye roved over the piny hills and dales as over fields of waving grain, and felt the light running in ripples and broad swelling undulations across the valleys from ridge to ridge, as the shining foliage was stirred by corresponding waves of air. Oftentimes these waves of reflected light would break up suddenly into a kind of beaten foam, and again, after chasing one another in regular order, they would seem to bend forward in concentric curves, and disappear on some hillside, like sea-waves on a shelving shore. The quantity of light reflected from the bent needles was so great as to make whole groves appear as if covered with snow, while the black shadows beneath the trees greatly enhanced the effect of the silvery splendor.

Excepting only the shadows there was nothing somber in all this wild sea   11
of pines. On the contrary, notwithstanding this was the winter season, the colors were remarkably beautiful. The shafts of the pine and libocedrus were
brown and purple, and most of the foliage was well tinged with yellow; the laurel groves, with the pale undersides of their leaves turned upward, made
masses of gray; and then there was many a dash of chocolate color from
clumps of manzanita, and jet of vivid crimson from the bark of the madroños,
while the ground on the hillsides, appearing here and there through openings
between the groves, displayed masses of pale purple and brown.

The sounds of the storm corresponded gloriously with this wild exuber-   12
ance of light and motion. The profound bass of the naked branches and boles
booming like waterfalls; the quick, tense vibrations of the pine-needles, now
rising to a shrill, whistling hiss, now falling to a silky murmur; the rustling of
laurel groves in the dells, and the keen metallic click of leaf on leaf—all this
was heard in easy analysis when the attention was calmly bent.

The varied gestures of the multitude were seen to fine advantage, so that   13
one could recognize the different species at a distance of several miles by this
means alone, as well as by their forms and colors, and the way they reflected
the light. All seemed strong and comfortable, as if really enjoying the storm,
while responding to its most enthusiastic greetings. We hear much nowadays
concerning the universal struggle for existence, but no struggle in the common meaning of the word was manifest here; no recognition of danger by any
tree; no deprecation; but rather an invincible gladness as remote from exulta-
tion as from fear.

I kept my lofty perch for hours, frequently closing my eyes to enjoy the   14
music by itself, or to feast quietly on the delicious fragrance that was streaming
past. The fragrance of the woods was less marked than that produced during
warm rain, when so many balsamic buds and leaves are steeped like tea; but,
from the chafing of resiny branches against each other, and the incessant at-
trition of myriads of needles, the gale was spiced to a very tonic degree. And
besides the fragrance from these local sources there were traces of scents
brought from afar. For this wind came first from the sea, rubbing against its
fresh, briny waves, then distilled through the redwoods, threading rich ferny
gulches, and spreading itself in broad undulating currents over many a flower-
enameled ridge of the coast mountains, then across the golden plains, up the
purple foot-hills, and into these piny woods with the varied incense gathered
by the way.

Winds are advertisements of all they touch, however much or little we may   15
be able to read them; telling their wanderings even by their scents alone.
Mariners detect the flowery perfume of land-winds far at sea, and sea-winds
carry the fragrance of dulse and tangle far inland, where it is quickly recognized, though mingled with the scents of a thousand land-flowers. As an il-

lustration of this, I may tell here that I breathed sea-air on the Firth of Forth, in Scotland, while a boy; then was taken to Wisconsin, where I remained nineteen years; then, without in all this time having breathed one breath of the sea, I walked quietly, alone, from the middle of the Mississippi Valley to the Gulf of Mexico, on a botanical excursion, and while in Florida, far from the coast, my attention wholly bent on the splendid tropical vegetation about me, I suddenly recognized a sea-breeze, as it came sifting through the palmettos and blooming vine-tangles, which at once awakened and set free a thousand dormant associations, and made me a boy again in Scotland, as if all the intervening years had been annihilated.

16   Most people like to look at mountain rivers, and bear them in mind; but few care to look at the winds, though far more beautiful and sublime, and though they become at times about as visible as flowing water. When the north winds in winter are making upward sweeps over the curving summits of the High Sierra, the fact is sometimes published with flying snow-banners a mile long. Those portions of the winds thus embodied can scarce be wholly invisible, even to the darkest imagination. And when we look around over an agitated forest, we may see something of the wind that stirs it, by its effects upon the trees. Yonder it descends in a rush of water-like ripples, and sweeps over the bending pines from hill to hill. Nearer, we see detached plumes and leaves, now speeding by on level currents, now whirling in eddies, or, escaping over the edges of the whirls, soaring aloft on grand, upswelling domes of air, or tossing on flame-like crests. Smooth, deep currents, cascades, falls, and swirling eddies, sing around every tree and leaf, and over all the varied topography of the region with telling changes of form, like mountain rivers conforming to the features of their channels.

17   After tracing the Sierra streams from their fountains to the plains, marking where they bloom white in falls, glide in crystal plumes, surge gray and foam-filled in boulder-choked gorges, and slip through the woods in long, tranquil reaches—after thus learning their language and forms in detail, we may at length hear them chanting all together in one grand anthem, and comprehend them all in clear inner vision, covering the range like lace. But even this spectacle is far less sublime and not a whit more substantial than what we may behold of these storm-streams of air in the mountain woods.

18   We all travel the milky way together, trees and men; but it never occurred to me until this storm-day, while swinging in the wind, that trees are travelers, in the ordinary sense. They make many journeys, not extensive ones, it is true; but our own little journeys, away and back again, are only little more than tree-wavings—many of them not so much.

19   When the storm began to abate, I dismounted and sauntered down through the calming woods. The storm-tones died away, and, turning toward the east, I beheld the countless hosts of the forests hushed and tranquil, tow-

ering above one another on the slopes of the hills like a devout audience. The setting sun filled them with amber light, and seemed to say, while they listened, "My peace I give unto you."

As I gazed on the impressive scene, all the so-called ruin of the storm was 20 forgotten, and never before did these noble woods appear so fresh, so joyous, so immortal.

Olive Schreiner

Sex-Parasitism

South African novelist Olive Schreiner was the daughter of a missionary father and a stern and rigid Victorian mother who believed in the superiority of the British over native black Africans and the Boers. Schreiner's parents met any show of sympathy for those two groups with severe punishment. Rather than adopt the same views, Schreiner resolved to spend her life defending the weak against the strong. In 1889 she met and married a cattle rancher, Samuel Cronwright, another anti-imperialist who, at her request, took her name when they married. The first novel Schreiner published, *The Story of an African Farm,* was an immediate best-seller. Her 1911 work *Women and Labour* is the volume from which this selection is taken. In this work Schreiner outlines the history and fate of any nation in which prosperity, because of the subjugation of a slavery class, leads to its women becoming useless except as vessels in which to breed the next generation.

THERE NEVER HAS BEEN, AND AS FAR AS CAN BE SEEN, there never will be, a time 1 when the majority of the males in any society will be supported by the rest of the males in a condition of perfect mental and physical inactivity. "*Find labour or die,*" is the choice ultimately put before the human male today, as in the past; and *this* constitutes his labour problem.

The labour of the man may not always be useful in the highest sense to his 2 society, or it may even be distinctly harmful and antisocial, as in the case of the robber-barons of the Middle Ages, who lived by capturing and despoiling all who passed by their castles; or as in the case of the share speculators, stockjobbers, ring-and-corner capitalists, and monopolists of the present day, who feed upon the productive labours of society without contributing anything to its welfare. But even males so occupied are compelled to expend a vast amount of energy and even a low intelligence in their callings; and, however injurious to their societies, they run no personal risk of handing down effete and enervated constitutions to their race. Whether beneficially or unbeneficially, the human male must, generally speaking, employ his intellect, or his muscle, or die.

3   The position of the unemployed modern female is one wholly different. The choice before her, as her ancient fields of domestic labour slip from her, is not generally or often at the present day the choice between finding new fields of labour, or death; but one far more serious in its ultimate reaction on humanity as a whole—it is the choice between finding new forms of labour or sinking into a condition of more or less complete and passive *sex-parasitism*!

4   Again and again in the history of the past, when among human creatures a certain stage of material civilization has been reached, a curious tendency has manifested itself for the human female to become more or less parasitic; social conditions tend to rob her of all forms of active conscious social labour, and to reduce her, like the field-bug, to the passive exercise of her sex functions alone. And the result of this parasitism has invariably been the decay in vitality and intelligence of the female, followed after a longer or shorter period by that of her male descendants and her entire society.

5   Nevertheless, in the history of the past the dangers of the sex-parasitism have never threatened more than a small section of the females of the human race, those exclusively of some dominant race or class; the mass of women beneath them being still compelled to assume many forms of strenuous activity. It is at the present day, and under the peculiar conditions of our modern civilization, that for the first time sex-parasitism has become a danger, more or less remote, to the mass of civilized women, perhaps ultimately to all.

6   In the very early stages of human growth, the sexual parasitism and degeneration of the female formed no possible source of social danger. Where the conditions of life rendered it inevitable that all the labour of a community should be performed by the members of that community for themselves, without the assistance of slaves or machinery, the tendency has always been rather to throw an excessive amount of social labour on the female. Under no conditions, at no time, in no place, in the history of the world have the males of any period, of any nation, or of any class, shown the slightest inclination to allow their own females to become inactive or parasitic, so long as the actual muscular labour of feeding and clothing them would in that case have devolved upon *themselves*!

7   The parasitism of the human female becomes a possibility only when a point in civilization is reached (such as that which was attained in the ancient civilizations of Greece, Rome, Persia, Assyria, India, and such as today exists in many of the civilizations of the East, such as those of China and Turkey), when, owing to the extensive employment of the labour of slaves, or of subject races or classes, the dominant race or class has become so liberally supplied with the material goods of life that mere physical toil on the part of its own female members has become unnecessary.

8   It is when this point has been reached, and never before, that the symptoms of female parasitism have in the past almost invariably tended to man-

ifest themselves, and have become a social danger. The males of the dominant class have almost always contrived to absorb to themselves the new intellectual occupations, which the absence of necessity for the old forms of
physical toil made possible in their societies and the females of the dominant class or race, for whose muscular labours there was now also no longer
any need, not succeeding grasping or attaining to these new forms of labour,
have sunk into a state in which, performing no species of active social duty,
they have existed through the passive performance of sexual functions
alone, with how much or how little of discontent will now never be known,
since no literary record has been made by the woman of the past, of her desires or sorrows. Then, in place of the active labouring woman, upholding
society—by her toil, has come the effete wife, concubine or prostitute, clad
in fine raiment, the work of others' fingers; fed on luxurious viands, the result of others' toil, waited on and tended by the labour of others. The need
for her physical labour having gone, and mental industry not having taken
its place, she bedecked and scented her person, or had it bedecked and
scented for her, she lay upon her sofa, or drove or was carried out in her vehicle, and, loaded with jewels, she sought by dissipations and amusements
to fill up the inordinate blank left by the lack of productive activity. And the
hand whitened and frame softened, till, at last, the very duties of motherhood, which were all the constitution of her life left her, became distasteful, and, from the instant when her infant came damp from her womb, it
passed into the hands of others, to be tended and reared by them; and from
youth to age her offspring often owed nothing to her personal toil. In many
cases so complete was her enervation, that at last the very joy of giving life,
the glory and beatitude of a virile womanhood, became distasteful; and she
sought to evade it, not because of its interference with more imperious duties to those already born of her, or to her society, but because her existence
of inactivity had robbed her of all joy in strenuous exertion and endurance
in any form. Finely clad, tenderly housed, life became for her merely the
gratification of her own physical and sexual appetites, and the appetites of
the male, through the stimulation of which she could maintain herself.
And, whether as kept wife, kept mistress, or prostitute, she contributed
nothing to the active and sustaining labours of her society. She had attained
to the full development of that type which, whether in modern Paris or New
York or London, or in ancient Greece, Assyria, or Rome, is essentially one
in its features, its nature, and its results. She was the "fine lady," the human
female parasite—the most deadly microbe which can make its appearance on
the surface of any social organism.

Wherever in the history of the past this type has reached its full development and has comprised the bulk of the females belonging to any dominant
class or race, it has heralded its decay. In Assyria, Greece, Rome, Persia, as in

Turkey today, the same material conditions have produced the same social dis-ease among wealthy and dominant races and again and again when the nation so affected has come into contact with nations more healthily constituted, the diseased condition has contributed to its destruction.

Henry David Thoreau

An Immoral Law

Henry David Thoreau (1817–1862) was known in his time as an odd sort of educated vagrant, rarely employed, who mostly kept to himself. He wrote voraciously in his journals at the suggestion of his most notable friend, Ralph Waldo Emerson. Occasionally, to earn extra money, he lectured about life in the backwoods, peppering his rather dry talks with folksy anecdotes. The one exception was when he spoke or wrote about slavery, when his laconic wit became an intense fire of emotion. In his most significant book, *Walden*, he expresses his seemingly contradictory individualist philosophy of civil responsibility. The following selection, from his jour-nal entry of June 16, 1854, is an application of the principles expressed in *Walden* to an event which deeply affected Thoreau's community—the enforcement of the Fugitive Slave Act by the forcible returning of a black man (possibly not even an escaped slave) to the South. The Fugitive Slave Act was never again enforced in Massachusetts.

1   THE EFFECT OF A GOOD GOVERNMENT IS TO MAKE LIFE MORE VALUABLE,—of a bad government, to make it less valuable. We can afford that railroad and all merely material stock should depreciate, for that only compels us to live more simply and economically; but suppose the value of life itself should be depre-ciated. Every man in New England capable of the sentiment of patriotism must have lived the last three weeks with the sense of having suffered a vast, indefinite loss. I had never respected this government, but I had foolishly thought that I might manage to live here, attending to my private affairs, and forget it. For my part, my old and worthiest pursuits have lost I cannot say how much of their attraction, and I feel that my investment in life here is worth many per cent, less since Massachusetts last deliberately and forcibly restored an innocent man, Anthony Burns, to slavery. I dwelt before in the illusion that my life passed somewhere only between heaven and hell, but now I can-not persuade myself that I do not dwell wholly within hell. The sight of that political organization called Massachusetts is to me morally covered with sco-riae and volcanic cinders, such as Milton imagined. If there is any hell more unprincipled than our rulers and our people, I feel curious to visit it. Life it-

self being worthless, all things with it, that feed it, are worthless. Suppose you have a small library, with pictures to adorn the walls,—a garden laid out around—and contemplate scientific and literary pursuits, etc., etc., and discover suddenly that your villa, with all its contents, is located in hell, and that the justice of the peace is one of the devil's angels, has a cloven foot and forked tail,—do not these things suddenly lose their value in your eyes? Are you not disposed to sell at a great sacrifice?

I feel that, to some extent, the State has fatally interfered with my just and proper business. It has not merely interrupted me in my passage through Court Street on errands of trade, but it has, to some extent, interrupted me and every man on his onward and upward path, on which he had trusted soon to leave Court Street far behind. I have found that hollow which I had relied on for solid. 2

I am surprised to see men going about their business as if nothing had happened, and say to myself, "Unfortunates! they have not heard the news"; that the man whom I just met on horseback should be so earnest to overtake his newly bought cows running away,—since all property is insecure, and if they do not run away again, they may be taken away from him when he gets them. Fool! does he not know that his seed-corn is worth less this year,—that all beneficent harvests fail as he approaches the empire of hell? No prudent man will build a stone house under these circumstances, or engage in any peaceful enterprise which it requires a long time to accomplish. Art is as long as ever, but life is more interrupted and less available for a man's proper pursuits. It is time we had done referring to our ancestors. We have used up all our inherited freedom, like the young bird the albumen in the egg. It is not an era of repose. If we would save our lives, we must fight for them. 3

The discovery is what matter of men your countrymen are. They steadily worship mammon—and on the seventh day curse God with a tintamarre from one end of the *Union* to the other. I heard the other day of a meek and sleek devil of a Bishop Somebody, who commended the law and order with which Burns was given up. I would like before I sit down to a table to inquire if there is one in the company who styles himself or is styled Bishop, and he or I should go out of it. I would have such a man wear his bishop's hat and his clerical bib and tucker, that we may know him. 4

Why will men be such fools as [to] trust to lawyers for a *moral* reform? I do not believe that there is a judge in this country prepared to decide by the principle that a law is immoral and therefore of no force. They put themselves, or rather are by character, exactly on a level with the marine who discharges his musket in any direction in which he is ordered. They are just as much tools, and as little men. 5

Student Essay

Maurice Johnson

Modern-Day Mobsters

For this essay, Maurice was assigned to use analogy to compare something old with something new. The result, a lighthearted look at today's banking practices, is very effective.

1   IN THE MEAN STREETS OF THE GREAT OLD CITIES like Chicago and New York, gangsters once ruled. Instead of acting like petty thieves or burglars, the gangsters formed syndicates which devised more and more complex schemes to extract ever greater sums of money from their victims. The simplest of these schemes was the "protection racket." Gangsters forced individuals and businesses in their territories to make weekly or monthly payments in exchange for "protection" against crime from rival gangs—or more commonly, from the gangsters themselves. Another common scheme was to lend money for gambling—at extraordinary interest rates. If you didn't pay up, the gang's henchmen would burglarize your home or break your bones. Using schemes like the protection racket, gangsters became wealthy, but at the expense of ordinary working people.

2   Today gangs still exist, but they behave much differently from the gangsters of old—they devote most of their attention to more serious criminal activities like prostitution and trafficking drugs. The modern institution that behaves most like the organized crime syndicates of the early twentieth century is your friendly, neighborhood bank.

3   Surprised? Look at the evidence. What modern institution is more like a protection racket than an Automated Teller Machine? In exchange for "protecting" your money by keeping it safe in the bank, the ATM charges extravagant fees—up to $4.50—every time you need $20 to go to the movies. If you dare let your bank balance fall below $3,000, the fees get higher, and you're charged an extra $20 a month! Just like Al Capone and his buddies, the bank makes money from you because you're frightened to carry around too much cash.

4   Credit cards, too, aren't much different from good old-fashioned loan sharks. Banks make the cards seem like easy money, just like gangsters used to do. They send them free in the mail, burying in fine print all the details about the 21 percent interest rates, the $15 late fees, and the $50 annual fee. And just like gangsters, if you don't pay, the banks will send their thugs to repos-

sess your furniture, your car, and even your home. Short of breaking your legs, the new loan sharks act just like the old ones.

Banks are now even getting into the gambling racket. It's almost impossi- 5
ble these days to open a simple bank account—the banker won't let you leave the building until you've set up a brokerage account so you can buy into the latest stock market fad. Don't have the money to invest? How about handing over your pension plan? You can even borrow money to invest. If the stock market crashes, it's no different from losing at the racetrack—just don't expect any sympathy from your banker.

Today's banks do everything yesterday's gangster did, but cloaked under 6
the authority of "FDIC" and "FNMA." Just like the gangsters, the bankers are getting rich at your expense. The only real difference is in the old days the gangsters came to you. Now you have to wait in line to get robbed.

9

Definition

Definition

1. **Use the type of definition that suits your purpose.** There are two types of definitions: concise "dictionary" or sentence definitions, and essay or extended definitions. Any essay may require a sentence definition if you introduce a specialized or technical term with which your readers may not be familiar. In those cases, simply define the word in a sentence or two and move on. This chapter mostly concerns itself with extended definitions, which not only provide a concise definition of a term or concept, but also build a fuller explanation of its object, using any of the other strategies in this book—example, description, analogy, and so on. When writing an extended definition, you may begin with dictionary definition, as D. H. Lawrence does in "Pornography," but the remainder of the essay should add something to, or even, as Lawrence does, completely contradict the standard definition.

2. **Select a writing strategy to develop your definition.** Depending on your purpose, any writing strategy can be effective in developing an extended definition. William Raspberry makes a powerful point about the word "black" by using examples. Margaret Atwood explains the term "pornography" largely by using narration. Because it can employ any writing strategy, definition is less of a strategy in itself than it is a goal. When writing an extended definition, you can use any strategy or combination of strategies to help you achieve your goal.

3. **Make your definition clear and unique.** Both dictionary and extended definitions must be clear enough for readers to understand, and precise enough to make a term or concept clearly different from all others. Defining "dog" as "an animal" is not unique because many other animals exist.

4. **Make sure your definition essay makes a point.** Like any other essay, definition essays should make a point. Usually this means you need a thesis sentence and a conclusion. For example, Marie Winn's point is that T.V. is as addictive as drugs or cigarettes, and Jason Gray suggests that intelligence is a complicated concept that can't be measured by a single number. Don't settle for the obvious definition of a term—that, after all, is what dictionaries are for.

D. H. Lawrence

Pornography

D. H. Lawrence (1885–1930) was a controversial figure in English literature because of the vivid descriptions of sex in his novels. His most famous work, *Lady Chatterley's Lover*, was banned in both England and the United States when it was published in 1928. In fact, the version published in 1928 was actually toned down by Lawrence in an attempt to elude censorship. After a widely publicized trial in 1960, the work was finally allowed to be published in unexpurgated form. Though the passages in question are actually quite tame by today's standards, some have even credited the re-release of *Lady Chatterley's Lover* in 1961 with causing the "free-love" movement of the 1960s. Here Lawrence defends his work by constructing a definition of pornography which carefully excludes his novels.

WHAT IS PORNOGRAPHY TO ONE MAN is the laughter of genius to another. The word itself, we are told, means "pertaining to harlots"—the graph of the harlot. But nowadays, what is a harlot? If she was a woman who took money from a man in return for going to bed with him—really, most wives sold themselves, in the past, and plenty of harlots gave themselves, when they felt like it, for nothing. If a woman hasn't got a tiny streak of harlot in her, she's a dry stick as a rule. And probably most harlots had somewhere a streak of womanly generosity. Why be so cut and dried? The law is a dreary thing, and its judgments have nothing to do with life. . . . 1

One essay on pornography, I remember, comes to the conclusion that pornography in art is that which is calculated to arouse sexual desire, or sexual excitement. And stress is laid on the fact, whether the author or artist *intended* to arouse sexual feelings. It is the old vexed question of intention, become so dull today, when we know how strong and influential our unconscious intentions are. And why a man should be held guilty of his conscious intentions, and innocent of his unconscious intentions, I don't know, since every man is more made up of unconscious intentions than of conscious ones. I am what I am, not merely what I think I am. 2

However! We take it, I assume, that *pornography* is something base, something unpleasant. In short, we don't like it. And why don't we like it? Because it arouses sexual feelings? 3

I think not. No matter how hard we may pretend otherwise, most of us rather like a moderate rousing of our sex. It warms us, stimulates us like sunshine on a grey day. After a century or two of Puritanism, this is still true of most people. Only the mob-habit of condemning any form of sex is too strong to let us admit it naturally. And there are, of course, many people who are gen- 4 uinely repelled by the simplest and most natural stirrings of sexual feeling. But these people are perverts who have fallen into hatred of their fellow men; thwarted, disappointed, unfulfilled people, of whom, alas, our civilisation contains so many. And they nearly always enjoy some unsimple and unnatural form of sex excitement, secretly.

5   Even quite advanced art critics would try to make us believe that any picture or book which had "sex appeal" was *ipso facto* a bad book or picture. This is just canting hypocrisy. Half the great poems, pictures, music, stories, of the whole world are great by virtue of the beauty of their sex appeal. Titian or Renoir, the Song of Solomon or *Jane Eyre*, Mozart or "Annie Laurie," the loveliness is all interwoven with sex appeal, sex stimulus, call it what you will. Even Michelangelo, who rather hated sex, can't help filling the Cornucopia with phallic acorns. Sex is a very powerful, beneficial and necessary stimulus in human life, and we are all grateful when we feel its warm, natural flow through us, like a form of sunshine. . . .

6   Then what is pornography, after all this? It isn't sex appeal or sex stimulus in art. It isn't even a deliberate intention on the part of the artist to arouse or excite sexual feelings. There's nothing wrong with sexual feelings in themselves, so long as they are straightforward and not sneaking or sly. The right sort of sex stimulus is invaluable to human daily life. Without it the world grows grey. I would give everybody the gay Renaissance stories to read; they would help to shake off a lot of grey self-importance, which is our modern civilised disease.

7   But even I would censor genuine pornography, rigorously. It would not be very difficult. In the first place, genuine pornography is almost always underworld, it doesn't come into the open. In the second, you can recognise it by the insult it offers, invariably, to sex and to the human spirit.

8   Pornography is the attempt to insult sex, to do dirt on it. This is unpardonable. Take the very lowest instance, the picture postcard sold underhand, by the underworld, in most cities. What I have seen of them have been of an ugliness to make you cry. The insult to the human body, the insult to a vital human relationship! Ugly and cheap they make the human nudity, ugly and degraded they make the sexual act, trivial and cheap and nasty.

9   It is the same with the books they sell in the underworld. They are either so ugly they make you ill, or so fatuous you can't imagine anybody but a cretin or a moron reading them, or writing them.

10   It is the same with the dirty limericks that people tell after dinner, or the dirty stories one hears commercial travellers telling each other in a smokeroom. Occasionally there is a really funny one, that redeems a great deal. But usually they are just ugly and repellent, and the so-called "humour" is just a trick of doing dirt on sex.

11   Now the human nudity of a great many modern people is just ugly and de-

graded, and the sexual act between modern people is just the same, merely ugly and degrading. But this is nothing to be proud of. It is the catastrophe of our civilisation. I am sure no other civilisation, not even the Roman, has showed such a vast proportion of ignominious and degraded nudity, and ugly, squalid dirty sex. Because no other civilisation has given sex into the underworld, and nudity to the w.c.

The intelligent young, thank heaven, seem determined to alter in these two respects. They are rescuing their young nudity from the stuffy, pornographical hole-and-corner underworld of their elders, and they refuse to sneak about the sexual relation. This is a change the elderly grey ones of course deplore, but it is in fact a very great change for the better, and a real revolution. 12

But it is amazing how strong is the will in ordinary, vulgar people, to do dirt on sex. It was one of my fond illusions, when I was young, that the ordinary healthy-seeming sort of men in railway carriages, or the smoke-room of an hotel or a pullman, were healthy in their feelings and had a wholesome, rough devil-may-care attitude towards sex. All wrong! All wrong! Experience teaches that common individuals of this sort have a disgusting attitude towards sex, a disgusting contempt of it, a disgusting desire to insult it. If such fellows have intercourse with a woman, they triumphantly feel that they have done her dirt, and now she is lower, cheaper, more contemptible than she was before. 13

It is individuals of this sort that tell dirty stories, carry indecent picture postcards, and know the indecent books. This is the great pornographical class—the really common men-in-the-street and women-in-the-street. They have as great a hate and contempt of sex as the greyest Puritan, and when an appeal is made to them, they are always on the side of the angels. They insist that a film heroine shall be a neuter, a sexless thing of washed-out purity. They insist that real sex-feeling shall only be shown by the villain or villainess, low lust. They find a Titian or a Renoir really indecent, and they don't want their wives and daughters to see it. 14

Why? Because they have the grey disease of sex-hatred, coupled with the yellow disease of dirt-lust. The sex functions and the excrementory functions in the human body work so close together, yet they are, so to speak, utterly different in direction. Sex is a creative flow, the excrementory flow is towards dissolution, decreation, if we may use such a word. In the really healthy human being the distinction between the two is instant, our profoundest instincts are perhaps our instincts of opposition between the two flows. But in the degraded human being the deep instincts have gone dead, and then the two flows become identical. *This* is the secret of really vulgar and of pornographical people: the sex flow and the excrement flow is the same to them. It happens when the psyche deteriorates, and the profound controlling instincts col- 15 lapse. Then sex is dirt and dirt is sex, and sexual excitement becomes a playing with dirt, and any sign of sex in a woman becomes a show of her dirt. This is the condition of the common, vulgar human being whose name is legion, and who lifts his voice, and it is the *Vox populi, vox Dei*. And this is the source of all pornography.

Margaret Atwood

Pornography

Margaret Atwood (b. 1939), a novelist, poet, and essayist, is best known as the author of novels such as *The Handmaid's Tale* (1986) and *Cat's Eye* (1989). In this essay, Atwood clearly has a much narrower definition of pornography than D. H. Lawrence. Instead of merely defining pornography, however, she is more interested in determining how to regulate it. The issues she brings up are not without consequence: how can we balance the need for freedom of expression against the rights of potential victims of rape or incest? If pornography incites people to violence, shouldn't it be banned? Should we define a movie depicting the horrible consequences of rape as "pornography" or "education"?

1   WHEN I WAS IN FINLAND A FEW YEARS AGO for an international writers' conference, I had occasion to say a few paragraphs in public on the subject of pornography. The context was a discussion of political repression, and I was suggesting the possibility of a link between the two. The immediate result was that a male journalist took several large bites out of me. Prudery and pornography are two halves of the same coin, said he, and I was clearly a prude. What could you expect from an Anglo-Canadian? Afterward, a couple of pleasant Scandinavian men asked me what I had been so worked up about. All "pornography" means, they said, is graphic depictions of whores, and what was the harm in that?

2   Not until then did it strike me that the male journalist and I had two entirely different things in mind. By "pornography," he meant naked bodies and sex. I, on the other hand, had recently been doing the research for my novel *Bodily Harm*, and was still in a state of shock from some of the material I had seen, including the Ontario Board of Film Censors' "outtakes." By "pornography," I meant women getting their nipples snipped off with garden shears, having meat hooks stuck into their vaginas, being disemboweled; little girls being raped; men (yes, there are some men) being smashed to a pulp and forcibly sodomized. The cutting edge of pornography, as far as I could see, was

no longer simple old copulation, hanging from the chandelier or otherwise: it was death, messy, explicit and highly sadistic. I explained this to the nice Scandinavian men. "Oh, but that's just the United States," they said. "Everyone knows they're sick." In their country, they said, violent "pornography" of that kind was not permitted on television or in movies; indeed, excessive violence of any kind was not permitted. They had drawn a clear line between erotica, which earlier studies had shown did not incite men to more aggressive and brutal behavior toward women, and violence, which later studies indicated did.

Some time after that I was in Saskatchewan, where, because of the scenes in *Bodily Harm*, I found myself on an open-line radio show answering questions about "pornography." Almost no one who phoned in was in favor of it, but again they weren't talking about the same stuff I was, because they hadn't seen it. Some of them were all set to stamp out bathing suits and negligees, and, if possible, any depictions of the female body whatsoever. God, it was implied, did not approve of female bodies, and sex of any kind, including that practised by bumblebees, should be shoved back into the dark, where it belonged. I had more than a suspicion that *Lady Chatterley's Lover*, Margaret Laurence's *The Diviners*, and indeed most books by most serious modern authors would have ended up as confetti if left in the hands of these callers.

For me, these two experiences illustrate the two poles of the emotionally heated debate that is now thundering around this issue. They also underline the desirability and even the necessity of defining the terms. "Pornography" is now one of those catchalls, like "Marxism" and "feminism," that have become so broad they can mean almost anything, ranging from certain verses in the Bible, ads for skin lotion and sex tests for children to the contents of *Penthouse*, Naughty '90s postcards and films with titles containing the word *Nazi* that show vicious scenes of torture and killing. It's easy to say that sensible people can tell the difference. Unfortunately, opinions on what constitutes a sensible person vary.

But even sensible people tend to lose their cool when they start talking about this subject. They soon stop talking and start yelling, and the name calling begins. Those in favor of censorship (which may include groups not noticeably in agreement on other issues, such as some feminists and religious fundamentalists) accuse the others of exploiting women through the use of degrading images, contributing to the corruption of children, and adding to the general climate of violence and threat in which both women and children live in this society; or, though they may not give much of a hoot about actual women and children, they invoke moral standards and God's supposed aversion to "filth," "smut" and deviated *preversion*, which may mean ankles.

The camp in favor of total "freedom of expression" often comes out howling as loud as the Romans would have if told they could no longer have innocent fun watching the lions eat up Christians. It too may include segments of the population who are not natural bedfellows: those who proclaim their God-given right to freedom, including the freedom to tote guns, drive when drunk, drool over chicken porn and get off on videotapes of women being raped and beaten, may be waving the same anticensorship banner as responsible liberals who fear the return of Mrs. Grundy, or gay groups for whom sexual emancipation involves the concept of "sexual theatre." *Whatever turns you on* is a handy motto, as is *A man's home is his castle* (and if it includes a dungeon with beautiful maidens strung up in chains and bleeding from every pore, that's his business).

7   Meanwhile, theoreticians theorize and speculators speculate. Is today's pornography yet another indication of the hatred of the body, the deep mind-body split, which is supposed to pervade Western Christian society? Is it a backlash against the women's movement by men who are threatened by uppity female behavior in real life, so like to fantasize about women done up like outsize parcels, being turned into hamburger, kneeling at their feet in slave-like adoration or sucking off guns? Is it a sign of collective impotence, of a generation of men who can't relate to real women at all but have to make do with bits of celluloid and paper? Is the current flood just a result of smart marketing and aggressive promotion by the money men in what has now become a multi-billion dollar industry? If they were selling movies about men getting their testicles stuck full of knitting needles by women with swastikas on their sleeves, would they do as well, or is this penchant somehow peculiarly male? If so, why? Is pornography a power trip rather than a sex one? Some say that those ropes, chains, muzzles and other restraining devices are an argument for the immense power female sexuality still wields in the male imagination: you don't put these things on dogs unless you're afraid of them. Others, more literary, wonder about the shift from the 19th-century Magic Woman or Femme Fatale image to the lollipop-licker, airhead or turkey-carcass treatment of women in porn today. The proporners don't care much about theory; they merely demand product. The antiporners don't care about it in the final analysis either; there's dirt on the street, and they want it cleaned up, now.

8   It seems to me that this conversation, with its *You're-a-prude/You're-a-pervert* dialectic, will never get anywhere as long as we continue to think of this material as just "entertainment." Possibly we're deluded by the packaging, the format: magazine, book, movie, theatrical presentation. We're used to thinking of these things as part of the "entertainment industry," and we're used to thinking of ourselves as free adult people who ought to be able to see any kind of "entertainment" we want to. That was what the First Choice pay-TV debate was all about. After all, it's only entertainment, right? Entertainment means fun, and only a killjoy would be antifun. What's the harm?

9   This is obviously the central question: *What's the harm?* If there isn't any

real harm to any real people, then the antiporners can tsk-tsk and/or throw up as much as they like, but they can't rightfully expect more legal controls or sanctions. However, the no harm position is far from being proven.

(For instance, there's a clear-cut case for banning—as the federal govern- 10 ment has proposed—movies, photos and videos that depict children engaging in sex with adults: real children are used to make the movies, and hardly anybody thinks this is ethical. The possibilities for coercion are too great.)

To shift the viewpoint, I'd like to suggest three other models for looking 11 at "pornography"—and here I mean the violent kind.

Those who find the idea of regulating pornographic materials repugnant 12 because they think it's Fascist or Communist or otherwise not in accordance with the principles of an open democratic society should consider that Canada has made it illegal to disseminate material that may lead to hatred toward any group because of race or religion. I suggest that if pornography of the violent kind depicted these acts being done predominantly to Chinese, to blacks, to Catholics, it would be off the market immediately, under the present laws. Why is hate literature illegal? Because whoever made the law thought that such material might incite real people to do real awful things to other real people. The human brain is to a certain extent a computer: garbage in, garbage out. We only hear about the extreme cases (like that of American multimurderer Ted Bundy) in which pornography has contributed to the death and/or mutilation of women and/or men. Although pornography is not the only factor involved in the creation of such deviance, it certainly has upped the ante by suggesting both a variety of techniques and the social acceptability of such actions. Nobody knows yet what effect this stuff is having on the less psychotic.

Studies have shown that a large part of the market for all kinds of porn, 13 soft and hard, is drawn from the 16-to-21-year-old population of young men. Boys used to learn about sex on the street, or (in Italy, according to Fellini movies) from friendly whores, or, in more genteel surroundings, from girls, their parents, or, once upon a time, in school, more or less. Now porn has been added, and sex education in the schools is rapidly being phased out. The buck has been passed, and boys are being taught that all women secretly like to be raped and that real men get high on scooping out women's digestive tracts.

Boys learn their concept of masculinity from other men: is this what most 14 men want them to be learning? If word gets around that rapists are "normal" and even admirable men, will boys feel that in order to be normal, admirable and masculine they will have to be rapists? Human beings are enormously flexible, and how they turn out depends a lot on how they're educated, by the society in which they're immersed as well as by their teachers. In a society that advertises and glorifies rape or even implicitly condones it, more women get raped. It becomes socially acceptable. And at a time when men and the traditional male role have taken a lot of flak and men are confused and casting around for an acceptable way of being male (and, in some cases, not getting much comfort from women on that score), this must be at times a pleasing thought.

15   It would be naïve to think of violent pornography as just harmless entertainment. It's also an educational tool and a powerful propaganda device. What happens when boy educated on porn meets girl brought up on Harlequin romances? The clash of expectations can be heard around the block. She wants him to get down on his knees with a ring, he wants her to get down on all fours with a ring in her nose. Can this marriage be saved?

16   Pornography has certain things in common with such addictive substances as alcohol and drugs: for some, though by no means for all, it induces chemical changes in the body, which the user finds exciting and pleasurable. It also appears to attract a "hard core" of habitual users and a penumbra of those who use it occasionally but aren't dependent on it in any way. There are also significant numbers of men who aren't much interested in it, not because they're undersexed but because real life is satisfying their needs, which may not require as many appliances as those of users.

17   For the "hard core," pornography may function as alcohol does for the alcoholic: tolerance develops, and a little is no longer enough. This may account for the short viewing time and fast turnover in porn theatres. Mary Brown, chairwoman of the Ontario Board of Film Censors, estimates that for every one mainstream movie requesting entrance to Ontario, there is one porno flick. Not only the quantity consumed but the quality of explicitness must escalate, which may account for the growing violence: once the big deal was breasts, then it was genitals, then copulation, then that was no longer enough and the hard users had to have more. The ultimate kick is death, and after that, as the Marquis de Sade so boringly demonstrated, multiple death.

18   The existence of alcoholism has not led us to ban social drinking. On the other hand, we do have laws about drinking and driving, excessive drunkenness and other abuses of alcohol that may result in injury or death to others.

19   This leads us back to the key question: what's the harm? Nobody knows, but this society should find out fast, before the saturation point is reached. The Scandinavian studies that showed a connection between depictions of sexual violence and increased impulse toward it on the part of male viewers would be a starting point, but many more questions remain to be raised as well as answered. What, for instance, is the crucial difference between men who are users and men who are not? Does using affect a man's relationship with actual women, and, if so, adversely? Is there a clear line between erotica and violent pornography, or are they on an escalating continuum? Is this

a "men versus women" issue, with all men secretly siding with the pro-porners and all women secretly siding against? (I think not; there *are* lots of men who don't think that running their true love through the Cuisinart is the best way they can think of to spend a Saturday night, and they're just as nauseated by films of someone else doing it as women are.) Is pornography merely an expression of the sexual confusion of this age or an active con-tributor to it?

Nobody wants to go back to the age of official repression, when even   20 piano legs were referred to as "limbs" and had to wear pantaloons to be de-cent. Neither do we want to end up in George Orwell's 1984, in which pornography is turned out by the State to keep the proles in a state of torpor, sex itself is considered dirty and the approved practise it only for repro-duction. But Rome under the emperors isn't such a good model either.

If all men and women respected each other, if sex were considered joyful   21 and life-enhancing instead of a wallow in germ-filled glop, if everyone were in love all the time, if, in other words, many people's lives were more satisfactory for them than they appear to be now, pornography might just go away on its own. But since this is obviously not happening, we as a society are going to have to make some informed and responsible decisions about how to deal with it.

Marie Winn

TV Addiction

Cookies or Heroin?

Born in Czechoslovakia, Marie Winn emigrated to the United States as a child. She has been a writer all her life, writing children's books, translating plays from her native Czech, and even writing a column on bird watching for the *Wall Street Journal*. In 1977, *The Plug-in Drug*, her first book for adults, gained her a national reputation as a careful observer of human nature.

THE WORD "ADDICTION" IS OFTEN USED LOOSELY and wryly in conversation.   1 People will refer to themselves as "mystery book addicts" or "cookie addicts." E. B. White writes of his annual surge of interest in gardening: "We are hooked and are making an attempt to kick the habit." Yet nobody really be-lieves that reading mysteries or ordering seeds by catalogue is serious enough to be compared with addictions to heroin or alcohol. The word "addiction" is here used jokingly to denote a tendency to overindulge in some pleasurable activity.

2   People often refer to being "hooked on TV." Does this, too, fall into the lighthearted category of cookie eating and other pleasures that people pursue with unusual intensity, or is there a kind of television viewing that falls into the more serious category of destructive addiction?

3   When we think about addiction to drugs or alcohol, we frequently focus on negative aspects, ignoring the pleasures that accompany drinking or drug-taking. And yet the essence of any serious addiction is a pursuit of pleasure, a search for a "high" that normal life does not supply. It is only the inability to function without the addictive substance that is dismaying, the dependence of the organism upon a certain experience and an increasing inability to function normally without it. Thus a person will take two or three drinks at the end of the day not merely for the pleasure drinking provides, but also because he "doesn't feel normal" without them.

4   An addict does not merely pursue a pleasurable experience and need to experience it in order to function normally. He needs to *repeat* it again and again. Something about that particular experience makes life without it less than complete. Other potentially pleasurable experiences are no longer possible, for under the spell of the addictive experience, his life is peculiarly distorted. The addict craves an experience and yet he is never really satisfied. The organism may be temporarily sated, but soon it begins to crave again.

5   Finally, a serious addiction is distinguished from a harmless pursuit of pleasure by its distinctly destructive elements. A heroin addict, for instance, leads a damaged life: His increasing need for heroin in increasing doses prevents him from working, from maintaining relationships, from developing in human ways. Similarly an alcoholic's life is narrowed and dehumanized by his dependence on alcohol.

6   Let us consider television viewing in the light of the conditions that define serious addictions.

7   Not unlike drugs or alcohol, the television experience allows the participant to blot out the real world and enter into a pleasurable and passive mental state. The worries and anxieties of reality are as effectively deferred by becoming absorbed in a television program as by going on a "trip" induced by drugs or alcohol. And just as alcoholics are only inchoately aware of their addiction, feeling that they control their drinking more than they really do ("I can cut it out any time I want—I just like to have three or four drinks before dinner"), people similarly overestimate their control over television watching. Even as they put off other activities to spend hour after hour watching television, they feel they could easily resume living in a different, less passive style. But somehow or other while the television set is present in their homes, the click doesn't sound. With television plea-

sures available, those other experiences seem less attractive, more difficult somehow.

A heavy viewer (a college English instructor) observes: "I find television almost irresistible. When the set is on, I cannot ignore it. I can't turn it off. I feel sapped, will-less, enervated. As I reach out to turn off the set, the strength goes out of my arms. So I sit there for hours and hours." 8

The self-confessed television addict often feels he "ought" to do other things—but the fact that he doesn't read and doesn't plant his garden or sew or crochet or play games or have conversations means that those activities are no longer as desirable as television viewing. In a way a heavy viewer's life is as imbalanced by his television "habit" as a drug addict's or an alcoholic's. He is living in a holding pattern, as it were, passing up the activities that lead to growth or development or a sense of accomplishment. This is one reason people talk about their television viewing so ruefully, so apologetically. They are aware that it is an unproductive experience, that almost any other endeavor is more worthwhile by any human measure. 9

Finally, it is the adverse effect of television viewing on the lives of so many people that defines it as a serious addiction. The television habit distorts the sense of time. It renders other experiences vague and curiously unreal while taking on a greater reality for itself. It weakens relationships by reducing and sometimes eliminating normal opportunities for talking, for communicating. 10

And yet television does not satisfy, else why would the viewer continue to watch hour after hour, day after day? "The measure of health," writes Lawrence Kubie, "is flexibility . . . and especially the freedom to cease when sated." But the television viewer can never be sated with his television experiences—they do not provide the true nourishment that satiation requires—and thus he finds that he cannot stop watching. 11

William Raspberry

The Handicap of Definition

William Raspberry (b. 1935) is a Pulitzer Prize-winning writer and a professor of journalism and communications at Duke University. His *Washington Post* column on minority affairs now appears in over 180 newspapers. While his columns often cover the difficult issues of race relations and social development, he remains cautiously optimistic. "I am a hopeful person," commented Raspberry in a 1995 interview, "and I think that there is a reasonable chance that people here and there, not all at once, will wake up to what we need to do and not sit around waiting for the politicians to come riding in to save us. It's the only way we're going to get anywhere." In this essay, he comments on the problems created by society's narrow definition of "black."

1   I KNOW ALL ABOUT BAD SCHOOLS, mean politicians, economic deprivation and racism. Still, it occurs to me that one of the heaviest burdens black Americans—and black children in particular—have to bear is the handicap of definition: the question of what it means to be black.

2   Let me explain quickly what I mean. If a basketball fan says that the Boston Celtics' Larry Bird plays "black," the fan intends it—and Bird probably accepts it—as a compliment. Tell pop singer Tom Jones he moves "black" and he might grin in appreciation. Say to Teena Marie or The Average White Band that they sound "black" and they'll thank you.

3   But name one pursuit, aside from athletics, entertainment or sexual performance in which a white practitioner will feel complimented to be told he does it "black." Tell a white broadcaster he talks "black" and he'll sign up for diction lessons. Tell a white reporter he writes "black" and he'll take a writing course. Tell a white lawyer he reasons "black" and he might sue you for slander.

4   What we have here is a tragically limited definition of blackness, and it isn't only white people who buy it.

5   Think of all the ways black children can put one another down with charges of "whiteness." For many of these children, hard study and hard work are "white." Trying to please a teacher might be criticized as acting "white." Speaking correct English is "white." Scrimping today in the interest of tomorrow's goals is "white." Educational toys and games are "white."

6   An incredible array of habits and attitudes that are conducive to success in business, in academia, in the non-entertainment professions are likely to be thought of as somehow "white." Even economic success, unless it involves such "black" undertakings as numbers banking, is defined as "white."

7   And the results are devastating. I wouldn't deny that blacks often are better entertainers and athletes. My point is the harm that comes from too narrow a definition of what is black.

8   One reason black youngsters tend to do better at basketball, for instance, is that they assume they can learn to do it well, and so they practice constantly to prove themselves right.

9   Wouldn't it be wonderful if we could infect black children with the notion that excellence in math is "black" rather than white, or possibly Chinese? Wouldn't it be of enormous value if we could create the myth that morality, strong families, determination, courage and love of learning are traits brought by slaves from Mother Africa and therefore quintessentially black?

10   There is no doubt in my mind that most black youngsters could develop their mathematical reasoning, their elocution and their attitudes the way they

develop their jump shots and their dance steps: by the combination of sustained, enthusiastic practice and the unquestioned belief that they can do it.

In one sense, what I am talking about is the importance of developing positive ethnic traditions. Maybe Jews have an innate talent for communication; maybe the Chinese are born with a gift for mathematical reasoning; maybe blacks are naturally blessed with athletic grace. I doubt it. What is at work, I suspect, is assumption, inculcated early in their lives, that this is a thing our people do well. 11

Unfortunately, many of the things about which blacks make this assumption are things that do not contribute to their career success—except for that handful of the truly gifted who can make it as entertainers and athletes. And many of the things we concede to whites are the things that are essential to economic security. So it is with a number of assumptions black youngsters make about what it is to be a "man": physical aggressiveness, sexual prowess, the refusal to submit to authority. The prisons are full of people who, by this perverted definition, are unmistakably men. 12

But the real problem is not so much that the things defined as "black" are negative. The problem is that the definition is much too narrow. 13

Somehow, we have to make our children understand that they are intelligent, competent people, capable of doing whatever they put their minds to and making it in the American mainstream, not just in a black subculture. 14

What we seem to be doing, instead, is raising up yet another generation of young blacks who will be failures—by definition. 15

Student Essay

Jason Gray

Questioning the Nature of Intelligence

Jason wrote this research paper for an advanced psychology course, but it is also relevant for general readers. Nearly everyone has been exposed to an IQ test at some point during their lives, but few of us understand what the concept of IQ really means. Jason clears up some of these iss ues by taking a historical approach to his definition, beginning with some of the pioneers of intellegence testing and finishing with contemporary research on the topic.

FROM A VERY YOUNG AGE, INDIVIDUALS BEGIN TO RECOGNIZE differences among their peers. Some friends are faster, some stronger, some taller, and others 1 shorter. Some friends have a different skin color. Some friends seem very bright and others seem never to understand. This incredible range of differences, which makes each human being unique, is the product of a number of different factors. Physical attributes, such as appearance, build, hair color, and eye color are primarily determined by inherited genetic make-up, even though environment can have many dramatic effects on early development (fetal alcohol syndrome, exposure to toxins in infancy, etc.). Mental attributes are much tougher to pin down and harder to accept as strictly the product of DNA. Is an enjoyment of Pearl Jam and chocolate ice cream over Mozart and vanilla really a matter of biochemistry or brain structure?

2   What about intelligence, where does it fit in? A much less arbitrary attribute than one's favorite ice cream flavor; however, individuals still have difficulty accepting brain power as 100% a matter of genes. Formal instruction and other environmental factors seem to affect how intelligent a person appears. Yet, the size of our brains is just as inherited as the size of our nose. Psychologists have been trying to make sense of this issue since the very beginning of the discipline.

3   The most recent and controversial addition to the debate has come from Herrnstein and Murray's publication, *The Bell Curve: Intelligence and Class Structure in American Life*. The book argues strongly in favor of the belief that intelligence is primarily inherited. They use the heritability argument as a explanation of class stratification in America. The poor are poor because they lack the inherited ability to be anything better. Conversely, the successful individuals have become wealthy because of their natural ability to take on more highly skilled professions such as medicine and the law, which pay better. Their theory is reminiscent of Social Darwinism, which was popular in the late 1800s but eventually fell out of favor. Herrnstein and Murray did not go as far as suggesting programs of eugenics, but the tone of their writing has much the same superior feel. However, this does not discount their argument that economic separation of the races is based on genetic differences in intelligence. Science seems to have come full circle. Might Social Darwinism have been correct all those years ago, just lacking significant evidence to back it up? Herrnstein and Murray present a convincing case for the modern equivalent and suggest that unless society is dramatically restructured the situation of the underclass is only going to get worse.

4   Many scholars from a variety of fields launched an all out assault on their work. Some writers, particularly Stephen Jay Gould, opened up a number of interesting holes in their theory which resulted in more unanswered questions. First, Gould points out that their entire argument is based on four principles of intelligence and should any one of them be proven false their entire argument falls apart. He says Herrnstein and Murray's four principles assert

that intelligence can be described as "a single number, capable of ranking people in linear order, genetically based, and effectively immutable" (Gould, 1994).

Once the accuracy of the four elements underpinning Herrnstein and Murray's notion of intelligence are analyzed, a better assessment of their overall argument can be made. In the end, more unanswered questions will be raised by this process than were started with and consideration will be given to these issues, as well as the direction of future work in the field of intelligence.

The earliest scientific investigations of the nature of intelligence are traced to Sir Francis Galton and his book *Hereditary Genius* (1869). Galton establishes the concept of the standard deviation curve (bell curve) and uses it to make clear to the reader what he means by superior intelligence. To Galton, truly superior intellects constituted only the very smallest part of the tail, those who scored more than three standard deviations above the mean on the Cambridge mathematical exams. Closely examining this very small population, he found that all of these people were somehow distantly related. From this he concluded that intelligence must run in families and therefore be an inherited trait.

Galton became a controversial figure for his suggestion of eugenics programs, where the best and brightest got together to have children and the less intelligent, lower classes are discouraged from having children (Weiten, 1995). Out of *Hereditary Genius* and Darwin's *Origin of Species*, Social Darwinism developed. Important to our modern debate about *The Bell Curve*, Galton argued that intelligence was immutable. He used the analogy of an athlete to describe mental abilities, saying that a man can work out for many years and gain strength and speed, but he inevitably reaches a maximum potential beyond which his strength cannot increase to match other men of greater size. He says that the same is true for mental ability (Galton, 1869).

The first test devised solely to be a measure of intelligence was put together by Alfred Binet and Theodore Simon in 1905 to help single out children in need of special assistance. The test turned out to be very good for predicting student success in school. Binet and Simon also developed the concept of mental age in relation to chronological age as a means of measuring whether a student was ahead or behind in their schooling. In 1916 Lewis Terman published his revision to the original Binet scale, called the Stanford-Binet Intelligence Scale. The test was revolutionary because of its incorporation of the new scoring system, developed by William Stern, which we still use today. The system introduced the "intelligence quotient" or IQ. This was defined as the child's mental age divided by their chronological age, multiplied by 100. The Stanford-Binet test became the standard of intelligence by which all future tests were correlated to ascertain their validity (Weiten, 1995).

9   Binet views intelligence as being more malleable than Galton and his athletic analogy. Binet is quoted as saying:

10   The intelligence of anyone is susceptible to development. With practice, enthusiasm and especially with method one can succeed in increasing one's attention, memory, judgement, and in becoming literally more intelligent than one was before (Weiten, 1995).

11   However, this statement does not directly refute what Galton said. Galton agreed that with work one could improve their intelligence, just that there was an upper limit to the amount of improvement and that this upper limit was set by our inheritance.

12   The next major development in the field of testing came from David Wechsler and his construction of the Wechsler Adult Intelligence Scale (WAIS). This was important for two reasons. First, he included problems that required non-verbal reasoning. Second, scoring was based on a normal distribution, akin to the modern day bell curve. Most IQ tests today use a normal distribution, but the term IQ remains. About his test, Wechsler said, "The subtests are different measures of intelligence, not measures of different kinds of intelligence" (Weiten, 1995). The importance of this concept will be brought to light when the modern approaches, suggesting multiple types of intelligences, are discussed.

13   Charles Spearman presented the final development in the historical view of intelligence. Using the method of factor analysis (which he developed), he looked at correlations among different tests that assessed specific cognitive abilities. Among all these correlations, he concluded that all the diverse tests shared a single core component, which he labeled g. g is often considered to be a general mental ability that is expressed through a variety of different mental tasks. Since the emergence of Spearman's theory, intelligence tests have attempted to correlate as highly as possible with g (Weiten, 1995).

14   Some modern theorists have separated from attempts to find a single overarching test and attempted to quantify the different components of intelligence separately. This will be discussed thoroughly in the next section. One other major modern development has been the use of completely non-verbal intelligence tests, the most widely used of these tests being the Raven's Progressive Matrices Test, which has been correlated with traditional intelligence tests in order to yield the same type of numerical value.

15   Already, the issues that Stephen Jay Gould raised in response to *The Bell Curve* are beginning to come to light. Is intelligence necessarily a single, immutable number? Binet and Galton seemed to be of different minds about the issue of immutability. Wechsler expressed the belief that intelligence is a single number that can be quantified in a number of different ways. Most im-

portantly, differences in testing are now being brought forward. The difference between the Stanford-Binet and Raven's test is dramatic. Yet, they each claim to be testing the same thing. Is it possible to make sense of which is better? In order to get a handle on this problem, a better definition of intelligence is necessary. If intelligence is just ability to abstract, then Raven's is likely to be a very good measure. If a broader view of intelligence is taken and acquired general knowledge is included in one's definition, then the Stanford-Binet might be considered to be more accurate. In addition to the knowledge vs. abstraction distinction, the tests also differ in their manner of presentation. The questions in the Stanford-Binet are all verbally based, whereas the Raven's requires no verbal ability to solve its matrices. Clearly, many questions still remained to be answered.

Robert Sternberg has pioneered one of the newest fields of assessment, called dynamic testing. The goal of dynamic testing is to quantify specifically the ability to learn, regardless of one's level of acquired knowledge. In most experiments, equal emphasis is put on testing and intervention, following the test-intervention-retest model. Much of this work has focused on assisting learning-disabled children or children who perform poorly in static testing situations.

Budoff conducted a study in which subjects were given a battery of different verbal and non-verbal IQ tests. They were then trained in problem solving techniques essential to achieving a good score and retested. Scores were found to improve (Grigorenko & Sternberg, 1998).

Another important distinction is the difference between academic intelligence (book smarts) and practical intelligence (street smarts). Individuals who exhibit complicated problem solving and abstraction skills on the job and in other settings but only have minimal education are considered primary examples in favor of practical intelligence as something distinct from academic intelligence. Racetrack handicappers and individuals who work on assembly lines are two specific cases where the average subject has no more than a high school education, but they are able to use complicated strategies to minimize the number of moves they have to make or maximize their profits, which more educated subjects can't figure out initially (Sternberg, et al., 1995).

However, challengers to the theory of practical intelligence suggest that it is no different from academic intelligence. They argue that individuals who failed to achieve in an academic setting but succeeded on the job may have lacked motivation or been facing other environmental issues when going through adolescence, etc. That does not change their ability to perform complex tasks. There is some experimental evidence against this. In a study of smart shoppers in California (individuals who could perform mathematical calculations quickly in their head to decide which size product is the best buy) conducted by Lave, et al., (1995) no relation was found between shopping accuracy and performance on the MIT mental arithmetic test.

20   Although dynamic assessment and practical intelligence are both very new fields, early studies have shown that there exist aspects of mental capacity that traditional psychometric tests fail to quantify. The dynamic tests are clearly better for distinguishing among lower achievers who still have potential and those that may still be beyond help. Psychometric testing, and in fact, pen and paper testing in general may be missing a whole field of cognitive problem solving that is now being defined as practical intelligence. This exposes a number of holes in Herrnstein and Murray's argument. Most importantly these tests seem to speak to the question of immutability of intelligence. For instance, why does academic intelligence increase with age until early adulthood when it begins to decline? Also, the traditional psychometric tests do not seem to be accurate predictors of some individuals' ability to learn, weakening their dismissal of the underclass as being unable to achieve.

21   Knowledge about the inner workings of inheritance has greatly improved since the time of Galton. The discovery of DNA and the implications that came along with understanding the mechanism of evolution revolutionized thinking in the fields of psychology and biology. Genetic theory along with other new technologies has sparked a feverish search for the physiological mechanisms connected with brain behavior. This trend can be seen in every field, from sensation and perception to the study of intelligence. The last ten years have been particularly fruitful in the search for what it is about the brain that makes someone smart.

22   These correlative and physiological findings suggest that Herrnstein and Murray are just wrong about the immutability of intelligence, even though a large portion of intelligence may be genetically determined. The data from Reed and Jensen, clearly showing that environmental effects not only manifest themselves as increased test scores but also as structural differences in the brain, can be explained away simply as a person maximizing their genetically given range. This is fine, but also inherent in the argument in *The Bell Curve* is that all people in the lower class are there because that's as smart as they can be. This certainly seems not to be the case. Scarr and Weinberg demonstrated otherwise by their study in which kids were taken into enriched environments and their scores improved. Given all the evidence that has come forward, even prior to the publication of *The Bell Curve*, it is difficult to believe Herrnstein and Murray would put forth the argument they did.

23   In light of the evidence, the four pillars of Herrnstein and Murray's argument do not seem as solid as the authors suggest in *The Bell Curve*. Their principle of immutability of intelligence has been brought into question. Modern methods of dynamic assessment have exposed weaknesses in the traditional tests used as the intelligence measure in *The Bell Curve*. Additionally, new the-

ories of practical intelligence have identified a different type of cognitive reasoning involving both problem solving and abstraction skills that is not quantified by traditional tests. Finally, physiological and correlational studies have shown that despite the large amount of heritability in intelligence, environment can produce dramatic cognitive and structural changes in the subject.

This is not to suggest that psychometric testing is dead, only that *The Bell Curve* presents a distasteful social argument based on a number of questionable assumptions about intelligence taken to be fact by the authors. This paper sought to illustrate the inaccuracy of these assumptions as a means of looking at the current work in the intelligence field. Psychometric testing remains, in fact, the best predictor of success that can be economically administered to large populations and give a rough estimate of an individual's ability. Modern methods of testing are more accurate, but cannot be administered efficiently to large populations. These traditional tests will most likely be used as the primary means of roughly assessing a subject's ability for many years to come. The danger of these IQ tests is when individuals such as Herrnstein and Murray attempt to read too much into what a single number tells. 24

The fact of the matter is that even psychologists are split over what the number represents. From Spearman's g to Sternberg's theory of practical intelligence, what exactly constitutes intelligence is still uncertain. Also, the new theories of dynamic assessment and practical intelligence have yet to be fully developed. A great deal of investigation into these fields is still necessary. The physiological field is another area which is quite new and has the potential for incredible expansion in the future. The intelligence field is undergoing a time of great change, likely to redefine the way mental capacity is discussed. 25

References

Carpenter, P., et al. (1990). What One Intelligence Test Measures: A Theoretical Account of the Processing in the Raven Progressive Matrices Test. *Psychological Review, 97(3),* 404–431.

Daniel, M.H. (1997). Intelligence Testing: Status and Trends. *American Psychologist, 52(10),* 1038–1045.

Galton, F. (1869). *Hereditary Genius: Its Laws and Consequences.* New York: D. Appleton & Co. pp. 45–88.

Gardner, H. (1994). Cracking Open the IQ Box. *The American Prospect,* Winter 1994.

Gould, S.J. (1994). Curveball. *The New Yorker,* Nov. 28, 1994.

Grigorenko, E. & Sternberg, R. (1998). Dynamic Testing. *Psychological Bulletin, 124(1),* 75–111.

Herrnstein R.J., & Murray, C. (1994). *The Bell Curve: Intelligence and Class Structure in American Life.* New York: Free Press. p. introduction-summaries-conclusions.

Myerson, J., Rank, M.R., Raines, F.Q., & Schnitzler, M.A. (1998). Race and General Cognitive Ability: The Myth of Diminishing Returns to Education. *Psychological Science, 9(2),* 139–142.

Neisser, U., et al. (1996). Intelligence: Knowns and Unknowns. *American Psychologist, 51(2),* 77–101.

Prabhakaran, V., et al. (1997). Neural Substrates of Fluid Reasoning: An fMRI Study of Neocortical Activation during Performance of the Raven's Progressive Matrices Test. *Cognitive Psychology, 33,* 43–63.

Reed, T.E. (1993). Effects of Enriched (Complex) Environment on Nerve Conduction Velocity: New Data and Review of Implications for the Speed of Information Processing. *Intelligence, 17,* 533–540.

Reed, T.E., & Jensen, A.R. (1991). Arm Nerve Conduction Velocity (NCV), Brain NCV, Reaction Time, and Intelligence. *Intelligence, 15,* 33–47.

Reed, T.E., & Jensen, A.R. (1992). Conduction Velocity in a Brain Nerve Pathway of Normal Adults Correlates with Intelligence Level. *Intelligence, 16,* 259–272.

Reed, T.E., & Jensen, A.R. (1993). A Somatosensory Latency Between the Thalamus and Cortex also Correlates with Level of Intelligence. *Intelligence, 17,* 443–450.

Saccuzzo, D. & Johnson, N. (1995). Traditional Psychometric Tests and Proportionate Representation: An Intervention and Program Evaluation Study. *Psychological Assessment, 7(2),* 183–194.

Sternberg, R.J., Wagner, R.K., Williams, W.M., & Horvath, J.A. (1995). Testing Common Sense. *American Psychologist, 50(11),* 912–927.

Weiten, W. (1995). *Psychology: Themes and Variations* 3rd Ed. Pacific Grove: Brooks/Cole Publishing Co. pp. 333–374.

10

Argument

Argument

1. **Formulate a clear thesis.** Argument is simply writing to convince someone either to agree with your point of view, or to change their behavior in the manner you desire. The best arguments, therefore, must clearly present the action or opinion the author would like the reader to adopt—a thesis statement. Virginia Woolf's thesis is (at least in part) "it would have been impossible, completely and entirely, for any woman to have written the plays of Shakespeare in the age of Shakespeare." Needless to say, you'll never convince your readers to do or think anything unless you know in advance what you want them to do or think.

2. **Anticipate your audience's response.** Will your readers be hostile to your argument? Generally agreeable? Depending on how you expect your audience to respond, you may want to state your thesis right away, or hold it back until the right moment.

3. **Appeal to your audience's emotions.** The theoretical discussion of argument began thousands of years ago with the ancient Greeks. Even then, philosophers realized that one of the most powerful methods of persuasion was to appeal to the audience's emotions. The same holds true today—for most of us, emotions are what make an argument *matter*. The most logical argument in the world won't convince anyone if it can easily be dismissed with "so what?"

4. **Support your argument with sound reasoning.** Logic is the basis for any sound argument. Volumes have been written about logic, but one of the most useful ways to use logic to support an argument is the data-claim-warrant model. This model, devised by the British philosopher Stephen Toulmin, suggests that any argument has three parts:

McGwire holds the single-
season home run record
data

Mark McGwire is the best
baseball player in history
claim

The best baseball player is the player who
can hit the most home runs in a single season
warrant

Any claim an author makes is based on a warrant, which is usually unstated. Only when the warrant is made explicit can the strength or weakness of a given argument be seen. It's a good idea to identify all three parts to each argument you make to ensure that your reasoning is sound.

Virginia Woolf

If Shakespeare Had Had a Sister

Virginia Woolf (1882–1941) was a poet, essayist, editor, and most notably, a novelist. She was the focus of the "Bloomsbury Group," a gathering of important thinkers, including T. S. Eliot, John Maynard Keynes, and E. M. Forster, who had wide influence in the early part of this century. In this passage from *A Room of One's Own* (1929), she builds a convincing case that a woman in Elizabethan England would never have been allowed the opportunity to create works like Shakespeare's plays.

IT IS A PERENNIAL PUZZLE WHY NO WOMAN WROTE A WORD of that extraordinary   1
[Elizabethan] literature when every other man, it seemed, was capable of song or sonnet. What were the conditions in which women lived, I asked myself; for fiction, imaginative work that is, is not dropped like a pebble upon the ground, as science may be; fiction is like a spider's web, attached ever so lightly perhaps, but still attached to life at all four corners. Often the attachment is scarcely perceptible; Shakespeare's plays, for instance, seem to hang there complete by themselves. But when the web is pulled askew, hooked up at the edge, torn in the middle, one remembers that these webs are not spun in midair by incorporeal creatures, but are the work of suffering human beings, and are attached to grossly material things, like health and money and the houses we live in. . . .

But what I find . . . is that nothing is known about women before the eigh-   2
teenth century. I have no model in my mind to turn about this way and that. Here am I asking why women did not write poetry in the Elizabethan age, and I am not sure how they were educated; whether they were taught to write; whether they had sitting-rooms to themselves; how many women had children before they were twenty-one; what, in short, they did from eight in the morning till eight at night. They had no money evidently; according to Professor Trevelyan they were married whether they liked it or not before they were out of the nursery, at fifteen or sixteen very likely. It would have been extremely odd, even upon this showing, had one of them suddenly written the plays of Shakespeare, I concluded, and I thought of that old gentleman, who is dead now, but was a bishop, I think, who declared that it was impossible for any woman, past, present, or to come, to have the genius of Shakespeare. He wrote to the papers about it. He also told a lady who applied to him for information that cats do not as a matter of fact go to heaven, though they have, he added, souls of a sort. How much thinking those old gentlemen used to save one! How the borders of ignorance shrank back at their approach! Cats do not go to heaven. Women cannot write the plays of Shakespeare.

3   Be that as it may, I could not help thinking, as I looked at the works of
Shakespeare on the shelf, that the bishop was right at least in this; it would
have been impossible, completely and entirely, for any woman to have written
the plays of Shakespeare in the age of Shakespeare. Let me imagine, since facts
are so hard to come by, what would have happened had Shakespeare had a
wonderfully gifted sister, called Judith, let us say. Shakespeare himself went,
very probably—his mother was an heiress—to the grammar school, where he
may have learnt Latin—Ovid, Virgil and Horace—and the elements of grammar and logic. He was, it is well known, a wild boy who poached rabbits, perhaps shot a deer, and had, rather sooner than he should have done, to marry
a woman in the neighbourhood, who bore him a child rather quicker than
was right. That escapade sent him to seek his fortune in London. He had, it
seemed, a taste for the theatre; he began by holding horses at the stage door.
Very soon he got work in the theatre, became a successful actor, and lived at
the hub of the universe, meeting everybody, knowing everybody, practising his
art on the boards, exercising his wits in the streets, and even getting access to
the palace of the queen. Meanwhile his extraordinarily gifted sister, let us suppose, remained at home. She was as adventurous, as imaginative, as agog to
see the world as he was. But she was not sent to school. She had no chance of
learning grammar and logic, let alone of reading Horace and Virgil. She
picked up a book now and then, one of her brother's perhaps, and read a few
pages. But then her parents came in and told her to mend the stockings or
mind the stew and not moon about with books and papers. They would have
spoken sharply but kindly, for they were substantial people who knew the conditions of life for a woman and loved their daughter—indeed, more likely than
not she was the apple of her father's eye. Perhaps she scribbled some pages up
in an apple loft on the sly, but was careful to hide them or set fire to them.
Soon, however, before she was out of her teens, she was to be betrothed to the
son of a neighbouring wool-stapler. She cried out that marriage was hateful to
her, and for that she was severely beaten by her father. Then he ceased to scold
her. He begged her instead not to hurt him, not to shame him in this matter
of her marriage. He would give her a chain of beads or a fine petticoat, he
said; and there were tears in his eyes. How could she disobey him? How could
she break his heart? The force of her own gift alone drove her to it. She made
up a small parcel of her belongings, let herself down by a rope one summer's
night and took the road to London. She was not seventeen. The birds that
sang in the hedge were not more musical than she was. She had the quickest
fancy, a gift like her brother's, for the tune of words. Like him, she had a taste
for the theatre. She stood at the stage door; she wanted to act, she said. Men
laughed in her face. The manager—a fat, loose-lipped man—guffawed. He bel-
lowed something about poodles dancing and women acting—no woman, he
said, could possibly be an actress. He hinted—you can imagine what. She

could get no training in her craft. Could she even seek her dinner in a tavern or roam the streets at midnight? Yet her genius was for fiction and lusted to feed abundantly upon the lives of men and women and the study of their ways. At last—for she was very young, oddly like Shakespeare the poet in her face, with the same grey eyes and rounded brows—at last Nick Greene the actor-manager took pity on her; she found herself with child by that gentleman and so—who shall measure the heat and violence of the poet's heart when caught and tangled in a woman's body?—killed herself one winter's night and lies buried at some cross-roads where the omnibuses now stop outside the Elephant and Castle.

That, more or less, is how the story would run, I think, if a woman in   4
Shakespeare's day had had Shakespeare's genius. But for my part, I agree with the deceased bishop, if such he was—it is unthinkable that any woman in Shakespeare's day should have had Shakespeare's genius. For genius like Shakespeare's is not born among labouring, uneducated, servile people. It was not born in England among the Saxons and the Britons. It is not born today among the working classes. How, then, could it have been born among women whose work began, according to Professor Trevelyan, almost before they were out of the nursery, who were forced to it by their parents and held to it by all the power of law and custom?

Anita K. Blair

Shattering the Myth of the Glass Ceiling

Anita K. Blair is the executive vice president of the Independent Women's Forum, a conservative women's lobbying group based in Arlington, Virginia. She has been outspoken as a defender of the status quo in the women's rights movement. As a trustee of the all-male Virginia Military Institute, she defended the college's decision not to admit women into its ranks. Here, she suggests that women have moved to a position of near-equality with men, and so no special efforts are necessary to "raise" the status of women any further.

WE OFTEN HEAR THAT WOMEN HAVE BEEN the biggest beneficiaries of affirma-   1
tive action. In fact, whether the credit belongs to affirmative action policies, the birth control pill, economic growth or a combination of factors, women have made remarkable progress in the last 30 years. Why have women succeeded so well while other minorities have not?

First, of course, women aren't a minority; they constitute more than 51%   2 of the U.S. population. But like racial and ethnic minorities, until the 1960s, women generally lacked access to educational and employment opportunities. What did they do when previously closed doors began to open for them? Government-gathered statistics tell the story.

3   Women went to college. In 1960, only 19% of bachelor's degrees were awarded to women. By 1992, women received 55% of bachelor's degrees and 54% of master's degrees. Note that these figures exceed the percentage of women in the population.

4   In 1960, women received only 5.5% of medical doctor degrees and 2.5% of juris doctor degrees. By 1992, women represented more than 35% of new physicians and 42% of new lawyers. Today, women constitute more than 22% of doctors and almost 25% of lawyers and judges.

5   Women also left home and went to work. Today, women constitute 46% of the civilian work force overall. Among women 25 to 54, 74% work outside the home. This includes 60% of married women, up from 32% in 1960.

6   We often hear about a "wage gap" between women and men. In 1992, the ratio of female to male, year-round, fulltime earnings was 71 cents to the dollar. This includes workers of all ages and all types of jobs. Among workers 25 to 34, the 1992 ratio was 82 cents on the dollar. And in a real "apples to apples" comparison, the gap narrows more. June E. O'Neill, director of the Congressional Budget Office, did a study based on the National Longitudinal Survey of Youth by Ohio State University's Center for Human Resources Research. O'Neill found that among people 27 to 33 who have never had a child, women's earnings were about 98% of men's. Similar results occur if you compare the earnings of women and men of the same education and experience in the same professions.

7   Women outnumber men in several significant job areas. For example, women far outnumber men in health and medicine management (79% female) and personnel and labor relations management (61% female). Women constitute 64% of workers in technical, sales and administrative support and about 60% of workers in service jobs. These are among the fastest growing occupations in America.

8   Consider, on the other hand, the jobs where men predominate. Women constitute only 24% of machine operators and laborers, 19% of farming, forestry and fishing workers and 9% of production, craft, and repair workers. The Bureau of Labor Statistics says these are among America's fastest declining occupations. Thus women are concentrated in occupations with good prospects for growth.

9   Women also have created jobs, for themselves and others. In 1980, there were about 2 million women-owned businesses with about $25 billion in sales. Today, according to the National Foundation for Women Business Owners, nearly 8 million companies with more than $2.25 trillion in sales are

owned by women. One in four American workers is employed by a
woman-owned business.

Should affirmative action policies receive the credit for women's success?   10
Assume it's true. What lessons can we learn about the future of affirmative action? First, merely opening doors—the classic meaning of "affirmative action"—can accomplish a lot if the people who walk through the doors have
done their homework by staying in school and getting the training necessary
to qualify for jobs they want.

Second, dictating results—as "affirmative action" has come to do through   11
quotas, goals, preferences and set-asides—not only doesn't help but probably
hurts. Suppose women had dedicated all their efforts to penetrating the
male-dominated trades mentioned above? They'd have a bleak future, as technology would have marched on anyway, and women would have missed the
new opportunities made possible by the technological revolution. Instead,
women today are well positioned to participate in the information age.

Finally, the era of affirmative action should teach us that any program pur-   12
portedly designed to achieve goals must achieve or die. If affirmative action
has served its purpose, it should be ended. If, after 30 years, it has not served
its purpose, it definitely should be ended.

Susan Bianchi-Sand

The Glass Ceiling Hurts Business Too

Susan Bianchi-Sand began her career path as an advocate of equal pay for equal work in 1969, when she took
a job as a stewardess for United Airlines. Appalled by the inequities she saw there, she ran for and won a seat
as president of the flight attendants union. Now Chair and Executive Director of the National Committee on Pay
Equity, she continues to work for equal pay and affirmative action.

IN RECENT MONTHS A CONSERVATIVE GROUP OF THINKERS has been passing off   1
the report *Women's Figures* as evidence that the glass ceiling is a myth, that the
wage gap doesn't exist and that feminists are on a mission to sucker the American woman into a victim mentality.

Debunking the backlash
This theory is circulating widely among the press—perhaps because it is con-   2
troversial and contradicts what has become rather boring to the media—but

what remains the real life experiences of women and people of color — no real change in the wage gap and no improvement in the glass ceiling.

3   Let's take a closer look at the glass ceiling "myth."

4   At the urging of former Secretary of Labor Elizabeth Dole, Republican President George Bush appointed a bipartisan Glass Ceiling Commission of leaders from a balanced constituency of the business community, civil rights groups and women's organizations to investigate the phenomenon of the "glass ceiling."

5   After two years of intensive study, focus groups, literature reviews and surveys of corporate America, the bipartisan Commission issued a fact-finding report, *Good for Business: Making Full Use of the Nation's Human Capital.* The report concluded that a serious problem exists within business that prevents highly educated and qualified women and people of color from reaching their potential in leadership positions within corporations. It said that the glass ceiling is experienced in various ways for women and people of color depending on their gender, race, ethnicity and national origin, and that it effectively results in the under-utilization of talent, skill and education of some of this nation's finest workers.

It's homogeneous at the top

6   The Commission found that less than five percent of all senior managers and executive positions were occupied by women. In addition, it found that 97% of the top male positions were held by white men.

7   The Commission went to great lengths to capture the subtle as well as overt experiences of discrimination in the workforce and its relationship to promotions and pay.

8   It looked at the "pipeline" to executive-level positions and found that highly-skilled, educated and otherwise qualified women and people of color were routinely denied admission to this training ground and "weeded out" while white male workers gained mentoring, assignments and career opportunities that put them on the right track to the top jobs.

9   Moreover, apart from the Commission's work, a mere perusal of the headlines of today's major newspapers indicates that workplace discrimination is hardly an issue of the past. Consider the problems within Mitsubishi, Texaco, the Citadel, the Navy and the Army, to name a few.

Gauging the wage gap

10   Actually, the glass ceiling begins very early, and can be measured through a number of different indicators. One measure is the earnings ratio between women and men—or the wage gap.

11   According to the U.S. Department of Commerce, Census Bureau, women earned only 71% of men's annual earnings in 1995. Even when one compares

earnings data for recent college graduates—as the U.S. Department of Education did in its recent report *Baccalaureate and Beyond,* women earn 15.7% less than men.

Another Education Department study, *Women at Thirtysomething,* found   12
that women who graduated from the class of 1972 failed to earn job opportunities and pay equal to men in all but seven occupations—even when they clearly had surpassed the men in the classroom.

That lower wage haunts women into their careers and becomes part of the   13
"objective" criteria that influences promotion decisions. Consider the case of two sales workers—according to the U.S. Bureau of Labor Statistics, the man who sells insurance earns on average $777 per week compared to the woman who sells insurance at an average weekly wage of $453. When a supervisory position comes open, the man looks better qualified, more "valuable" on paper, simply because he earns higher wages. The woman's lower earnings contribute to the glass ceiling effect.

A foot in the door

Overcoming the glass ceiling means more than just getting the right credentials   14
for the job. Because the reality of the labor market is not just *what* you know, and what you can do, but *who* you know and who will give you a chance.

Affirmative action has never been about substituting opportunity and fair-   15
ness for credentials and qualifications. It simply is ludicrous to maintain that all businesses should hire women and people of color just for representational purposes. Such a policy does no one any good.

Rather, affirmative action is the policy of giving opportunity to all who are   16
qualified. Not only has it been to the advantage of families and individuals, but it has been good for business. Just ask Xerox, Johnson and Johnson, Hewlett Packard and others.

The bottom line

Bottom line—the increased growth of women and people of color into the   17
marketplace has been a bonus and helped to create the strong economy we enjoy currently. The only choice we have is to open the door wider to en-courage talent of all shapes, sizes and colors to walk through.

In fact, propagating the glass ceiling as a myth steers a good business prac-   18
tice down a narrow one-way alley of limited talent and potential. Businesses that fail to reach beyond the glass ceiling barrier to effectively utilize all of our nation's talent and skills will cheat only themselves.

Patricia Curtis

The Argument Against Animal Experimentation

In 1978, Patricia Curtis shocked many readers of *The New York Times* with her graphic depiction of the world of animal experimentation. Today the animal rights movement is well known, and many of the practices Curtis describes have been banned. Now an author of children's books on animals, Curtis's most recent book is *Animals You Never Even Heard Of*.

1   THE PROFESSOR WAS LATE LEAVING THE MEDICAL SCHOOL because he'd had to review papers by his third-year students in experimental surgery. It was well after 11 when he wearily drove his car into the garage. The house was dark except for a hall light left on for him. His wife and youngsters were already asleep, he realized, and the professor suddenly felt lonely as he fit his key in the lock. But even as he pushed open the door, Sabrina was there to welcome him. She was always waiting for him, lying on the rug just inside the door.

2   The little dog leaped up ecstatically, wagging her tail and licking the professor's hand. The professor stroked her affectionately. She flopped on her back and grinned at him as he tickled her chest and belly; then she jumped to her feet and danced around his legs as he walked into the kitchen to get something to eat. Sabrina's exuberant joy at his return never failed to cheer him.

3   Early next morning, the professor drove back to the medical school and entered the laboratory. He noticed that a dog on which one of his students had operated the previous afternoon still had an endotracheal tube in its throat and obviously had not received pain medication. He must be more strict in his orders, he thought to himself. Another dog had bled through its bandages and lay silently in a pool of blood. Sloppy work, the professor thought—must speak to that student. None of the dogs made any sounds, because new arrivals at the laboratory were always subjected to an operation called a ventriculocordectomy that destroyed their vocal cords so that no barks or howls disturbed people in the medical school and surrounding buildings.

4   The professor looked over the animals that would be used that day by his surgery students. He came across a new female dog that had just been delivered by the dealer. Badly frightened, she whined and wagged her tail ingratiatingly as he paused in front of her cage. The professor felt a stab. The small dog bore an amazing resemblance to Sabrina. Quickly he walked away. Nev-

ertheless, he made a note to remind himself to give orders for her vocal cords to be destroyed and for her to be conditioned for experimental surgery.

American researchers sacrifice approximately 64 million animals annually. Some 400,000 dogs, 200,000 cats, 33,000 apes and monkeys, thousands of horses, ponies, calves, sheep, goats and pigs, and millions of rabbits, hamsters, guinea pigs, birds, rats and mice are used every year in experiments that often involve intense suffering. The research establishment has generally insisted that live animals provide the only reliable tests for drugs, chemicals and cosmetics that will be used by people. Researchers also believe that animal experiments are necessary in the search for cures for human illnesses and defects. There is no question that many important medical discoveries, from polio vaccine to the physiology of the stress response, have indeed been made through the use of animals. Thus universities, medical and scientific institutions, pharmaceutical companies, cosmetics manufacturers and the military have always taken for granted their right to use animals in almost any way they see fit.

But increasing numbers of scientists are beginning to ask themselves some hard ethical questions and to re-evaluate their routine use of painful testing tools such as electric shock, stomach tubes, hot plates, restraining boxes and radiation devices. A new debate has arisen over whether all such experiments are worth the suffering they entail.

Strongly opposing curtailment of animal experimentation are groups such as the National Society for Medical Research, which insists that any such reduction would jeopardize public safety and scientific progress. The N.S.M.R. was formed to resist what it considers the threat of Government regulation of animal research and to refute the charges of humane societies. Many scientists, however, although they firmly believe that some animal research is necessary, no longer endorse such an absolutist approach to the issue.

"Some knowledge can be obtained at too high a price," writes British physiologist Dr. D. H. Smyth in his recent book *Alternatives to Animal Experiments*.

"The lives and suffering of animals must surely count for something," says Jeremy J. Stone, director of the Washington-based Federation of American Scientists, which has devoted an entire newsletter to a discussion of the rights of animals.

According to physiologist Dr. F. Barbara Orlans of the National Institutes of Health, "Within the scientific community there's a growing concern for animals that has not yet had a forum." Dr. Orlans is president of the newly formed Scientists' Center for Animal Welfare, which hopes to raise the level of awareness on the part of fellow scientists and the public about avoidable suffering inflicted on lab animals, wildlife, and animals raised for meat. "We will try to be a voice of reason. We can perhaps be a link between scientists and the humane organizations," Dr. Orlans explains. "We hope also to provide solid factual data on which animal-protection decisions can be based."

11   Another link between researchers and humane organizations is a new committee comprising more than 400 doctors and scientists that has been formed by Friends of Animals, a national animal-welfare group. Headed by eight M.D.s, the committee is making a survey of Federally funded animal-research projects. Friends of Animals hopes that the study will expose not only needless atrocities performed on animals, but also boondoggles involving taxpayers' money.

12   One reason scientists are no longer so indifferent to the suffering they inflict on animals is the discoveries that science itself has made. We now know that many animals feel, think, reason, communicate, have sophisticated social systems, and even, on occasion, behave altruistically toward each other. Communication by sign language with higher primates, demonstrations of the intelligence of dolphins and whales, observations of the complex societies of wolves and other animals, and many other investigations have narrowed the gap between ourselves and the rest of the animal kingdom, making it more difficult to rationalize inhumane experiments. Dr. Dallas Pratt, author of *Painful Experiments on Animals,* points out that "among the rats and mice, the computers and oscilloscopes, there is Koko"—referring to the young gorilla whom a California primatologist has taught a working vocabulary of 375 words and concepts in sign language and who has even learned to take snapshots with a Polaroid camera. It's hard not to feel squeamish about subjecting animals to inhumane experiments when they possess almost-human intelligence.

13   The thinking of researchers is also beginning to be affected by the growing movement for animal rights. The rising concern for the welfare of animals is seen by some people as a natural extension of contemporary movements promoting civil rights, women's rights, homosexual rights, human rights, and children's rights. Public interest in preserving endangered species is based first on an increasing awareness of the complexity and fragility of ecosystems, and second on the notion, still much debated, that any species of plant or animal, from the lowly snail darter to the blue whale, has the right to continue to exist. From here it is only a short logical step to the belief that animals have the right to exist without suffering unnecessarily.

14   Near the top of the list of animal-welfare activists' causes is putting an end to inhumane experiments on laboratory animals. In Great Britain, where a vigorous antivivisection movement has existed for more than a century, a clandestine group called the Animal Liberation Front conducts commando-style raids on laboratories, liberating animals and sabotaging research equipment. A.L.F. members have also been known to slash tires and pour sugar in the gas tanks of trucks used by animal dealers who supply labs. To be sure, this group of zealots hasn't made much of a dent in England's vast research community, but it does appeal to a gut reaction on the part of many Britons against animal research.

Animal-rights activists are not merely sentimental do-gooders and pet-   15
lovers. They have mounted a philosophical attack on the traditional Western attitude toward animals, branding it as "speciesist" (like racist or sexist),
a term derived from the word "speciesism," coined by psychologist and author Dr. Richard Ryder. The Australian philosopher Peter Singer, in his influential 1975 book *Animal Liberation,* argued that the "speciesist" rational-
ization, "Human beings come first," is usually used by people who do nothing for either human or nonhuman animals. And he pointed out the parallels between the oppression of blacks, women, and animals: Such oppression is usually rationalized on the grounds that the oppressed group is infe-
rior.

In 1977, when outraged antivivisectionists heard about some highly un-   16
pleasant electric-shock and burn experiments conducted on young pigs in Den-
mark, they wasted no time in pointing out the irony that the tests were being
conducted by Amnesty International, the human-rights organization. Amnesty
International was attempting to prove that human prisoners could be tortured
without leaving any marks, and pigs were used because of the similarity of their
skin to ours. (The tests were subsequently discontinued.)

Paradoxically, the public tends to be "speciesist" in its reaction to animal   17
experimentation: For many people, a test is permissible when it inflicts pain
on a "lower" animal like a hamster, but not when the victim is a dog. When
it was discovered in the summer of 1976 that the American Museum of Natural History was damaging the brains of cats and running painful sex experiments on them, hundreds of people picketed in protest. The museum's Animal Behavior Department defended itself on the grounds that the research
was intended to gain a better understanding of human sexual responses. Animal-rights groups, scientists among them, were not convinced of the necessity
of the tests, which came to an end only when the chief researcher retired. But
the protesters made no stir about the pigeons, doves, and rats that suffered in
the same laboratory.

If United States Army researchers had used guinea pigs instead of beagles   18
when they tried out a poison gas, they probably would not have provoked the
public outcry that resulted in the curtailment of their funding in 1974. When
a few Avon saleswomen quit their jobs last spring after reading about painful
eye-makeup tests the company conducts on rabbits, they did not complain
about the thousands of guinea pigs and rats Avon routinely puts to death in
acute-toxicity tests.

It is not known whether any single vertebrate species is more or less im-   19
mune to pain than another. A neat line cannot be drawn across the evolu-
tionary scale dividing the sensitive from the insensitive. Yet the suffering of
laboratory rats and mice is regarded as trivial by scientists and the public alike.
These rodents have the dubious honor of being our No. 1 experimental ani-

mals, composing possibly 75 percent of America's total lab-animal population. As Russell Baker once wrote, "This is no time to be a mouse."

20　　Rats and mice are specifically excluded from a Federal law designed to give some protection to laboratory animals. The Animal Welfare Act, passed in 1966 and amended in 1970, is administered by the Department of Agriculture and covers only about 4 percent of laboratory animals. Animal advocates worked hard for the bill, which sets some standards for the housing of animals in laboratories and at the dealers' facilities from which many of them are obtained. But the law places no restrictions on the kinds of experiments to which animals may be subjected. It does indicate that pain-relieving drugs should be used on the few types of animals it covers—but it includes a loophole so as not to inhibit researchers unduly. If a scientist claims that pain is a necessary part of an experiment, anesthetics or analgesics may be withheld.

21　　One standard test conducted on rats by drug companies is called the "writhing test" because of the agonized way the animals react to irritants injected into their abdomens. Paradoxically, this test assesses the efficacy of pain-killers, which are administered only after the rats show signs of acute suffering.

22　　Equally common are psychological experiments in "learned helplessness" that have been conducted on rats, dogs, and other kinds of animals. In some of these tests, caged animals are given painful electric shocks until they learn certain maneuvers to obtain their food. As they become adept at avoiding the shocks, the researchers keep changing the rules so that the animals have to keep learning more and more ways to avoid shocks. Ultimately no way remains to escape, and the animals simply give up and lie on the floors of their cages, passively receiving shock after shock. Researchers have attempted to draw parallels between "learned helplessness" and depression in human beings, but some critics have difficulty perceiving their necessity. "What more are we going to learn about human depression by continuing to produce immobility in animals?" asks former animal experimenter Dr. Roger Ulrich, now a research professor of psychology at Western Michigan University.

23　　Electric shock is widely used on many different kinds of animals in various types of research. In one experiment typical of a series that has been under way since 1966 at the Armed Forces Radiobiology Research Institute in Bethesda, Md., 10 rhesus monkeys were starved for 18 hours and then "encouraged" with electric prods to run rapidly on treadmills. This went on for several weeks before the monkeys were subjected to 4,600 rads of gamma-neutron radiation. Then they were retested on the treadmills for six hours, and subsequently for two hours each day until they died. Mean survival time for the vomiting, incapacitated monkeys was recorded in A.F.R.R.I.'s report as 37 hours. Dogs have been used in similar experiments, whose purpose is to get an idea of the effects of radiation on human endurance.

Now A.F.R.R.I. and other American research facilities are having to look   24
for new sources of monkeys. In March 1978, the Government of India banned
further export of rhesus monkeys to the United States. The native population
was dwindling and Prime Minister Morarji R. Desai cited violations of a previous agreement that restricted the use of rhesus monkeys to medical research
under humane conditions. "There is no difference between cruelty to animals
and cruelty to human beings," the ascetic Prime Minister stated. The International Primate Protection League, a four-year-old watchdog group whose
members include many scientists and especially primatologists (Jane Goodall,
for one), had spread word in the Indian press that American scientists were
using rhesus monkeys in grisly trauma experiments. According to the Primate
Protection League, these tests included dipping monkeys in boiling water at
the University of Kansas, shooting them in the face with high-powered rifles
at the University of Chicago, and slamming them in the stomach with a can-
non-impactor traveling at a speed of 70 miles per hour at the University of
Michigan.

"I feel justified in stating that fully 80 percent of the experiments involv-   25
ing rhesus monkeys are either unnecessary, represent useless duplication of
previous work, or could utilize nonanimal alternatives," wrote Illinois Wes-
leyan University biologist Dr. John E. McArdle, a specialist in primate func-
tional anatomy, in a letter to Prime Minister Desai, who so far has held firm
despite pressure from the American scientific community to rescind the ban.
In the meantime, researchers are making do with non-Indian rhesus monkeys
and a close relative, the crab-eating macaque.

One of the arguments in favor of animal tests is that under the controlled   26
circumstances of the experimental laboratory they are likely to be objective
and consistent. But the results of the same tests conducted on the same kinds
of animals often differ from one laboratory to the next. When 25 cooperating
companies, including Avon, Revlon, and American Cyanamid, conducted a
comprehensive study of eye- and skin-irritation tests using rabbits, the results
varied widely. The study concluded that these tests "should not be recommended as standard procedures in any new regulations" because they yielded
"unreliable results."

One of these tests, the Draize Ophthalmic Irritancy Test, is used to evalu-   27
ate the effect upon the eyes of household and aerosol products, shampoos,
and eye makeup. Rabbits are used because their eyes do not have effective tear
glands and thus cannot easily flush away or dissolve irritants. The animals are
pinioned in stocks and their eyes are exposed to a substance until inflamma-
tion, ulceration, or gross damage occurs.

Many investigators concede that the data provided by such experiments   28
are often inconsistent and that the stresses caused by crowded cages, callous
treatment, pain, and fear can affect animals' metabolisms and thus confuse

test results. "Since there is hardly a single organ or biochemical system in the body that is not affected by stress," says Dr. Harold Hillman, a British physiologist, "it is almost certainly the main reason for the wide variation reported among animals on whom painful experiments have been done."

29   Very often, different species respond differently to substances or situations. The rationale for many animal tests is that they predict human reactions, but thalidomide, for example, did not produce deformities in the fetuses of dogs, cats, monkeys, and hamsters. On the other hand, insulin has been proved harmful to rabbits and mice although it saves human lives.

30   Researchers are becoming increasingly dubious about the efficacy of the LD/50, a test for acute toxicity that consists of force-feeding a group of animals a specific substance until half of them die, ostensibly providing a quantitative measure of how poisonous the substance is. In *Painful Experiments on Animals,* Dr. Pratt asks what we learn from forcing hair dye or face powder into a dog or rat through a stomach tube until its internal organs rupture.

31   One small victory for animal-welfare activists that was hailed by many American scientists was the 1975 Canadian ban on the use of vertebrate animals by students participating in science fairs. Children had been awarded prizes for attempting heart-transplant surgery on unanesthetized rabbits, amputating the feet of lizards, performing Caesarean operations on pregnant mice, bleeding dogs into a state of shock and blinding pigeons. Remarking that such "experiments" were a distortion of the spirit of research, science fair officials ruled out all such projects except observations of the normal living patterns of wild or domestic animals.

32   In this country, the search for adequate substitutes for laboratory animals was officially launched last summer when the year-old American Fund for Alternatives to Animal Research made its first grant—$12,500 to a biology professor at Whitman College in Walla Walla, Wash. The award to Dr. Earl William Fleck will help finance his development of a test substituting one-celled organisms called tetrahymena for animals in screening substances for teratogens, agents that can cause birth defects. It is expected that the test, if and when perfected, will be cheaper, quicker, more accurate, and certainly more humane than putting thousands of pregnant animals to death.

33   According to veterinarian Thurman Grafton, executive director of the National Society for Medical Research, people who talk about alternatives to animals are creating false hopes. "These new technologies can only be adjuncts to the use of animals," he claims. "While they serve a purpose in furnishing clues as to what direction a type of research might take, you will always ultimately need an intact animal with all its living complications and interchanging biochemical functions to properly assay a drug."

34   "Not so," says Ethel Thurston, administrator of the American Fund for Al-

ternatives. "Enough progress has already been made to indicate that certain techniques can completely replace animals."

Several of these techniques have been developed over the last five years in Great Britain, where the Lord Dowding Fund for Humane Research has given grants totaling more than $400,000 to dozens of scientists engaged in research aimed at finding experimental substitutes for animals. Dowding is currently financing several developmental studies of the Ames Test, a promising technique invented by a Berkeley biochemistry professor, Dr. Bruce Ames, that uses salmonella bacteria rather than animals to determine the carcinogenic properties of chemicals. (It was the Ames Test that recently revealed the possible carcinogenic dangers of certain hair dyes.) Another Dowding Fund recipient, research physician Dr. John C. Petricciani, now with the Food and Drug Administration, has devised a method of assessing how tumors grow by inoculating the tumor cells into skin from 9-day-old chicken embryos instead of into living animals. 35

Animal tests are frequently replaced by other methods discovered and developed by scientists like Dr. Ames who are not trying to avoid the use of animals per se but are simply searching for simpler and more cost-efficient ways to achieve their goals. Dr. Hans Stich, a Canadian cancer researcher, for example, has devised a new test for detecting carcinogenicity in chemicals; it uses human cells, takes one week and costs only about $260. The traditional method, using rats and mice, takes three years and costs approximately $150,000. 36

In addition to egg embryos, bacteria, and simple organisms, possible substitutes for animals include tissue cultures, human and other mammal cells grown in test tubes, and organ banks. Preserved human corneas, for instance, might be used to spare rabbits the agony of the Draize test. Computers could also play a role if researchers used them fully to analyze experimental data, predict the properties of new drugs, and test theoretical data. Computers can even be programmed to simulate living processes. Mechanical models and audio-visual aids can and do substitute for animals as teaching instruments. Simulated human models could provide valid information in car-crash tests. 37

Last winter, Representative Robert F. Drinan, Democrat of Massachusetts, introduced a bill authorizing the Department of Health, Education and Welfare to fund projects aimed at discovering research methods that would reduce both the numbers of animals used in laboratories and the suffering to which they are subjected. 38

Meanwhile, medical and military research and an unending stream of new pharmaceutical, cosmetic, and household products are resulting in an ever-increasing use of animals in the laboratory. 39

The most recent and thorough exploration of alternatives is Dr. D. H. Smyth's book *Alternatives to Animal Experiments*, which examines every option 40 and weighs its pros and cons. He concludes that there is certainly reason to hope that the numbers of laboratory animals can be drastically reduced, but also warns that it is unlikely a complete phasing out of animal experimentation will happen soon. "By the time we can produce complete alternatives to living tissue," Dr. Smyth writes, "we will not need those alternatives because we will already understand how living tissues work."

41   Still, Dr. Smyth asks, "Does this mean we can perpetrate any cruelty on animals to satisfy scientific curiosity in the hope that it will one day be useful? To me it certainly does not. . . . Everyone has a right to decide that certain procedures are unacceptable."

42   Richard Ryder calls animal experimenters to task for trying to have it both ways: Researchers defend their work scientifically on the basis of the *similarities* between human beings and animals, but defend it morally on the basis of the *differences*.

43   And there's the rub: The differences aren't as reassuringly clearcut as they once were. We now know that some animals have a more highly developed intelligence than some human beings—infants, for example, or the retarded and the senile. Dr. Ryder asks, "If we were to be discovered by some more intelligent creatures in the universe, would they be justified in experimenting on us?"

Linda Hasselstrom

The Cow versus the Animal Rights Activist

People often ask Linda Hasselstrom (b. 1943) why she doesn't devote herself full-time to either writing or ranching, although she's been quite successful doing both. Her response is characteristically down-to-earth: "I'm often tired, but never bored. When I'm confronted with a job I detest, six other jobs I prefer can delay it another day." Her writings often focus on her own connection to the land and the lessons she has learned from that association. While the result, in less apt hands, would soon devolve into dogmatic drivel, Hasselstrom somehow strikes the right balance—she rarely sounds like she's preaching. In this excerpt from *Land Circle*, Hasselstrom again uses her own experience as a rancher to dispute animal rights activists' claims that raising and killing animals for food is immoral.

1   I'M A RANCHER; BEEF CATTLE PROVIDE MOST OF MY MONEY and food. I *like* cows; I've had a warm partnership with them for thirty-five years. I admire a cow's instincts, and suspect her of having a sense of humor, as well as of knowing

more than we think. I envy her adaptation to the arid plains, and her apparent serenity in emergencies.

I also love to cut into a tender sirloin steak with a hint of pink in the center, and dip each bite into the luscious brown juice surrounding the potatoes on my plate. I relish each mouthful, thinking dreamily of the cow whose flesh I'm eating; I remember when she was born, how she became crippled so that her destiny became the dark freezer in my basement rather than the meat department of a brightly lighted supermarket. I have always considered that the relationship between me and my cattle was a little like a good marriage, with good days and bad days, but considerable satisfaction on both sides.   2

Suddenly my personal paradox has frightening possibilities, because animal rights activists are declaring in sizeable headlines that it is not possible to love animals and also kill them. Anyone who says so, they declare, is vicious, sadistic, and untrustworthy. Some extremists declare that doing anything at all with an animal but letting it follow its normal patterns is immoral, and others declare that we have no right to experiment with animals even to save human lives. Ranchers are targets because we confine cattle in pastures, brand them with hot irons, and cut sections out of their ears to show ownership. Those, say the activists, are the actions of exploiters, unfit to be environmentalists or associate with your daughter. Activists have destroyed research labs to free the animals, sometimes loosing dangerous bacteria. Some deer and bison lovers follow hunters into the woods, shouting to frighten the game. One screaming activist repeatedly whacked and poked a bison hunter with the point of a ski pole; the hunter, a model of nonviolence, neither screamed back nor made threatening gestures with his Rolling Block .45-70, capable of decimating an activist with one shot. In a middle-sized town near our ranch, activists scream obscenities and spit on women in fur coats. At a National Cattlemen's Association meeting, a speaker warned ranchers that new employees may work undercover for animal rights groups. An auction yard in Dixon, California, and a meatpacking plant in San Jose were torched by arsonists, and an unlit Molotov cocktail lobbed into the offices of the California Cattlemen's Association. A popular country singer, k.d. lang, was part of a "Meat Stinks" campaign supported by People for the Ethical Treatment of Animals, a group that opposes using animals "other than for companionship." Radio and television stations in beef-producing areas, including South Dakota, promptly stopped playing all of lang's records. I was disappointed; watching lang croon sweet nothings into the ear of a dairy cow—in no danger of being eaten because she is too valuable as a milk factory, and tough as guitar strings—was the highlight of my television watching.   3

Her problem, and the difficulty of the ski pole-wielding activist confronting the bison hunter, is lack of information. The beef cattle industry has three major phases. First, farmers and ranchers own basic herds and   4 produce breeding cattle, or yearlings sold as feeders. They keep the breeding cattle, and sell the yearlings at a sale market where the price is determined by supply and demand, and by bidders. When the ranchers sell, they have no opportunity to add costs of materials to the product, passing expenses on to the consumer as most businesses do. Ranchers take the price offered on sale day, or take the cattle home—where they will require more care, more expense.

5   The second phase of the beef cattle industry consists of stocker operators whose pastures put additional weight on feeder cattle before they enter feedlots, the third phase. Confined in muddy, stinking feedlots, cattle consume huge quantities of pesticide-laced grain designed to make the meat fat enough for consumer preference, and produce immense amounts of polluted runoff. The dangers posed to humans by the chemicals in both the meat and runoff have drawn environmentalists' attention to the cattle industry—but they are attacking the wrong end of production. Feedlots are generally operated by corporations that control feeding, butchering, and in some cases supermarket sales of meat, grain, and associated products. In 1988, three companies—Iowa Beef Packing (IBP, owned by Occidental Petroleum), ConAgra, and Excel (Cargill)—accounted for 70 percent of all fed cattle slaughtered in the United States. These monopolies, which also control a considerable amount of the nation's grain, flour, pork, egg, and poultry production, do pass costs to the consumers, hiking prices far above what ranchers get for their labor. But enormous corporations are tough to find and difficult to move; it's easier to attack individual hunters and ranchers.

6   I'm afraid that one day I'll be sweating and swearing in the corral, struggling to brand calves twice my weight, and suddenly find I'm surrounded by people with no sense of humor who have come to "liberate" my cows.

7   I'd like to discourage that kind of behavior, partly because some ranchers are impatient and armed, and partly because it's based on lack of information. Unchecked ignorance and paranoia can escalate misunderstandings to bloodshed. And some of my cows, unaccustomed to noise and rudeness, might kick the strangers, who would sue me, not the cows.

8   I recognize the difficulty many people face in reconciling their love of animals with their love of meat, but I believe the problem is increasing because we are getting further from the realities of human existence. As we developed our large brain, we also built a complicated set of desires that seems to imply that enough wealth will allow us to sit still. We want our food to be easily obtainable; now that we no longer have to run it down and beat it to death, many of us buy it precooked. When someone markets predigested dinners, there will be buyers. But many of us will continue to wear leather shoes, lust after leather skirts and jackets and leather upholstery on our car seats, and relish a good steak or hamburger. As long as humans have such desires but re-

main unwilling or unable to slaughter and skin the animals that can satisfy them, ranchers will be needed.

In defense, beef industry representatives say a pregnant woman produces four hundred thousand times as much estrogen every day as she would get from the average serving of beef injected with growth-inducing hormones. I've spent my life doing hard physical labor while eating organically raised cattle, so I understand the healthy properties of red meat, and I despair at the perception among many Americans that this tasty stuff isn't good for them. I am part of an industry that requires me to donate one dollar from each animal sold to the Beef Check-Off plan, which promotes the facts about eating beef and health—a group defense instituted, reluctantly, by cattle ranchers in response to misinformation spread by antibeef activists. In part, this idea comes from paranoia about cholesterol and growth hormones; in part, it's a result of government-subsidized campaigns by producers of other foods. In many countries, the beef I eat in a year would make a family wealthy, but I am frustrated by being unable to sell directly to consumers beef raised on grass that is the natural product of my land.   9

Like most ranchers, I work more closely with cows than any animal rights activist I've ever met. I kneel in steaming cow manure and hot urine while talking kindly to a cow and urging a calf from her birth canal. I must brand calves so they won't stray or be stolen; castrate bulls to make them edible steers and protect bloodlines. I've cut cows' throats, helped gut and skin them, and canned every edible part of them for my family's use; in the process I've gained a deep appreciation for what killing our own meat can mean to humans. Because of this close involvement with the lives of cows, I feel I have worked hard for the right to eat their flesh. My relationship with cows is intimate, balanced—the cow is capable of killing or injuring me—and demands the most complete responsibility from the human half of the equation. The relationship is reviewed by both parties almost daily, and its implications carefully considered at least by the human half. Who knows what the cows are thinking?   10

Animal rights activists seem to me guilty of simplistic thinking and tunnel vision, although I envy people who forswear *all* killing and eating of flesh; I believe they have an easier road than those of us who try to strike a balance between exploitation and love. Similarly, I don't consider strolling along behind a fur-wearing woman screaming epithets, or shooting a cow, or burning a packing plant, to be meaningful activism; such actions are too simplistic, and too close to terrorism. During the easy environmentalism of the 1960s, one could lie on the lawn smoking grass on "Gentle Thursdays," sing "We Shall Overcome" and shout "No More War," and go back to class, one's pacifist duty done for the week. During that period, a few hard-working environmentalists passed strict laws which gave us a sense of power, but were some-   11 times as narrow and poorly thought out as the actions behind the corporate greed that made them necessary.

12   All of us—ranchers, environmentalists, and animal rights activists—if we expect to be taken seriously, should put as much work into defining and achieving realistic, fair goals as ranchers spend trying to keep cows alive. Few of us are born with that kind of dedication; we have to develop an interest in detail, a respect for our fellow animals—even Democrats, feminists, and snail darters—and an understanding of our responsibilities to the whole spectrum of life on the planet. What E. B. White wrote nearly sixty years ago is still true:

13   Before you can be an internationalist you have first to be a naturalist and feel the ground under you making a whole circle. It is easier for a man to be loyal to his club than to his planet; the by-laws are shorter, and he is personally acquainted with the other members.

14   The effect of any organization of a social and brotherly nature is to strengthen rather than to diminish the lines which divide people into classes; the effect of states and nations is the same, and eventually these lines will have to be softened, these powers will have to be generalized. It is written on the wall that this is so. I'm not inventing it, I'm just copying it off the wall.

15   Statistics from a few years ago declared that the average American ate fourteen cows in a lifetime, but consumption will drop to a twenty-five-year low in 1990 as hysterical and ill-informed folks screech about the dangers of beef. I've eaten more than my share in an effort to make up for vegetarian relatives and friends. When I calculated this my own family consisted of my parents, and my husband and me; we would butcher two animals, usually heifers, per year. Assuming each of us ate about one-fourth of each animal, I was eating an entire cow every four years, which means I've gobbled upwards of ten so far. If I live to be eighty, as I hope to do, I'll have eaten at least twenty of my own herd, not to mention the beef I eat in restaurants when I'm upholding the honor and economy of ranchers while surrounded by midwesterners lying about how good the frozen fish tastes. I am willing to take responsibility for the deaths of those twenty bovines, because I've saved the lives of many more than that.

16   Vegetarians may whittle the number of beefeaters down, but I'm confident beef will remain part of the American diet. Ranchers are learning to produce lean meat; I believe we will soon begin to move away from the dangerous chemicals and growth hormones we've been talked into using in order to raise productivity above sensible limits. At the same time, we are becoming aware of growing criticism of the damage cattle do to public lands by poorly controlled grazing. Little has been done, however, to control the meat and grain

monopolies which will eventually control our food supplies and determine grocery prices.

It's a popular pastime now to debunk the myth of the independent cowboy and the cattle baron, and rightly so in many ways. Although there's truth to the legends, they were popularized and distorted by dime novels and bad movies; and some cow folk even bought their own advertising campaign or fantasy, and played their roles more eagerly than pulp heroes. They deserve to be reminded of reality. 17

But simply pronouncing the death of the age of the cattle baron and cowboy is too simple. Sure, those men—and their womenfolk—treated the West as if it was their kingdom. They battled its hardships, "civilized" it as they thought best—because they were given a challenge to do so by the wisest spirits of their age. Where I live was "the Great American Desert," shunned by all but the hardiest explorers. Later, the thinkers in their comfy New England offices decided that "rain follows the plow," and all that was needed to make the desert bloom were a few hardy souls to build claim shanties and plow to the horizon. The New England philosophers had no idea what difficult conditions westerners faced, but the westerners went right on working until they controlled everything but the weather. 18

We now see their errors, but we might have been guilty of the same actions, now seen as abuse, had we been cattle barons in those days. And some changes have been made not out of lack of concern, but through economic necessity. Cowboys, paid "forty a month and found," used to ride the range constantly, moving cattle around so that grazing was spread evenly over a wide area. Today workers who might once have become cowboys and cowgirls are instead making big wages in a city, and many ranchers operate alone, or assisted only by their smaller number of children or seasonal help. They have tried to adapt the advice given to farmers by agricultural experts within the government to invest more money, get big, and become efficient, but it didn't work as well on mobile cattle as on rows of corn; it didn't work on corn either, but that's another story, and Wes Jackson is telling it in his sustainable agriculture research at The Land Institute. 19

This generation's heroes are people who work to save our environment: the dead Saint Ed Abbey, Wendell Berry, Wes Jackson, Annie Dillard, Ann Zwinger, Gary Snyder, Barry Lopez, Gretel Ehrlich, Bil Gilbert, Kim Stafford, and other writers who contemplate humanity and nature. Some have attained almost mythical stature themselves, and we all try to learn from and imitate them. We believe, fervently, that they are right; those old ranchers believed in Manifest Destiny and the American Way just as passionately. What if we're wrong again? 20

Instead of blaming ranchers and farmers for doing what they were told to do, environmentalists need to show us what's wrong with the way we graze cat- 21 tle, if they know. Most of the complainers have never been personally introduced to a cow, have no clear idea what's wrong with her grazing habits, and wouldn't know a good stand of native grass if they were lying in it reciting poetry or reading Abbey. They're willing to take someone else's word—just as the ranchers took the government's word for how to use the land. Too many environmentalists condemn without knowledge. None of the rhetoric changes the fact that the grasslands are in trouble, and only the people who own the land are likely to resolve the problems.

22   When I left the ranch, bound for a life of comfortable academic superiority in some ivory tower, I cared considerably less about cows than I do now, though I already knew more than the average American about the brutal facts of bovine life. Living beside a packing plant for a few months made a temporary vegetarian out of me. I saw cows unloaded daily, heard the thud as the knacker's maul struck their foreheads, the bawl of pain as they were swung, only stunned, off their hooves by a hook thrust into an ankle. Sometimes, I could hear the bubbling, choking screech cut short as a worker finally opened a steer's throat. My cat grew sleek dragging home fleshy bones larger than he was, and I watched smugly when a steer escaped and ran through the streets, ineffectually pursued by a police force with little experience in cattle management. But as soon as I moved back to South Dakota, where I look out on my walking larder through every window, I went back to eating meat without hesitation. I earn every mouthful. The outmoded butchering practices used in packing plants have been changed; animals are killed with a gun, rather than stunned, before butchering begins. Other changes in the beef industry show increased awareness of public scrutiny.

23   When I returned to the ranch, I had shed some of the narrow attitudes with which I grew up, and I became involved in the complicated process of keeping a cow alive. I've learned, but I've remained a part of a wider world. Critics think ranch men read only *Farm Journal* and their wives do nothing but cook and raise children, but many are college graduates, and even those who aren't read more widely than their ancestors did. They also watch television; the rest of the world is no longer distant and inaccessible to them. They are informed about conditions in the "outer" world, and aware that most consumers know little about ranching or the food processing industry. For example, while farmers and ranchers know a good deal about what happens to their products—meat, grains, hay—when these leave the land, many folks who buy those products or by-products neatly wrapped in polyethylene haven't a clue about their production, and don't want to. Knowing the origins of our food and frivolities helps us make sensible choices about what we really want; in some cases, the sacrifice is not worth the benefit. When I shop for groceries, I carry a booklet that categorizes products by how socially responsible the producer is. I avoid products if the Council on Economic Priorities re-

ports no reductions in animal testing by those companies, and no company contributions toward alternative research. On the other hand, I wouldn't hesitate to use any compatible animal heart to save the life of a child. But if the child was cocaine-addicted in the womb, and the operation was at taxpayers' expense, I could not support it.

Cattle have been domesticated for centuries, and belong in a separate 24 category from animals bred for laboratory tests, and from wildlife; we are not likely to stop eating and managing cattle herds, nor should we. Wild cattle herds would be hardly more aesthetically satisfying than tame ones, as Indians have discovered while dodging sacred cows. A poorly managed herd of cattle can be as repugnant as Edward Abbey insisted, but that's the fault of the human manager, not the cows. With adequate feed and water and space to move while grazing selectively, a herd of cattle can be at least as acceptable in polite society as the average dog or child. Cattle do attract flies; before poisonous sprays and other costly forms of fly control existed, we built "oilers," slinging old feed sacks on a wire between two posts. We poured used crankcase oil on the cloth (recycling!) and cows rubbed oil on their bodies to discourage flies and lice. When the chemical companies noticed us using a product we didn't buy, they developed spray, injections, and fly-killing ear tags.

But most folks don't know this, because they spend more time with do- 25 mesticated cats and dogs, and half-savage children, than with cows; and it is the activities that result from ignorance that bother me. Since I have become moderately well known as an articulate ranch woman, I've been questioned several times about animal rights.

What do I think of proposed laws to make branding illegal, for example? 26 My reply: the folks who pass that law can find and return or replace the stolen cattle, catch and prosecute the thieves, and pay the costs of the confusion and crime. Branding does hurt, but it places a permanent mark on a cow, so even if she's illegally butchered, an owner has some chance of proving it. No other method is as useful, and I'll consider another method of marking my cattle when we stop licensing cars to identify them and prevent their theft. Every few years, someone suggests that acid brands are more merciful; I'd like that idea tested on the folks who suggest it: which hurts most, a burn with a hot iron, or an acid burn? Even if they are less painful, acid brands might not be enough; local old-timers talk about the days when government agencies used them. Enterprising cowboys sometimes roped the cows, smeared axle grease on the brands to neutralize the acid, turned the cows out until the hair grew back, and a few months later branded cows that appeared ownerless. Speaking of pain, what about breeds of dogs—Boxers, Doberman Pinschers, Schnauzers—not considered attractive unless their ears and tails are chopped off? Poodles, among the most widely popular dog breeds, just have their tails trimmed, though dogs with extremities intact are now allowed in some shows. What about the thousands of pets killed each year because owners couldn't be bothered with them any longer? Is it more merciful to keep a wild predator like a cat confined to an apartment for its entire life than to brand a cow once? So-called "pet" cats slaughter wild songbirds by the millions in most cities, but few animal rights activists picket pet owners. Why do suburbanites let their dogs run loose to chase and kill wildlife and calves?

27   Today's cattle live very well compared to their ancestors, perhaps too well for the health of the species; some old breeds are dying out. We may need their genetic diversity in coming years, if we continue to breed cattle for beef and milk production instead of their ability to survive, coddling them with medications until they can no longer resist disease. The average calf is observed and protected from predators at birth, and quickly vaccinated against many diseases. When necessary operations like branding, earmarking, castration, and dehorning occur, they are done with sterile equipment, supplemented with healing sprays to keep flies and maggots from the wounds. In the wild, only the fittest animals would survive a tough winter; modern cattle operators carefully control herd feed throughout the year for maximum gain, and maximum protection of pasture. Sick, weak, crippled, or otherwise unfit animals are culled from the herd, instead of being allowed to suffer and pass on their genes and illnesses. Ranchers who habitually abuse their cattle damage their own income and endanger themselves, both indirectly—by hurting their own profits—and directly; an abused or frightened cow can be a dangerous proposition.

28   As the rancher's awareness of chemical dangers increases, and as costs climb, some of us are realizing that we could raise organic, lean beef with less effort and expense, with the help of a real demand in the market from an informed public. Some ranchers already nervous about growth hormone implants would give them up if the steers didn't gain; heavier steers mean more income. As I write this, several tuna-packing companies have finally instituted policies that will make the killing of dolphins unprofitable. If the public demands chemical-free beef, it will be produced; ideally, South Dakota could encourage the sale of cattle straight from the organic grass of our pastures to the hungry customer—rather than selling the land for garbage dumps. I have heard of no state-sponsored efforts to keep native grass unplowed and grazed by cows for organic beef. If state officials put half the energy and cash spent on tourism into promoting the state's ranchers—whose product can keep the land relatively undamaged—we might discover a strong demand for grass-fed beef. And why not give tourists the chance to visit real, working ranches?

29   So if you like beef but don't like chemicals, cholesterol, or high food prices, get acquainted with a rancher who raises cattle on grass. Get a few

friends together, buy a fat young "beef," and butcher it yourself—or ask a hunter to help. If one person does it, you'll just be a well-fed oddity. If two people do it, or five, it might become a movement. Think of it! Ranchers and beef eaters, joining together to beat chemical companies and monopolies; why, it's the stuff democracy is made of.

I'll say it again: I love cows, and consider my care and understanding of them superior to the treatment they'd get at the hands of the average animal rights activist. 30

Student MLA Essay

Eileen Williams

Mandatory AIDS Testing for Job Applicants

There is no need to shy away from controversial topics in research papers. Here, Eileen puts forth a very convincing case for banning AIDS testing of job applicants. Note that her case is consistently supported by research—she doesn't just make undocumented assertions.

AIDS IS A RAPIDLY SPREADING DISEASE that is reaching epidemic proportions. According to a brochure entitled *Facts About AIDS* put out by the Public Health Service, AIDS was first reported in the United States in 1981. By early 1987, an estimated 1.5 million Americans had been infected with the AIDS virus, more than 30,000 had developed AIDS, and 17,000 had died from it. Researchers are predicting that by 1991, these latter two figures will be ten times as high. An issue evolving from the AIDS problem is that of whether or not employers can require job applicants to take a blood test for AIDS before the employers will consider hiring them. Although many workers feel they have the right to refuse to work with an AIDS victim because they do not want to risk contracting the illness, and although an employer might not want to invest in a person whose condition ends in death, these tests should not be made mandatory. They will only lead to discrimination in both the workplace and with insurance, and they are an invasion of privacy. 1

Once an AIDS test for a job applicant has come back positive, discrimination is likely to start. Many employees feel they do not have to work with a person infected with AIDS because they risk contracting the disease. This shows ignorance because over and over the U.S. Public Health Service has as- 2 sured the public that AIDS cannot be transmitted through casual contact. The only ways known to transmit the virus are through sexual contact, the sharing of needles for intravenous drugs, blood transfusions, and rarely, a mother's breast milk (Facts). One cannot contract the AIDS virus from a toilet seat or from sharing someone's eating utensils. These concerned employees have no logical or medical evidence to support them, only emotional input.

3   An employer might also want to require AIDS testing so he'll know if he wants to invest in a person whom he expects always to be sick and to have a short life expectancy. But in the Facts About AIDS brochure, it is stated that it might be up to five years after a person is infected with the virus before he starts experiencing symptoms. So even though he may have several good years to live and work, the employer will probably label him an AIDS victim and not hire him. This is discrimination because a person's life should not end the moment he or she is diagnosed as having AIDS. As long as he can, he should be allowed to lead a normal life, including working for as long as he is able. Fortunately, according to the article, "Workplace AIDS," most authorities feel that people with AIDS are included in the laws that protect the handicapped from discrimination. So if they don't have any symptoms that interfere with their work ability, they cannot be fired. In all fairness, this should apply to hiring as well.

4   Discrimination doesn't remain only in the workplace, though. If job applicants' test results are passed on to insurance companies, they sometimes discriminate also. Fortunately, as stated in a U.S. News and World Report article, "contract law forbids insurers from barring newly diagnosed AIDS patients from group health plans". Yet, according to another U.S. News article, a man in Colorado sent a copy of his negative AIDS test to his insurance company, and they still refused him "on the basis that the fact he got tested at all made him too great a risk". These companies are presently fighting bills that would keep them from refusing AIDS victims.

5   Along with causing discrimination, the AIDS tests are invading persons' privacy. Employers, by testing job applicants for AIDS, are prying into their personal lives. Employers don't test prospective employees for other diseases that aren't contagious through casual contact such as cancer, syphillis, and cerebral palsy, and for that matter, for diseases that are more easily contagious, such as hepatitis and pneumonia, so why should AIDS be an exception? Besides, once employers explore all aspects of applicants' health and discover positive AIDS tests, what's to stop employers from looking into causes and discriminating against the applicants, not necessarily because of AIDS, but perhaps because they are homosexual? That is quite a generalization, and perhaps most employers are more unbiased than this, but it is certainly possible that discrimination could become this out-of-hand.

Yes, the population of AIDS victims is rapidly growing, and it is frighten-   6
ing because everyone is afraid of contracting this dreadful illness. But if we refrain from the activities known to transmit AIDS, we have no need to worry,
even in the workplace. AIDS victims—like everyone else—have the right to live
normal lives, and as long as they are able to perform their job duties, they
should not be discriminated against. So, until the medical community finds
any evidence that AIDS can be transmitted through casual contact, I don't see
any risk with an AIDS victim in the workplace. Therefore, mandatory blood
tests to check for AIDS in job applicants are unnecessary.

Works Cited

"AIDS: No Need for Worry in the Workplace." *Newsweek* 25 Nov. 1985: 51.
"AIDS: What We Know Now." *McCall's* Apr. 1987: 143-44.
Facts About AIDS. U.S. Dept. of Health and Human Services, Spring 1986.
"Mandatory Tests for AIDS?" *U.S. News & World Report* 9 March 1987: 62.
"Workplace AIDS." *Nation's Business* Nov. 1986: 30.

James Zigarelli

Hand It Over

James Zigarelli teaches G.E.D. and Adult Basic Education classes in Philadelphia. He graduated with a B.A. in English from Rutgers University in 1998. He has worked as a reporter and a freelance writer while studying abroad in South Africa. He has also been an editorial assistant at The Village Voice. Currently, he is working on a collection of short fiction. "Hand It Over" originally appeared in the online magazine citypaper.net.

IT'S NOT SOMETHING THAT HAPPENS AT YOUR FAVORITE Fairmount pub every   1
night: two young men, appearing at the open front door, guns pointed, demanding that the cash register be open.

It happens quickly. A short, dark figure is swiftly behind the bar, remov-   2
ing the contents of the cash drawer. The other man is three feet behind me,
over my right shoulder. In a heavy, demanding voice, he says, "All the money,
everybody's money on the table!" Everyone empties the cash from their wal-
lets onto the table. I drop my money, and in an act of spirited self-preserva-
tion, let my eyes gaze, out of focus, at the counter.

3   They flee. My friend alertly pulls the door shut and locks it. Out of a window on the side of the bar one patron sees them get into a red getaway car.

4   The bartender calls the police. There are 10 of us in the bar, not counting the bartender.

5   After the initial crash that follows any rush or release, we all agree that the job took under a minute.

6   "Those guys are making about $60,000 an hour."

7   "Not a bad wage!"

8   The volume of conversation continues to rise. Repeatedly, the bartender is imploring us to keep it down.

9   But containing people's vigor is not easy. A liveliness and grand camaraderie begins to inhabit the bar. People are at once intimates, caused by one unchangeable swoop of chance.

10   When the bartender hangs up, he announces that drinks are on the house. We all have to wait for the detectives to arrive and question us.

11   "I feel like I've experienced something," someone says. "I feel like we've all bonded," someone else says across the bar.

12   "I just finished peddling all night delivering pizzas," one guy says. He plopped his hard-earned $80 down on the table when the robbers requested, but didn't seem to mind very much. "I can earn it again tomorrow," he says with a shrug and a smile.

13   This cool nonchalance to victimization expressed by the pizza deliverer is the prevailing sentiment. None of the money just stolen from us is irreplaceable. Much of it would have been dropped at the bar anyway. The only irreplaceable thing in all of our lives at this moment seems to be a warped sense that being robbed is some sort of extreme-sport gut-check. We are all taking inventory, asking ourselves how we fared. If that were lights, camera, action, was I ready to go?

14   An hour passes as we wait for the detectives. The cops have already arrived, but this sort of thing is mundane for them, and I gain a new sense of awe for the life of a cop. One of them finds a television screen perched in a high corner of the bar far more absorbing than the details of the armed robbery we are all discussing.

15   While we sit, drinking mugs of ale and porter, I begin to consider the other people involved, the two gunmen. It seems they had given us so much, an intense experience that will last a lifetime; and we have given them so little, enough money perhaps to live for a week. My more Marxist leanings beg me to understand the robbery as a very natural occurrence, just a simple redistribution of wealth in a capitalist society. Yet beyond textbooks and theories, I had seen the horror in the turbulent face of the young man, not a day over 18, who was robbing the cash register. The delight I had taken from the

incident was perverse, I knew, but to what degree was I complicit in this robbery? Was I a witness or a participant? How badly did he wish he didn't have to walk into that bar with a gun to get what America says we can all have?

I found my answer moments later, when the bartender, in the voice of a 16 victor, revealed that in his haste, the young gunman had not even grabbed the twenties out of the register.

Apparently, his gaze was as out of focus as mine. 17

Credits

ATWOOD: "Pornography" by Margaret Atwood © 1983. Reprinted with permission of the author.

BAKER: Reprinted from *Growing Up* by Russell Baker, © 1985. Used with permission of NTC/Contemporary Publishing Group, Inc.

BIANCHI-SAND: "The Glass Cieling Hurts Business Too." Copyright © 1997 by Susan Bianchi-Sand. As first appeared in *Intellectual Capital*. Reprinted by permission of the author.

BLAIR: "Shattering the Myth of the Glass Ceiling" by Anita K. Blair, from *The Los Angeles Times*, May 7, 1996. Copyright © 1996, Los Angeles Times. Reprinted by permission of the author.

CARTON: Carton, Barbara. "Why Does 'Everybody' Now Put 'Everything' in Quotation Marks?" from *The Wall Street Journal*. Reprinted by permission.

COFER: Judith Ortiz Cofer. "Advanced Biology." From *The Latin Deli: Prose & Poetry* by Judith Ortiz Cofer. University of Georgia Press, 1993. Copyright © 1993 by Judith Ortiz Cofer. Reprinted by permission of the University of Georgia Press.

CROCKETT: "'Haven't We Met . . .?': The Pickup Line Just Goes On and On" by Stephanie A. Crockett. Copyright © 1995 by the Washington Post Writers Group. Reprinted by permission of the author.

CURTIS: Curtis, Patricia. "The Argument Against Animal Experimentation." From *The New York Times*, December 31, 1978. Copyright © 1978 by The New York Times Company. Reprinted by permission.

DILLARD: Excerpt from *An American Childhood* by Annie Dillard. Copyright © 1987 by Annie Dillard. Reprinted by permission of HarperCollins Publishers, Inc.

EHRENREICH: Ehrenreich, Barbara. "What I've Learned From Men." © 1995 Time Inc. Reprinted by permission.

ELBOW: From *Writing Without Teachers* by Peter Elbow. Copyright © 1973, 1998 by Peter Elbow. Used by permission of Oxford University Press, Inc.